World-Class Accounting

for

World-Class Manufacturing

Edited by

Lamont F. Steedle

National Association of Accountants
Montvale, New Jersey

Published by

National Association of Accountants
10 Paragon Drive, Montvale, NJ 07645-1760

Claire Barth, Editor
Mandel & Wagreich, Cover
NAA Publication Number 90255
ISBN 0-86641-193-3

Foreword

In March 1989 we discussed with Al King, NAA's managing director of professional services, the need for NAA to develop new course materials for NAA's professional education program. These courses would incorporate many of the new cost concepts that had surfaced in the last three or four years. We concluded that the development of new strategies such as total quality control, just-in-time technologies, activity-based costing, and factory automation, and new techniques in performance measurement and investment management, had led to the recognition that previous approaches to cost accounting may no longer suffice to meet management needs. What was needed now for the NAA practitioner was a current synthesis of the published work in the new areas of cost and management accounting.

That same month a letter was sent to members of the management accounting section of the American Accounting Association inquiring as to their interest in developing materials for NAA. Among the responses was an outline from Professor Lamont Steedle, then of James Madison University (now of Towson State University), that proposed the idea that NAA should publish

a monograph reflecting these new and emerging strategies. It would be designed to be a highly organized single source reference guide for the NAA member practitioner.

With that objective in mind, Professor Steedle was asked to draft this work using key articles selected from NAA's *Management Accounting*. The volume contains eight sections, each consisting of three articles written by noted professionals and practitioners, covering subjects from factory automation to activity accounting to product costing. The introduction to each section gives additional readings from *Management Accounting*, which also are included in a bibliography at the end of the book. NAA members should find *World-Class Accounting for World-Class Manufacturing* a useful guide in their efforts to improve cost management practices in their firms.

This report, the introductions to each section, and the articles selected reflect the views of the researcher and article authors and not necessarily those of the National Association of Accountants or its Committee on Research.

Fred J. Newton
Chairman, Committee on Research
Defense Contract Audit Agency
Alexandria, Virginia

Patrick L. Romano
Director of Research
National Association of Accountants

Preface

"World-class" is a term that has become widely used to define the level of excellence required for competition in the international marketplace. World-class manufacturing is a management philosophy committed to producing high-quality, low-cost products on time. This new manufacturing environment is characterized by changes in objectives and methods that cause traditional management accounting systems to become outdated and that lead to the development of new management accounting systems to meet the information needs of the manufacturer competing in the international marketplace.

The National Association of Accountants (NAA) has played a leading role in the dissemination of information concerning world-class management accounting systems through its conferences, seminars, and sponsorship of research projects and through its monthly publication, *Management Accounting*. To further that role, the NAA's Committee on Research is publishing this collection of articles on the subject. A synthesis of published work on world-class management accounting systems, the collection presents recent research in a form convenient for use in both the continuing education of accounting practitioners and the education of accounting students.

The articles selected for this publication all appeared in *Management Accounting* and represent the on-going thinking and research in the development of modern management accounting systems. The authors include leading academics, management consultants, and accounting practitioners. An intentional effort was made to capture the latest thinking; all of the works were published in the last five years. Many of the articles contain numerous references to earlier works as well as to materials published elsewhere. Space limitations caused many useful and relevant articles to be excluded. They are listed, according to theme, at the end of the introductory comments accompanying each section; they also are included in the bibliography.

The articles are grouped in three parts. Section 1 provides an overview of the inadequacies of current manufacturing accounting systems and the changes occurring in the world-class manufacturing environment. Sections 2 through 5 describe in more depth four of the most important of these changes: factory automation, just-in-time and bar code technologies, quality cost measurement, and activity accounting. Sections 6 through 8 review the implications for future management accounting systems in three management accounting areas: product costing, performance measurement, and investment management.

Much of the text discusses the key role of management accountants in the new manufacturing environment. The first step in fulfilling this role is an awareness of the environment and its implications for future cost accounting systems. The objective of this collection is to facilitate that first step.

Lamont F. Steedle

Acknowledgments

I would like to thank all of those at NAA who helped with this work. I am especially grateful for the support and guidance provided by Patrick Romano, director of research, as well as for the suggestions and the enthusiastic support given by the Committee on Research and its chairman, Fred Newton.

About the Author

Lamont F. Steedle received a Ph.D. degree in accounting from The Pennsylvania State University in 1978 and a CMA in 1982. He served as managing editor of the *Journal of Accounting Education* from 1986 to 1989. He is currently professor of accounting at Towson State University, having taught previously at The Pennsylvania State University, Lehigh University, and James Madison University.

Dr. Steedle was coauthor of the NAA monograph *NAA Student Affiliate Groups: Current Status and Future Direction*. Some of his other research has been published in *Management Accounting* and other leading practitioner journals.

Since joining NAA in the 1970s, he has been active in the Lehigh Valley and Virginia Skyline Chapters. He has served as director of manuscripts, director of CMA activities, and director of communications. While at James Madison University, he was adviser to an outstanding NAA Student Affiliate Group for two consecutive years.

Table of Contents

Section 1

Overview and Introduction

The three works presented in Section 1 review the development of current manufacturing accounting systems, question their relevance to the new manufacturing environment, and introduce the reader to the world of world-class manufacturing and the factory of the future. The readings show which organizations are world-class manufacturers, how they are distinguishable from traditional manufacturers, and what unique changes are occurring in their environment and within their management accounting systems.

While the theme for this publication focuses on the views of those experts who believe that dynamic changes are required for world-class accounting, there are other experts who do not believe dramatic conceptual changes are required. An example of that perspective was published by NAA in *Management Accounting*. (See the Porter and Akers article referenced in the additional readings list.)

The opening article, by H. Thomas Johnson and Robert S. Kaplan, calls for management accounting systems that are radically different from those currently in practice. The authors state that management accounting reports are of little help to operating managers in attempting to reduce costs and improve productivity; that management accounting systems fail to provide accurate costs; and that managers' horizons contract to the short-term cycle of their monthly profit and loss statement. In the view of the authors, current management accounting systems are driven by financial reporting systems and management accounting information is too late, too aggregated, and too distorted to be relevant to users' needs.

Johnson and Kaplan trace the roots of management accounting practice and in so doing identify the root of the current problem. They chronicle the development, through 1925, of virtually all of today's practices. They then cite the dominance of external accounting reports and the demand for periodic audited statements at a time when information technology did not make parallel systems cost effective. They also blame academics led astray by economic models and chief executives driven by financial numbers for the perpetuation of the problem. They believe that experimentation and communication will bring knowledge, which, when combined with today's information technology and innovative spirit, will bring about necessary changes.

Robert A. Howell and Stephen R. Soucy describe the new environment of the world-class manufacturer. They outline six major trends that reflect a commitment to producing high-quality, low-cost products on time and a significant shift in traditional management philosophy. These six trends—higher quality, lower inventory, flexible flow lines, automation, product line organization, and effective use of information—are discussed in turn, with examples from current world-class organizations.

Howell and Soucy review some of the implications of these trends for current methods of process control and product cost determination. They cite the decrease in labor costs, the increase in overhead costs, and the resulting impact on traditional overhead allocation methods, as well as the increasing spread between variable costs and full cost. They state that management accountants need to reassess traditional methods and search for alternative measures in the areas of product costing, performance measurement, and decision-making analysis, thus grasping the opportunity to play a key role in the rebirth of American manufacturing.

In the final article, James A. Brimson sounds the alarm for changes in cost management systems in response to those in factory automation. He asserts that current systems do not provide the necessary financial information to manage the factory of the future. Brimson summarizes some of the more significant trends reshaping the manufacturing environment: capital decay relationships changing competition in individual industries; an unending technology explosion; decreasing product life cycles and increasing engineering changes; improved availability of accurate data and increased importance of computerized information; integrated approaches with significant investments and long implementation cycles; and more fixed production costs associated with increased capital intensity.

In reiterating his argument that changes in cost management systems are needed, Brimson reviews those cost management issues becoming most prominent. He discusses the changing patterns in cost components, decreases in labor and increases in equipment and information, and the resultant impact on cost allocation methods and product costs. He recognizes the need for new strategic cost measures in the area of operational performance measurement and for identification of cost drivers influencing the cost of individual manufacturing processes. Some of the other issues examined by Brimson include direct and indirect cost classifications, depreciation methods, life cycle reporting, investment analysis, and the paperless environment.

Additional Readings from *Management Accounting*

Edwards, James B., "At the Crossroads," September 1985, pp. 44-50.

Jayson, Susan, "Goldratt and Fox: Revolutionizing the Factory Floor," May 1987, pp. 18-22.

Johansson, Henry J., "Preparing for Accounting System Changes," July 1990, pp. 37-41.

Keller, Donald E. and Paul Krause, "'World-Class' Down on the Farm," May 1990, pp. 39-45.

Krause, Paul and Donald E. Keller, "Bringing World-Class Manufacturing Accounting to a Small Company," November 1988, pp. 28-33.

Mackey, James T., "Eleven Key Issues in Manufacturing Accounting," January 1987, pp. 32-37.

Porter, Grover L. and Michael D. Akers, "In Defense of Management Accounting," November 1987, pp. 58-62.

Schiff, Jonathan B. and Allen I. Schiff, "High-Tech Cost Accounting for the F-16," September 1988, pp. 43-48.

Tatikonda, Lakshmi U., "Production Managers Need a Course in Cost Accounting," June 1987, pp. 26-29.

Vangermeersch, Richard, "Reviewing Our Heritage," July 1987, pp. 47-49.

Whitt, Sue Y. and Jerry D. Whitt, "What Professional Service Firms Can Learn from Manufacturing," November 1988, pp. 39-42.

Williams, Kathy, "CAM-I: On the Leading Edge," June 1989, pp. 18-21.

Overview and Introduction

By H. Thomas Johnson and Robert S. Kaplan

The Rise and

Driven by the procedures and cycle of the organization's financial reporting system, management accounting information is produced too late, too aggregated, and too distorted to be relevant for managers' planning and control decisions. With increased emphasis on meeting quarterly or annual earnings targets, internal accounting systems focus too narrowly on producing a monthly earnings report. And despite the considerable resources devoted to computing a monthly or quarterly income figure, this figure fails to measure the actual increase or decrease in economic value that has occurred during this period. Consequently:

Management accounting reports are of little help to operating managers attempting to reduce costs and improve productivity. Frequently, the reports decrease productivity because they require operating managers to spend time trying to understand and explain reported variances that have little to do with the economic and technological reality of their operations. Management accounting systems do not provide timely and detailed information on process efficiencies, or they focus too narrowly on inputs, such as direct labor, that are relatively insignificant in today's production environment. Thus, the system not only fails to provide relevant information to managers, but it also distracts them from noticing the key factors important for production efficiencies.

The management accounting system fails to provide accurate product costs. Costs get distributed to products by simplistic measures, usually direct-labor based, that do not represent the demands made by each product on the firm's resources. While simplistic and aggregate product costing methods are adequate for financial reporting requirements—the methods yield values for inventory and for cost of goods sold that satisfy external reporting and auditing requirements—these methods systematically bias and distort product costs at the individual product level. The standard product cost systems, which are typical of most organizations, usually lead to enormous cross-subsidies across products. When such distorted standard product cost information represents the only available data on "product costs," a dangerous opportunity exists for misguided decisions on product pricing, product sourcing, product mix, and responses to rival products. Many firms seem to be falling victim to this trap.

Managers' horizons contract to the short-term cycle of their monthly profit and loss statement. The financial accounting system treats many cash outlays as expenses of the period in which they are made even though these outlays will benefit future periods. Discretionary cash outlays for new products and improved processes, for preventive maintenance, for long-term marketing positioning, for employee training and morale, and for developing new systems all can produce substantial cash inflows for future periods. Managers under pressure to meet short-term profit goals, on occasion, can achieve these goals by reducing their expenditures on such discretionary investments. Thus, short-term profit pressures can lead to a decrease in investment for the long-run. Monthly accounting statements, using practices mandated for external reporting, can signal increased profits even when the long-term economic health of the firm has been compromised.

There could be many valid short-term measures that would be appropriate for motivating and evaluating managerial performance. It is unlikely, however, that monthly or quarterly profits, especially when based on the practices mandated and used for external constituencies, would be one of these.

Today's management accounting systems provide a misleading target for managerial attention. They fail to provide the relevant set of measures that appropriately reflect the technology, products, processes, and competitive environment in which the organization operates. Originally designed earlier in this century to help coordinate the diverse activities of emerging vertically integrated enterprises, financial measures such as return on investment (ROI) have become for many organizations the only measure of success. Financial managers, relying exclusively on periodic financial statements for their view of the firm, get isolated from the real value-creating operations of the organization and fail to recognize when the accounting numbers are no longer providing relevant or appropriate measures of the organization's operations.

The Challenge

Vigorous global competition, rapid progress in product and process technology, and wide fluctuations in currency exchange rates and raw material prices demand excellence from corporate management accounting systems. An organization's management accounting system must provide timely and accurate information to facilitate efforts to control costs, to measure and improve productivity, and to devise improved production

Fall of Management Accounting

Management accounting information is too late, too aggregated, and too distorted to be relevant.

processes. The management accounting system also needs to report accurate product costs so that pricing decisions, introductions of new products, abandonments of obsolete products, and responses to the appearance of rival products can be made with the best possible information on product resource demands. Finally, large decentralized organizations require systems to motivate and evaluate the performance of their managers. These systems should provide appropriate incentives and signals to managers working in different functions, with diverse products and processes, amid globally dispersed operations.

The organization's management accounting system serves as a vital two-way communication link between senior and subordinate managers. It is the means by which senior executives communicate to subordinate and decentralized managers the goals and objectives of the organization. In the reverse direction, the management accounting system is the channel by which information about the firm's product performance and production efficiencies get reported to upper levels of management. Further, managerial compensation and promotion decisions are usually based on the numbers reported by management accounting system.

An excellent management accounting system will not by itself guarantee success in today's economy. Ultimately, success depends on products that meet customers' needs, on efficient production and distribution systems for these products, and on effective marketing efforts. However, an ineffective management accounting system can undermine even the best efforts in product development, process improvement, and marketing policy. With an ineffective management accounting system, the best outcome occurs when managers understand the irrelevance of their system and bypass it by developing personalized information systems. But danger lurks if managers do not recognize the inadequacies in their management accounting system and erroneously rely on it for managerial control information and product decisions.

The Opportunity

Fortunately, the increased demands for excellent management accounting systems occur at a time when the costs for collecting, processing, analyzing, and reporting information have been decreasing. With many production processes under direct control of digital computers, information can be recorded in real time for analysis of operating performance. In highly automated environments, virtually every transaction can be captured for subsequent analysis. Automated parts recognition and tracking systems combined with Local Area Network technology can provide continual status reports on work-in-process. Thus, extensive systems now can accurately measure and attribute the resource demands made by each product in a diverse product line. Timely and relevant managerial performance measures can be computed and disseminated throughout the organization.

Today's designers of management accounting systems can use sophisticated electronic technology to devise reporting and control systems that are more accurate, more timely, and, hence, more effective than those designed by their predecessors. Simplified and aggregate procedures that were adopted in earlier decades because more relevant and timely procedures would have been too costly or even infeasible no longer need to be tolerated. The computing revolution of the past two decades has so reduced information collection and processing costs that it has removed virtually all barriers to the design and implementation of effective management accounting systems.

Management Accounting's Roots

Historians have demonstrated that accounting reports have been prepared for thousands of years. Bookkeeping records, dating back to ancient civilizations, have been found engraved in stone tablets. Five hundred years ago, a Venetian monk, Fra Pacioli, described the basics for a well-functioning, double-entry bookkeeping system. Thus, the demand to record information on commercial transactions has existed for as long as people traded with each other in market exchanges.

But the demand for management accounting information, for information about transactions occurring within organizations, is a much more recent phenomenon. Before the early 19th century, virtually all exchange transactions occurred between an owner/entrepreneur and individuals who were not part of the organization: raw material suppliers, labor paid by piece-work, and customers. There were no "levels of management," nor were there long-term salaried employees of the organization. Transactions occurred in the market and measures of success were easily obtained. The owner/entrepreneur needed to collect more cash from sales to customers than was paid out to suppliers of the input factors of production, primarily labor and material.

As a consequence of the Industrial Revolution and the ability to achieve gain through economies of scale, it became efficient for 19th century enterprise owners to commit significant sums of capital to their production processes. In order to gain maximum efficiency from their capital investment, owners hired workers on a long-term basis, rather than bearing the costs and risks of continual spot contracting in the labor market. The long-term viability and success of these "managed" organizations revealed the gains that could be earned by managing a hierarchical organization, as opposed to conducting all business through market transactions. Examples of such successful, hierarchical organizations are the textile mills founded in the first half of the 19th century, the railroads formed around mid-century, and the steel companies created in the second half of that century.

H. Thomas Johnson is the Zulauf Alumni Professor of Accounting at Pacific Lutheran University in Tacoma.

The emergence, more than 150 years ago, of managed, hierarchical organizations created a new demand for accounting information. As conversion processes, which formerly were supplied at a price through market exchanges, became performed within organizations, a demand arose for measures to determine the "price" of output from internal operations. Lacking price information on the conversion processes occurring within their organizations, owners devised measures to summarize the efficiency by which labor and material were converted to finished products. These measures also served to motivate and evaluate the managers who supervised the conversion process. Such measures were especially important because frequently, the factories were located a considerable distance away from the central office of the owners. Thus, management accounting developed to support the profit-seeking activities of entrepreneurs for whom multi-process, hierarchical, managed enterprises were more efficient than managing conversion processes through continual transactions in the marketplace.

The early management accounting measures were simple but seemed to serve well the needs of owners and managers. They focused on conversion costs and produced summary measures, such as cost per hour or cost per pound produced, for each process and for each worker. The measured costs included labor and material and involved some attribution of overhead costs. The goal of these systems was to identify the costs for the intermediate and final products of the firm, and to provide a benchmark to measure the efficiency of the conversion process. In effect, the management accounting information provided a substitute or a surrogate for the market prices that were absent in managed enterprises.

By the middle of the 19th century, great advances in transportation and communication, especially the invention of the railroad and the tele-

Is Management Accounting Irrelevant?

In *Relevance Lost: The Rise and Fall of Management Accounting,* Professors Tom Johnson and Bob Kaplan state that contemporary trends in competition, technology, and management demand major changes in the way organizations measure and manage costs and in how they evaluate short- and long-term performance. They conclude that if companies fail to make modifications in their management accounting systems, their ability to be effective and efficient global competitors will be inhibited. Recently, we asked Professors Johnson and Kaplan questions on some of the issues raised in their soon-to-be released book.

When and how did you become aware that management accounting systems were failing to provide relevant information for management planning and control decisions?

Around 1981 I began meeting regularly with corporate financial executives to discover "real-life" material that would enliven my university courses in management accounting. To my surprise, these executives concentrated their attention on problems that did not relate directly to topics that we customarily teach in the classroom. The problems that these managers considered very important are not even broached in the usual management accounting curriculum. For example, problems such as managing overhead costs or managing product quality. Moreover, conversations with these executives revealed that the information supplied by their accounting departments—often resembling the information that we ask management accounting students to analyze—does not solve the problems that mattered to them. (Johnson)

My personal journey started about four years ago when I became aware of the major changes occurring in the organization and technology of manufacturing operations: zero defect total quality control systems, just-in-time inventory systems, and computer-integrated-manufacturing, for example. It seemed to me that such radical changes undermined the intellectual basis of almost all we teach and research in management accounting. During the next two years, I attempted to study how innovative organizations were adapting their management accounting systems to the new competitive and operating environment. I found, first, that the accounting systems were lagging far behind the manufacturing process changes being implemented by innovating companies in manufacturing and in deregulated service industries. But more importantly, I found that even companies with traditional manufacturing technologies, who had not made major changes in their operations and equipment, also had management accounting systems that were completely inadequate for cost control and for product planning decisions. That's when the obsolescence of virtually all companies' management accounting systems became apparent to me. (Kaplan)

How do you think management accountants in industry and academe will respond to your book?

I expect management accountants in industry to respond favorably to the book. The book discusses problems and solutions to problems with which people in real-life industrial organizations can

graph, provided further opportunities for gain to large, hierarchical organizations. These enterprises could now coordinate the acquisition of raw materials and the distribution of final products over much larger geographical areas than had previously been possible. But without a corresponding increase in the quantity and quality of management accounting information, these organizations would not have been able to capture the full potential gains from increased scale of operations. In fact, effective management accounting systems were necessary to coordinate, efficiently, the logistical, conversion, and distribution activities of these enterprises and to provide summary measures of performance for decentralized and dispersed managers.

Perhaps the best examples of effective management accounting systems could be found in the railroad corporations of the mid-19th century. At the time, they were the largest enterprises ever created by man. To oversee their diverse and dispersed operations, new procedures were invented just to control the receipt and disbursement of cash. In addition to these significant financial recording or bookkeeping innovations, however, the railroads also developed extensive summaries of their internal operations and performance. Measures such as cost-per-ton-mile were created and reported for each major segment of operations. The operating ratio, the ratio of revenues to operating costs, was developed, both to measure the profitability of various segments of business—passenger vs. freight, region by region—and to evaluate the performance of managers.

Improved transportation and communication combined with economies of scale also permitted the growth of large distribution enterprises, particularly retail store chains such as Marshall Field, Sears, and Woolworth. These retailers developed their own measures of internal performance to support their managerial planning and control activities. Obviously, measures of conversion costs, such as cost per hour or cost per pound, or the operating measures of the railroads, the cost-per-ton mile, were not relevant for these distribution enterprises. These organizations required information on the effectiveness and efficiency of their purchasing, pricing, and retailing activities. For these activities, measures such as gross margin by department—selling revenues less purchases and operating costs—and inventory stockturn were created.

These examples reveal that management accounting information was developed to expedite the management of process-type industries such as textile and steel conversion, transportation, and distribution. The management accounting measures were designed to motivate and evaluate the efficiency of internal processes. There was little concern with measuring the overall "profit" of the enterprise. These organizations really had only one activity they had to do well: convert raw materials into a single final product such as cloth or steel, move passengers or freight, or re-sell purchased goods. If this basic activity were per-

Robert S. Kaplan is the Arthur Lowes Dickinson professor of accounting at the Harvard Business School and former dean of the Graduate School of Industrial Administration at Carnegie-Mellon University, where he still holds a teaching appointment.

identify. It is more difficult to predict how management accountants in academe will respond to the book. I hope it will be embraced by those academics who view management accounting as a vital management tool that can be understood only in the context of the organizations that use it. However, I am not optimistic about the reception the book will receive from those academics who view management accounting information solely in the context of economic decision theory. (Johnson)

That's an interesting question because I predict the reaction will be quite different by the two audiences you ask about. I find virtually no resistance from industry management accountants to the message being made in the book. They know that their current systems are inadequate for today's and tomorrow's environment. They may not know what the systems were designed for, or by how much the systems are influenced by financial reporting requirements and cycles, but they understand that the systems do a poor job of computing product costs and are too late and too aggregate for being helpful for measuring production performance. I sense a real interest in looking for new approaches for design of their systems. Perhaps the most convincing evidence of this occurred at the NAA Conference, Cost Accounting for the '90s. We had two full days of new ideas and directions for management accounting systems. The message was enthusiastically received; not one of the more than 250 in attendance spoke up to defend existing systems or to declare that the speakers were advocating change from a system that was not broken.

The academic response has been quite different. For one thing, most of our academic colleagues are not staying abreast of the radi-

cal changes occurring in contemporary organizations. They tend not to appreciate how the simple models and procedures they are teaching produce distorted product costs and dysfunctional performance incentives when applied to complex production processes in companies producing hundreds and thousands of different products. Thus, they are more skeptical than we about the need for rethinking the traditional approach to management accounting teaching and research. (Kaplan)

Is it a controversial book?

Yes, we hope so; for a number of reasons. We are challenging a number of conventions and assumptions that have gone unchallenged for many years, if not decades. For one, we show that management accounting systems worked better for their organizations in the nineteenth century than they do today. Many probably feel that with all the knowledge produced during the past century, with more than 65,000 MBAs and 200,000 undergraduates in business graduating each year, and with the great advances in information technology, that our organizations should be better managed than organizations operating 60 to 100 years ago. We show, that at least along the important dimension of how well management accounting systems function in organizations, this belief is unfounded. In effect, we are saying that the emperor has no clothes. All these computerized cost accounting systems are producing highly distorted, dysfunctional information. The management accounting systems used by railroads in the 1860s, in the Carnegie Steel company in the 1880s, and in DuPont and General Motors earlier in this century served their owner-managers much better than most systems in existence today. We also

formed efficiently, then the organization could be confident that it would be profitable in the long run. Thus, the management accounting system was created to promote efficiency in the key operating activity of the organization. There could be an alternative, transactions-based, system that recorded receipts and expenditures and produced periodic, probably annual, financial statements for the owners and creditors of the firm. But these two systems, management and financial, operated independently of each other.

Further advances in the technology of management accounting systems were made in conjunction with the scientific management movement. This movement started in metal fabricating companies during the last two decades of the 19th century. While the goal of the scientific management engineers, such as Frederick Taylor, was to improve the efficiency and utilization of labor and materials, the physical standards they developed, such as labor grade and labor hours per unit, and material quantities per unit, were easily converted into standards for labor and material costs. Eventually, these labor and material costs, often combined with an allocation of indirect or overhead costs, were aggregated together into a finished product unit cost that could be used for pricing decisions. With fluctuations in the price paid for labor and materials, the standards were frequently updated to reflect the most recent purchases. Thus, finished product standard costs were often closer to what we now call replacement cost than to any measure of historic cost. As with the measures of conversion efficiency developed earlier in process industries, finished product unit costs were calculated to aid managerial decisions (pricing in this case), and not to produce external financial statements. Therefore, there was little demand for having the unit cost information be "consistent" with the books of transactions used to prepare summary financial statements.

The final developments in management accounting systems occurred in the early decades of the 20th century to support the growth of multi-activity, diversified corporations. The DuPont Powder Company, formed in 1903 as a combination of previously separate family-run or independent companies, was the prototype of this new organizational form. The managers of the new DuPont Company faced the problem of coordinating the diverse activities of a vertically integrated manufacturing and marketing organization and of deciding on the most profitable allocation of capital to these different activities. Before DuPont, organizations engaged in only a single type of activity. The only important capital choice was whether to expand the scale of one homogeneous operation, not which of several diverse operations should be expanded.

A number of important operating and budgeting activities were devised by the senior managers of DuPont to coordinate the activities of their diverse operating groups. But the most important and the most enduring management accounting

are exposing the degree to which financial accounting practices have come to dominate the design and implementation of the organization's internal accounting system. And we also are challenging the academic accountants' use of single product, single process models for illustrating cost accounting concepts in their teaching and research. So there are many opportunities for controversy to arise from the messages in the book. (Kaplan)

What should management accountants do to facilitate the creation of relevant management accounting and control systems? And, why is it important that engineers and operating managers work with accountants in modifying management accounting and control systems?

As in any crisis, the first step is awareness and overcoming defensiveness and denial. After that, and assuming that senior management enthusastically supports their efforts—a necessary condition to implement any major organizational change—management accountants will need to talk with operating personnel, with marketing people, with product managers having profit responsibility, and with general managers to learn what factors are critical to their success. They need to understand that management accounting systems exist to promote operating efficiency, encourage excellent product designs, and provide insight on where profits are being earned and where losses are being incurred in the organization. The use of cost accounting information to value inventory for financial statements is a detail that can be handled by relatively simple systems, and should not be the driving force in the design of cost systems. The management accounting system has to track, support, and encourage the value-adding activities of the organization.

The environment for effective product design and process technology has changed radically during the past decade and will continue to evolve rapidly in the years ahead. Management accountants have to understand the impact of their systems on the product design activities of engineers, of the payoffs that accrue from investment in flexible automated process technology (CIM), and the change in local performance measures that arise when organizations move to zero defect and zero inventory production systems. These changes are occurring today in most organizations. Management accountants who leave their offices will not find it difficult to discover where these changes are occurring in their organizations and the engineers who are in the forefront of implementing these changes. The big intellectual step management accountants have to make is recognition: recognition that the old way of counting the beans and keeping score is inadequate in today's organizations.

Our book also documents that innovative ideas in management accounting were made by engineers, not professionally trained accountants. People like Andrew Carnegie, Alexander Hamilton Church, Alfred Sloan, and Donaldson Brown had great insights into the design of effective management accounting systems. Somehow, in the past 60 years, the growth of the "accounting profession" with its emphasis on external reporting demands, has prevented ideas from outside the profession from influencing the design of internal accounting systems. We need to again learn from engineers how to design more effective internal measurement systems. (Kaplan)

In your book you chronicle the history of management accounting. What can management accountants learn from their "roots" that will help them create relevant management accounting systems?

The ultimate purpose of historical writing is to describe the past and to explain the conditions that made things as they were. Historians don't study the past in order to prescribe solutions for the present. However, astute individuals realize that knowledge about the past provides important insight into the options that we face in the preinnovation was the return-on-investment (ROI) measure. Return-on-investment provided an overall measure of the commercial success of each operating unit and of the entire organization. Because capital allocation remained a central management function in the early DuPont company, departmental managers were not held responsible for ROI performance. These managers took their scale of operations as given and concentrated solely on promoting efficiencies in their internally-managed processes, just as their 19th century counterparts had done. Only top managers used ROI, to help direct their allocations of capital and to evaluate the performance of the operating department (which could be different from the performance of the manager of that department). Donaldson Brown, the chief financial officer of DuPont, decomposed the ROI measure into its component parts and demonstrated that the ROI measure could be viewed as a combination of two efficiency measures—the operating ratio (return on sales) and stock turn (sales to assets)—used by single activity organizations.

Use of the ROI measure was expanded in the 1920s as the multidivisional form of organization evolved in the DuPont and the newly reorganized General Motors corporation. The decentralized, multidivisional corporation developed to capture economies of scope—the gains from sharing common organizational functions across a broad spectrum of products. But the enormous diversity in the product markets served by these giant corporations required new systems and measures to coordinate dispersed and decentralized activities. Division managers were responsible for the profitability and return on capital employed in their divisions and had authority to generate capital requests. It was no longer possible for the corporate-level departments of marketing, purchasing, and finance to have the requisite information to function effectively or efficiently in all the markets being served by their organization. Decentralization was necessary and each operating division required its own staff functions to support its activities. Thus, central managers were now in the position of providing capital to diverse operating units and attempting to coordinate, motivate, and evaluate the performance of their divisional managers. The ROI measure played a key role in permitting this internal market for managers and for capital to function.

Lost Relevance

By 1925, virtually all management accounting practices that are practiced today had been developed: cost accounts for labor, material, and overhead; budgets for cash, income, and capital; flexible budgets, sales forecasts, standard costs, variance analysis, transfer prices, and divisional performance measures. These practices had evolved to serve the informational and control needs of the managers of increasingly complex and diverse organizations. But the pace of innovation seemed to stop in the mid-1920s. Perhaps

sent. For instance, knowledge about the historic conditions that prompted manufacturing managers to account for unit direct labor cost of products may help us evaluate the relevance of that type of accounting information under present-day conditions. If the technological and market conditions no longer exist that made managing direct labor a strategic source of profits, then perhaps it is time to create new information that is more relevant to new strategies. Understanding their "roots" will help management accountants consider carefully the conditions that make particular systems relevant. If systems that management accountants currently use are relevant to technological and market conditions that no longer exist, it may be time to ask what might be more relevant to current conditions. But history can only help management accountants raise that question; it can't help them answer it. The answer requires them to go where no one has been before. (Johnson)

Any time you are advocating major organizational changes, as we are in this book, you need to understand how we acquired the systems and procedures in use today. After all, the people running our organizations are not foolish, unmotivated individuals. It would be a normal and correct response to initially deny the claims by a couple of academics that a system as fundamental to the organization as the management accounting system could be as inadequate as we claim. The value of tracing the roots of today's system is to show that these systems were eminently sensible and useful for the environment in which they were designed: an era of high direct labor content, relatively limited product lines, simple production flow processes, and, most importantly, expensive information processing technology. We can then see that these factors are not valid today. And when we add in the impact of today's global economy, with rapid technology transfer to factories in less developed nations, with worldwide capital markets, and extremely efficient bulk transportation and communications around the globe, it should not take a genius to recognize that perhaps new systems for measuring product costs and motivating performance may be called for. (Kaplan)

What are some typical examples of problems caused by the failure of management accounting systems to provide relevant data for management planning and control decisions?

A partial list of the most serious problems includes the following: misdirected marketing efforts that result from poor information about the profitability of a company's diverse products; inability to manage "overhead" costs; a misplaced emphasis on cost-cutting programs as the way to increase productivity; the use of modern flexible machining systems to produce standard parts in high volume, not custom parts in small lots; and underinvestment by manufacturers who fail to consider the full strategic consequences of investments in computer-aided production systems. (Johnson)

There are a number of problems that arise from the failure of management accounting systems. Perhaps most basic is that virtually no multiproduct organization today knows the costs of each of its products. The cost accounting system is the only system for estimating product costs. Today's systems do a miserable job of tracing the consumption of indirect or overhead resources to products. Large cost categories, such as marketing, distribution, and engineering support may not even be attributed to products or product lines.

The systems also provide misleading targets for manufacturing managers. We see in many organizations, operating managers producing products in excessively large batch sizes so that they can have favorable volume variances and high labor and machine utilization measures. That they are producing inventory that is not easily stored or sold is not evaluated. Nor is the lack of customer respon-

Ironically, as management accounting systems became less relevant to corporate operations and strategy, many firms began to be dominated by executives who liked to run the firm 'by the numbers.'

there was little incentive to continue to develop innovative management accounting procedures because the corporate organizational forms developed by companies such as DuPont and General Motors proved to be the model for many corporations for the next half-century.

Even without significant innovations in organizational forms, however, the diversity of products and complexity of manufacturing processes continued to increase in the decades after 1920. Thus, the need for accurate product costs and effective process control should have imposed new demands on organizations' management accounting systems. Yet the evolution of management accounting systems after 1920 did not keep pace with the improvement in corporations' product and process technologies. This lag eventually led to today's problems: distorted product costs, delayed and overly aggregated process control information, and short-term performance measures that do not reflect the increases or decreases in the organization's economic position.

In part, this stagnation can be attributed to the dominance of the external or financial accounting statements during the 20th century. With more widespread public ownership of corporations' securities, the demand for periodic, audited financial statements increased. Auditors, mindful of potential liability to users of financial statements, preferred conservative accounting practices based on objective, verifiable, and realized financial transactions. When measuring cost of goods sold

and valuing inventory, auditors insisted on product costs based on the historical transactions recorded in the firms' ledger accounts. Further, they wanted the income statement and balance sheet to "articulate"—that is, the two financial statements had to be based on the same transactions and events. It did not matter for the summary financial statements if the inventory costing procedures distorted or cross-subsidized product costs as long as the total value recorded in the inventory accounts was sufficiently accurate. Thus, simple methods were used to assign direct and period costs to products.

In principle, of course, early 20th-century managers did not have to yield the design of their cost accounting systems to their financial accountants and auditors. They could have maintained separate systems for managerial purposes and for external reporting. But the information technology in the early 20th century may not have made such parallel systems cost effective.

Perhaps the product line of 1920s' organizations was more focused than that of today's organizations so that the distorting effect from using simplistic methods to attach costs to products was not as severe as it has become today. Also the cost of collecting data and providing prompt reports to production managers may have been too high to permit the real-time process control that is now possible. Thus, the decision by managers to not invest in management accounting systems separate from those already mandated by the demands

siveness caused by keeping labor and machines busy producing unwanted inventory penalized. The monthly variance measures produced by typical management accounting systems also arrive too late and are too aggregate to be helpful for operating managers attempting to control their production processes and make productivity improvements.

Finally, monthly and quarterly income figures provide a poor target for the value-creating activities of organizations. Recording product design, process improvement, employee training, and prototype development activities as expenses of the current period completely distorts the value being created by these long-term investments in the organization's knowledge base.

Basically, when complex, diversified organizations do not produce valid information about the effectiveness and efficiency of their internal operations, they become vulnerable to smaller and more focused competitors. Focused enterprises have much simpler information needs, they can become highly efficient in their narrow product segments or range of production processes and will outperform diversified organizations that, because of inadequate management accounting information, cannot assess the relative profitability of their varied activities. Whatever scale economies large diversified enterprises attempt to achieve will be dissipated by their inability to manage complexity and diversity. (Kaplan)

Did you find any innovative organizations developing new and relevant management accounting systems?

Yes. There are a number of organizations in the process of developing and instituting new management accounting systems. We interact with the movers and shakers for these new systems in organizations such as the Association for Manufacturing Excellence (AME) and Computer-Aided-Manufacturing, International (CAM-

I). It's interesting that the professional organizations in the forefront of promoting change in management accounting systems are basically production and engineering organizations, such as AME and CAM-I. They have given up waiting for management accountants to implement change on their own; they are establishing projects under their influence and control to stimulate new ideas in management accounting systems design.

Companies such as Hewlett-Packard, IBM, General Electric, Caterpillar, and Motorola are developing and implementing innovative management accounting systems at least in parts of their organization. Another source of innovation, of course, arises in newly deregulated service industries: banking, transportation, health care, and telecommunications. Given the major changes in their environment, the companies in these industries now worry much more about operating efficiencies and, more importantly, now need to know the cost of each of their major products or services so that they can learn where they are making and where they are losing money. Before, many of these companies earned regulated rates of return on their entire product mix and did not have to be concerned about profit or loss at the individual product level. Thus, many companies in service industries are now developing, for the first time, product costing systems. (Kaplan)

You point out that companies can't be run entirely "by the numbers." What nonfinancial measures should be developed and implemented to improve decision making?

Each organization has to decide for itself those measures that will promote its tactical and strategic goals. It is unlikely that monthly income will be one of these measures. Organizations stressing total quality control and zero defect policies will want to measure yields, the incidence of failures internal and external to the organization,

for audited, periodic financial statements may have been the correct economic decision. The benefits from a more accurate and more responsive management accounting system may not have been worth the cost of maintaining such a separate system.

Over the years, however, as corporations' product lines expanded, as production technology changed, as product life cycles shortened, as global competitive conditions shifted, and, most importantly, as great advances in information technology occurred, we should have expected a reconsideration of the decision to not invest in a more relevant and more timely management accounting system. But by the time these events unfolded, the spirit and knowledge of management accounting systems design that occurred throughout the hundred-year 1825-1925 period had disappeared. Organizations had fixated on the cost systems and management reporting methods of the 1920s. In fact, when cost systems became automated on digital computers, starting in the mid-1960s, the system designers basically automated the manual systems they found in the factory. Left unquestioned was whether these systems were still sensible given the great expansion in information technology represented by electronic, digital computers.

Academics Led Astray

Why did university-based researchers fail to note the growing obsolescence of organizations' management accounting systems? And, why did they not play a more active or stimulative role to improve the art of management accounting systems design?

We believe academics were led astray by focusing too narrowly on a simplified model of firm behavior. Influenced strongly by economists' one-product, one-production process model of the firm, management accounting academics found little value in the cost allocations imposed on organizations by financial accounting procedures.

Sixty years of literature emerged advocating the separation of costs into fixed and variable components for making good product decisions and for controlling costs. This literature, very persuasive when illustrated in the simple one-product settings used by academic economists and accountants, never fully addressed the question of where fixed costs came from and how these costs needed to be covered by each of the products in the corporations' repertoire. Nor did the academic researchers attempt to implement their ideas in the environment of actual organizations, with hundreds or thousands of products and with complex, multistage production processes. Thus, the academic literature concentrated on elegant and sophisticated approaches to analyzing costs for single product, single process firms while companies tried to manage with antiquated systems in settings that had little relationship to the simplified model assumed for analytical convenience by researchers.

the percentage of items produced that required no rework, etc. Organizations attempting to impelement just-in-time production systems may want measures such as average setup times, days production in inventory, and average travel distance for products. One measure that leading Japanese companies are now stressing is throughput time: how long from the time an item is first started into production until the time it is shipped, or at least ready to be shipped, to the customer. The overall performance of an entire factory is judged by its throughput time. In effect, innovating Japanese companies are now managing time, not costs. This could be a profound change for U.S. management accountants, especially those trained to think only about financial measures.

There are all kinds of nonfinancial measures that can provide much better indicators of a company's success than monthly or quarterly income. Product launch times, percentage of delivery commitments met, product design measures, marketing and distribution performance measures provide superior targets for motivating and measuring short-term performance. We don't think that the financial accounting model for measuring periodic profits was ever designed to measure firm-wide performance during short time periods. Certainly, this was not the intention of DuPont and General Motors executives when they devised return on investment (ROI) measures, earlier in this century.

Many of the most difficult problems faced by the Financial Accounting Standards Board arise from attempting to time the recognition of income and expense or allocate long term costs and benefits to arbitrarily short periods. Whatever the outcome of these deliberations, they are unlikely to be able to capture the outcome of all the wealth creating activities of the organization in a single number, like net income. If we can get this point generally accepted, perhaps the pressures to measure all performance through a measure created by financial accountants will lessen. (Kaplan)

Can you speculate on the characteristics of future management accounting systems?

Future management accounting systems should distinguish clearly between two types of information—strategic profitability information and process control information—that most management accountants today derive from the same system, the financial accounting system. There must be one system to provide information about the strategic variables that create value for an organization. In particular, this system should identify the long-run contribution that each product or service makes to an organization's profitability. This information is virtually non-existent in today's management accounting systems. Second, there must be a system that provides relevant information for controlling an organization's operating processes. Here there must be timely and detailed information about the myriad economic events through which an organization efficiently creates value for the customer. Much of that information, referred to in the previous question, will not come from the accounting system *per se.*

In the final analysis, the management accounting system must help managers answer one fundamental question: why does this organization exist?

A proper management accounting system should reveal whether an organization conducts its internal economic activities more efficaciously than another organization or unaided market exchange might conduct the same activities. That is the ultimate strategic question. A proper management accounting system must be designed to answer that question. (Johnson) □

Ironically, as management accounting systems became less relevant and less representative of the organization's operations and strategy, many companies became dominated by senior executives who believed they could run the firm "by the numbers." Early 20th century organizations, such as DuPont, General Motors, and General Electric, had been created by owners who well understood the technology of their products and processes.

In succeeding decades, however, chief executives were selected whose entire careers were spent in staff functions, such as finance and legal. Lacking knowledge and uncomfortable with their firms' underlying technology, these CEOs increasingly looked at what the projected short-term impact would be on financial measures when making decisions—especially earnings-per-share and return-on-investment. But as product life cycles are shortened, and more costs are incurred before production begins (research and development, product and process design, capital investment, software development, and education and training), directly traceable product costs become a much lower fraction of total costs. Consequently, traditional financial measures, such as periodic earnings and accounting ROI, become less useful measures of corporate performance.

Accounting for Caravans

In some respects, this is not a new phenomenon. If we return to the 15th century and the publication of perhaps the original accounting book by Fra Pacioli, we can ask what kinds of events were occurring that led to a demand for accounting information. Undoubtedly, merchants in Venice were trading goods with other countries. Consider a group of Venetian investors who acquired goods produced in Northern Italy and chartered an expedition to sell these goods in India. Once the goods were sold in India, the traders purchased tea, traveled back to Venice, and then sold the tea. At the end of the expedition, the accountant subtracted the cost of the caravan and the cost of acquiring the initial load of merchandise from the revenues received from the sale of tea in Italy to compute a profit for the entire trip, a profit to be distributed among the investors in the venture.

This was a worthwhile role for accounting—to compute the overall profitability of the venture and to distribute the net proceeds (the retained earnings) among the initial investors. However, did the investors or the Venetian version of the SEC or FASB also ask the accountant to compute the expedition's profits during the third quarter of 1487 when the caravan was traversing the Persian desert enroute to India? Probably not. Because even in the early unsophisticated days of account-ing 500 years ago, investors understood that allocating the total profits of expeditions to periods as short as three months was not a meaningful exercise. Yet isn't the value of preparing monthly income statements for many of today's organizations not unlike an attempt to allocate the profits of a long venture to every month within that venture?

Arguing that it is meaningless to allocate project profitability to short-time periods within the life of a project does not imply that we believe it fruitless to attempt to obtain valuable indicators of short-term progress. Returning to our Venetian expedition, there probably are many measures of the caravan's performance during the third quarter of 1487 that the investors would be interested in knowing. For example, what distance did the caravan cover, and in what direction? How many provisions are left? What is the condition of the inventory being transported? Are the workers content or rebellious? There are many potentially useful indicators of the caravan manager's performance during the third quarter, 1487. But quarterly profits is not one of them!

And given the current competitive, technological environment, there are probably many better indicators of a company's short-term performance than its quarterly earnings. Certainly, cash flow is important and we would want to know the pattern and structure of a company's cash receipts and cash expenditures. But knowing sources and uses of cash is very different from working hard every month and every quarter to produce complete income statements and balance sheets, replete with amortizations, capitalizations, and many other accruals.

Needed: Innovation

The challenge and opportunity for contemporary organizations is clear. Management accounting systems can and should be designed to support the operations and the strategy of the organization. The technology exists to implement systems radically different from those being used today. What is lacking is knowledge. But this knowledge can emerge from experimentation and communication.

The innovative spirit of 100 years ago at the outset of the scientific management movement can be recaptured by creative managers and academic researchers who are committed to developing the new concepts for designing relevant management accounting systems. ☐

This article was excerpted from a new book, Relevance Lost: The Rise and Fall of Management Accounting, *by H. Thomas Johnson and Robert S. Kaplan, published by Harvard Business School Press.*

THE NEW MANUFACTURING ENVIRONMENT:
Major Trends
For Management Accounting

BY ROBERT A. HOWELL AND
STEPHEN R. SOUCY

U. S. manufacturing is in the midst of dramatic change. From the end of World War II to the mid-seventies, the United States was the most prolific producer in the world. American plants churned out large quantities of goods willingly consumed by an expanding global market. From 1950 to 1979, the U.S. gross national product rose from $641 billion to $1,860 billion (1975 dollars) and foreign consumption of U.S. goods rose from $22 billion to $134 billion. In 1985, U.S. manufacturers exported only $108 billion while U.S. consumers imported $172 billion (1975 dollars), and the U.S. share of total output has dropped from over 40% in 1962 to approximately 25% in 1980.

The shifting competitive balance from domestic to foreign producers commonly is blamed on an expensive labor force, trade barriers to foreign markets, unfavorable exchange rates, and foreign and domestic government interference. These macroeconomic fundamentals are significant, but they are beyond management's direct control. But to say the problem is exoge-

Automation is impacting production—and management.

Photo by Don Carroll/The Image Bank.

Editor's Note:
"The New Manufacturing Environment: Major Trends for Management Accounting," first in a series of five articles, addresses the impact of changes in manufacturing. Subsequent articles will focus on product and process costing, operating controls, investment justification, and entity performance management.

nous to the business community overlooks two serious failures of U.S. manufacturers—the failure to recognize shifts in consumer demands and the complacent acceptance of antiquated manufacturing processes and management philosophies.

Some companies, however, are recognizing what must be done to be competitive in today's global market. These world class manufacturers are using techniques developed both locally and abroad that dramatically change the way they manage their businesses.

Although there are a number of ways to categorize the changes made by these leading U.S. manufacturers, we find it helpful to think in terms of six major trends:

1. Higher quality,
2. Lower inventory,
3. Flexible flow lines,
4. Automation,
5. Product line organization, and
6. Effective use of information.

Together they reflect a commitment to producing high quality goods, on time, at the lowest possible cost. These trends also reflect a significant shift in traditional management philosophies. For example, world class manufacturers do not view high quality and low cost as alternative strategies—a popular, but misguided, view of the 1970s. Rather, high quality is viewed as totally consistent with low cost. Nor do world class manufacturers focus on labor utilization or overhead absorption as measures of efficiency or productivity. Measures such as these encourage overproduction and result in excessive inventory balances.

Instead, world class manufacturers strive to eliminate inventory and are introducing new arrangements of equipment, product lines, and organizations. They are breaking with traditional patterns in order to achieve more focus and better results.

It is essential to understand that the resurrection of U.S. manufacturing is a long-term effort.

The management accountant has an opportunity to play a key role in the rebirth of U.S. manufacturing. Understanding how the factory is changing is a start.

THE MAJOR TRENDS

Higher quality is clearly a driving force in the new manufacturing environment. In the 1950s and 1960s, low price served as the primary basis for competition, and quality was defined as a standard level of acceptability.

During the past two decades, foreign competitors have provided markets with higher quality goods at competitive, if not cheaper, prices than their U.S. counterparts. While first ignored by U.S. manufacturers, continual erosion in the export and domestic markets placed pressure on them to either meet the higher quality in the marketplace or drop out.

The electronics and home appliance industries provide a contrasting example of the impact of quality on U.S. manufacturing. In electronics, America's share of the world market has fallen to 10%, less than a third of what it was in 1965. Foreign competitors are providing a higher quality product at a lower cost, forcing U.S. producers to respond in kind. Many have failed to do so. In contrast, the home appliance industry has been nearly impregnable from foreign competition. The industry's success is not the result of quotas, tariffs, or trade agreements, but is due to the high level of quality produced by U.S. manufacturers such as GE, Whirlpool, Maytag, and others.

A second explanation for higher quality is the realization that poor quality is a significant cost driver for the manufacturer. The absence of good materials, highly trained labor, and well-maintained equipment will dramatically increase the costs of nonquality such as scrap, rework, excess inventories, process and equipment breakdowns, field service, and product warranty claims.

For example, purchasing typically has been evaluated on a purchase price variance (actual price versus standard). This motivates purchasers to use suppliers that provide the least expensive material. Yet, low-cost, low-quality materials often result in manufacturing costs such as scrap, rework, and schedule disruptions. Purchasing rarely is accountable for these costs. By motivating purchasers to focus on price, the rest of the company incurs costs of nonquality that often exceed the price "savings" achieved.

Quality is not expensive, nonquality is. Harold K. Sperlich, presi-

Before the management accountant can play a key role in the rebirth of U.S. manufacturing, he must understand how the factory is changing.

dent of Chrysler, reported that "to put value into the marketplace and meet the competitive challenge, you have to run a cost effective business dedicated to constant, never ending improvement. Quality is the main doorway to improving productivity and running a tighter ship."[1]

Lower Inventories is the second major trend in the new manufacturing environment. Companies are sharply reducing their inventory levels while maintaining delivery schedules and customer service. The impetus behind inventory reduction is threefold. First, inventory requires significant capital and the real cost of capital is dramatically higher today than in the 1950s and 1960s. Secondly, companies are recognizing the traditional reasons for holding inventory may no longer be valid. Finally, some companies, both foreign and domestic, are obtaining significant cost savings through reductions in inventory.

The cost of inventory traditionally is viewed as a financing cost—the inventory on hand times the cost of capital. While the direct financial cost to carry inventory can be significant, there are other indirect and qualitative costs associated with holding inventory that often are less explicitly identified. Examples include: increased space requirements, increased materials handling costs, increased record-keeping costs, increased insurance and tax obligations, slower throughput, higher scrap and obsolescence, and more costly inventory write-downs.

Efforts to quantify these indirect costs often result in estimates that match or exceed the financing cost of holding inventory. If the financial cost is 10%, then a more accurate estimate of the total cost may be 20 to 25%. By reducing inventory, a company obviously frees up cash to be invested in productive assets, but the savings associated with eliminating the indirect costs can greatly improve a company's short- and long-term profitability performance.

World class manufacturers also argue that the reasons for holding high inventories are not valid and simply mask organizational deficiencies in sales, engineering, and procurement as well as manufacturing. By reducing the level of inventory, the issues are identified, and with management's effort, resolved.

For example, companies hold raw material inventories because vendor quality and delivery are not reliable. Qualifying vendors on the basis of quality and delivery performance eliminates the need for these buffer stocks. Work-in-process inventory builds up because of schedule changes, production imbalances, worker mistakes, and equipment breakdowns. Tighter process controls eliminate these deficiencies. Sales forecast errors often result in excess finished goods inventory. Shorter production cycles reduce the need for long-term forecasts, which are historically inaccurate.

The final explanation behind the push for lower inventories comes from witnessing the success of manufacturers that sharply lowered their inventory and increased inventory turns. Many Japanese companies are turning their inventories 25 to 30 times a year with some even exceeding 100 times. American companies also have been very successful in this area. Harley-Davidson increased its annual turns from 3.5 to 20. Ford Motor Co. reduced its inventory by $2 billion from 1979 to 1982. Westinghouse Transportation Division reduced its inventory space requirements from 66% of available space to 15%. Allen-Bradley's World Contactor facility operates with zero end-of-day, work-in-process and finished goods inventory.

Flexible Flow Lines is a third trend in the new manufacturing environment. Flow lines represent the physical path a product takes through the manufacturing process from raw material receipt to product shipment. Companies are redesigning their manufacturing flow lines to shorten cycle time—the length of time it requires to produce a product, and increase product variety.

The trend is to establish multiple product flow lines within a factory as contrasted to functionally organized process flows. A functional plant layout requires products to be moved from one group of like machines to another, oftentimes across the manufacturing plant or even to another building. This re-

sults in extensive material handling costs as well as increased work-in-process inventory.

In a product line flow, all the different types of equipment required in the manufacturing process are brought together, splitting up large groups of similar equipment, creating multiple "mini" product line factories. This layout minimizes material handling and inventory. Due to the tightened process flow,

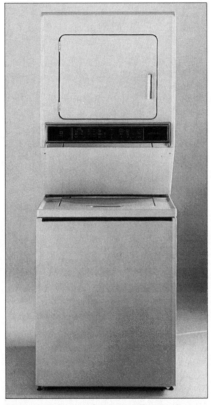

Maytag is known for its quality products.

it moves the product quickly through the process, reinforces quality, and instills employee identification with the end product.

At AMC Jeep, production lines at its Toledo plant are broken at several places, causing partially assembled car bodies to be dragged manually from one line to the next as the assembly proceeds. By focusing on simplified product flow lines and producing a completed product rather than performing a specific function, world class manufacturers are achieving increased quality, throughput and productivity, reducing inventory levels, and getting more product and process improvement suggestions from employees.

Once the plant layout is established, management can then leverage its benefits by focusing on the objective of maintaining a continuous flow. This requires that the entire process work in concert. The central idea is that product is pulled through the manufacturing process starting with customer demand and working back to incoming materials. This is in contrast to developing a production plan, buying material, releasing it to the factory floor and pushing it through the plant, and then notifying sales as to what is available to sell or more accurately what there is too much of and needs to be sold.

The "pull" concept is most commonly referred to as just-in-time (JIT) production, but other terms including continuous flow manufacturing (CFM) and pull-through

Ford reduced its inventory by $2 billion from 1979 to 1982 (above, 1987 Taurus).

production (PTP) reflect the same objective. Each requires a tremendous amount of discipline because the program is totally dependent upon an effective coordination of the process and the availability of materials.

If machines are not operable, workers are poorly trained, materials are unavailable or of poor quality, the absence of buffer stocks of inventory brings the production line to a halt. Therefore, pull-through production requires a high degree of stability, reliability, and quality in the manufacturing process. This is very much in contrast with the idea that production is a constant crisis environment. For many manufacturers, expediting orders, changing schedules, and fighting fires are virtually standard operating procedures.

The benefits of pull-through production include the elimination of inventories between stages of production, the reduction of space required to accommodate inventories,

and low material handling and storage expenses. Because it is so tight a system, it forces all the components of the manufacturing process to work together to produce quality goods.

The trend toward flexible flow lines also reflects the emphasis on making the process more flexible, allowing it to produce more than one product on a production line. The implication of this major trend is that a production process need not be dedicated to any particular product.

Henry Ford's assembly line for the Model T was a product flow line, but it was not very flexible. A customer could have any color provided it was black. Today, Nissan produces both cars and trucks, of different colors, and with some variation of components on the same assembly line. Allen-Bradley can produce hundreds of variations of an electrical contactor on one assembly line in its "factory within a factory."

*A*utomation is probably the most visible change taking place in the new manufacturing environment. Some large U.S. manufacturers in the automotive, aerospace, heavy equipment, and high technology industries such as GE, Rockwell International, IBM, Apple Computer, and General Motors have invested heavily in automated equipment to increase quality and productivity and meet the competitive challenge of the global market.

While automation provides significant opportunities to manufacturers, companies should not rely on automation to solve their competitive problems. Rather, automation should be used to leverage the progress made in the areas discussed above. Quality, inventory, and flexible flows require management to address the fundamental issues of how business is conducted. Many companies have in fact realized disappointing returns from automation resulting from poor

Apple Computer has invested heavily in automated equipment to increase production.

planning, neglect of basic shop floor controls, and unrealistic expectations. A more focused organization and a simpler, more streamlined factory removes the temptation to automate a process that should be eliminated.

A typical example is the automation of material handling. Some companies proudly exhibit highly automated material transfer and storage systems that cost millions of dollars to install but are "reaping" tremendous returns. Other companies, instead, proudly exhibit that they have no inventory to store. For these companies, the returns have been realized without the investment.

The investment in automation can be thought of as consisting of three levels: the stand-alone piece of equipment, the cell, and the fully integrated factory. At each level, automation may allow an organization to increase capacity, reduce inventory and costs as well as contribute to the productive aspects of quality, flexibility, reliability, throughput, and delivery.

Representative stand-alone pieces of equipment include CNC (computer numerically controlled) machines, computer-aided design technology, and robots. The nature of most automated pieces of equipment is that they perform a limited number of tasks (often only one) in repetitive operations and/or undesirable work conditions. Given the limited impact on the factory as a whole, the investment is frequently justified on the basis of labor and materials savings. While the generalization may be reasonable, the introduction of automated equipment often can generate benefits that are qualitatively oriented.

Unfortunately, most capital investment analyses do not attempt to quantify the qualitative benefits. These benefits include improved quality, delivery, service and flexibility, reduced product development time, and improved competitive position and can generate significant cost savings and higher sales. Attributing a value of zero to qualitative benefits is clearly less correct than using a reasonable, well-founded estimate. Companies that are quantifying these benefits assert that it is critical to be generally right than absolutely wrong. The new approach to investment evaluation is undoubtedly an area

of significant opportunity for the management accountant.

In one example, the Yamazaki Machinery Company in Japan installed an $18 million flexible manufacturing system. The benefits included: a reduction in machines from 68 to 18, in employees from 215 to 12, in the floor space required for production from 103,000 square feet to 30,000, and in average processing time from 35 days to 1.5.

While traditional capital investment techniques would have considered only the labor savings and the reductions in inventory and equipment, such an analysis would likely provide a return of slightly over 10%, a return unlikely to exceed most companies' established hurdle rates or provide a payback fast enough to justify the investment.[2] Yet, benefits resulting from improved quality, lower process and product variability, greater throughput, and increased schedule attainment clearly need to be considered in an investment of this nature.

Stand-alone pieces of equipment have been steadily introduced into the factory since the seventies. However, the new trend in manufacturing is to integrate machines and systems in an effort to make domestic manufacturing economically viable.

Flexible manufacturing systems, as they commonly are called, produce a particular product or major component from start to finish. A flexible manufacturing system may be a series of electronically interlocked machining centers that perform a set of prescribed operations controlled by a computer using robots or one machine performing a complex series of machining tasks. Flexible manufacturing systems normally provide additional benefits of reduced material handling and work-in-process, as well as in-

creased quality, flexibility, and throughput.

There are already many examples of flexible manufacturing systems in use. One example is GE's Erie, Pa., locomotive plant. A $16 million FMS produces motor frames and gear boxes and has cut throughput times from 16 days to 16 hours.

The highest level of capital investment, is the integrated factory. Examples include Allen-Bradley's World Contactor "factory within a factory" facility in Milwaukee, IBM's Proprinter facility in Charlotte, N.C., Apple Computer's Macintosh plant in Fremont, Calif., and GE's Dishwasher factory in Louisville, Ky.

While automation is not considered the cure-all, neither is the decision to automate a casual alternative. One executive from GE noted that "automation is not a trendy corporate thrust for us. In most of our manufacturing businesses it is survival." GE has realized a competitive advantage through its investments. For example, in its dishwasher plant in Kentucky, management has been able to reduce inventory by 60%, service calls by 53%, cycle time from 5 to 6 days to 18 hours, and increased employee productivity by 25% and production capacity by 20%. Thus, the integrated factory contributes to a company's bottom line on the basis of a significant competitive advantage in terms of product quality, deliverability, and variety, which translates into more sales and lower costs.

Product line organization calls for the scaling down of centralized service departments and reassigning people with specialized skills directly to the product lines. This reorganization results in mini-organizations that focus on a few products.

One company increased manufacturing efficiency by dividing its 12,000-person work force into four separate smaller manufacturing groups concentrating on a limited number of products.

In contrast, the conventional manufacturing organization structure is characterized by a number of centralized service departments—purchasing, production scheduling and inventory control, industrial and manufacturing engineering, maintenance, quality control and personnel—providing support to the various production departments.

The rationale for centralized support functions is that maximizing the parts through economies of scale will maximize the whole. According to Harvard Professor Wickham Skinner, however, "the result more often is a hodgepodge of compromises, a high overhead, and a manufacturing organization that is constantly in hot water with top management." He also noted: "An organization that focuses on a narrow product mix will outperform the conventional plant. Because a focused factory or organization's equipment, supporting systems, and procedures can concentrate on a limited task for one set of customers, its costs and especially its overhead are likely to be lower than those of the conventional plant."[3]

The advantage of a product line organization is the direct identification of the resources required to support a particular product line. Relatively straightforward and easy to manage product lines have limited support resources. Product lines that are more complex have more resources directly assigned to them.

Disaggregating overhead costs helps management understand and control its business better. The typical cost accounting process would have to allocate the service department's costs, by one of several routines, to the production department's. These allocated costs then become a part of the production department's costs. In turn, these costs are assigned to the products going through the department. By the time the allocation process is complete, the final product cost numbers are far removed from the source of the cost and have little value for decision-making purposes.

Unfortunately, these figures often are the basis for out-sourcing production, dropping product lines, or even closing plants. Although product line organizations will not eliminate allocations, they provide a clearer picture of which products use more resources under a disaggregated factory arrangement.

Examples of companies reorganizing their management structure include S.C. Johnson, Hewlett-Packard, and Kollmorgon. S.C. Johnson, the privately held consumer goods company, has increased manufacturing efficiency by dividing its 12,000 person work force in its Racine, Wis. plant into four separate, smaller manufacturing groups concentrating on a limited number of products.

Hewlett-Packard cites people-related factors as a primary reason for going to smaller plants. HP is among a handful of companies that have long held "small is beautiful" and have minimized layers of management, emphasized team approaches to problems, and shortened the lines of communication between departments in order to increase efficiency and profitability.

The *effective use of information technology* is the final major trend in the new manufacturing environment. While many companies have been using information technology for years, advancements in integrated systems allow companies to exert greater control over the factory floor through more flexible, real-time, computer-based communications networks. Better information is obtained faster, and often provides the company with a competitive edge.

While systems for operating control and financial/external reporting are traditionally completely separate systems, the world-class manufacturer needs to use technology to create a single database, maintained on a real-time basis, that can be used for both purposes. This capability is not yet a reality because of the incompatibility of most available systems. However, as equipment and systems are purchased with this objective in mind, manufacturing machines and processes are being linked. This enables CNC machines to communicate between each other and with a master control program. It allows a problem arising at one location in the process to be communicated to other operations, thus preventing a build-up of work-in-process inventory until the problem is corrected.

Computers also are being extensively used to monitor and control operations. Computers, using statistical process control, can automatically monitor a process and make adjustments to ensure the consistency and quality of the output.

An integrated factory, such as Allen-Bradley's World Contactor facility, is dependent upon the computer for guidance. As the hardware becomes increasingly integrated, the computer's ability to communicate with multiple systems and between pieces of equipment becomes essential.

The computer also is being used to generate operational and financial data on what is happening on the factory floor and converting it into useful managerial information, such as units produced, material utilized, scrap, cost by operation, and cost by individual

> *We believe companies should not rely on automation to solve their competitive problems.*

Whirlpool quality products, such as the Electra III refrigerator, have been able to withstand foreign competition.

product, if appropriate. The computer affords management the opportunity to analyze real-time information regarding the inputs to and outputs of the manufacturing process. Through the application of bar codes and other tracking mechanisms, it is possible to record costs on a unit of one basis.

In a highly competitive environment, managers no longer can wait until the end of the month to get a sense of how things are going. Production managers need to know before the end of a period whether a department's scrap rate is significantly out of line with expectations. Also, strategic decisions are often made using data compiled specifically for financial statement purposes. In most cases, this information fails to reflect these economic realities in ways that enable a manager to make well-informed decisions.

Technology also results in substantial productivity savings as well as financial returns. At Exxon USA, getting the right information to the right person at the right time is a major company objective. According to Michael C. Wilser, Exxon's officer automation coordinator, the company able to do this better than its competitors will

achieve a significant strategic advantage in the marketplace.

IMPLICATIONS

Product oriented flow lines, automation, and information technology demand that management accountants reassess the traditional method of process control and product cost determination. Automation and increasing reliance on "information workers" in the factory are removing labor and increasing overhead in product costs, pushing labor based overhead rates to extraordinary heights. Product line organizations may bring many overhead costs closer to the product, but flexible flow lines make traditional allocation methods more unworkable. Certainly, methods for allocating costs to products must change.

Automation is increasing the spread between variable costs and full costs, heightening the need to distinguish between contribution margins and full cost profit margins. Decreased labor and increased process reliability will change the shape of traditional, labor oriented variance analysis. Changing management methods for the control of inventory and quality are going to

force management accountants to give up labor efficiency oriented performance measures; the search for alternative measures of overall process control has already begun in many plants.

The factory of the future requires the accountant to identify and address many nonfinancial areas of manufacturing performance. Measures such as customer complaints, vendor performance, defect free units, cycle time, schedule attainment and others need to be developed to measure the critical factors of quality, service and cost.

Capital investments are more complex and expensive. In the new manufacturing environment, investments also improve quality, lower inventory, improve flexibility, and achieve more effective use of information. Greater emphasis must be placed on identifying and including these intangible benefits in the decision-making process.

Traditional methods of analyzing a company's performance need to change to reflect the changing fundamental characteristics of a business. Financial statements provide a fundamental basis for appraising managerial performance as well as establishing security value. The preparers of financial statement information need to spearhead changes in financial statement presentation that reflect the new manufacturing environment.

Management accountants will play a key role in the turnaround of American manufacturing. But they need to get out into the factory and understand what changes are taking place before redesigning and updating the control and reporting mechanisms that will advance their organizations to world-class status. ∎

[1]Harold K. Sperlich, "The State of Quality in the U.S. Today," *Quality Progress,* April 1985.
[2]Robert S. Kaplan, "Must CIM be Justified by Faith Alone," *Harvard Business Review,* March-April 1986, p. 87. Example cross-referenced to *American Market,/Metalworking News,* October 26, 1981.
[3]Wickham Skinner, "The Focused Factory," *Harvard Business Review,* May-June 1974.

Robert A. Howell, DBA, CMA, is president of Howell Management Corp., and professor of management and accounting at the Graduate School of Business Administration, New York University.
Stephen R. Soucy, MBA, CPA, is a consultant at Howell Management Corporation.

Photo by Steve Niedorf/The Image Bank.

"Automation is increasing the spread between variable costs and full costs."

How Advanced Manufacturing Technologies Are Reshaping Cost Management

Today's cost management systems are failing to provide companies with the financial information they need to manage their factories of the future successfully.

By James A. Brimson

Manufacturers worldwide now find themselves at a crossroad. In order to compete effectively, companies must simultaneously strive to manufacture sophisticated products at an exceptionally low cost while maintaining high quality with outstanding customer service (short lead times). They also must have tremendous flexibility to meet short product life cycles and increased competition from abroad.

The problem facing most manufacturers is that their facilities are not structured to meet these demands, and there are many roadblocks that make the transition to an automated factory difficult. One of the most important but least understood of these roadblocks is current cost management systems. These systems do not provide companies with the financial information necessary to manage the transition to a factory of the future.

Technology: The Problem and the Solution

The reality of the factory of today is that it is significantly different, both physically and functionally, from the factory of the past. The difference will become more acute as factories continue to automate. Here are some of the most significant trends that are reshaping the manufacturing environment.

Advanced manufacturing technologies, through capital decay, are changing the basis of competition in the marketplace.

Companies are becoming increasingly aware that a manufacturing facility can be either a competitive weapon or a corporate millstone. Significant improvements in product and shop floor capabilities can change the basis of competition and force other companies in an industry to improve their performance or risk loss of market share.

The impact of automation on changing the basis of competition is most evident when you consider:

- Improvements in material science and microcomputers have resulted in products with capabilities not achievable without automation;
- Reduction in manufacturing costs will occur when an automated process is substituted for a less efficient, nonautomated process;
- Products with higher levels of quality are possible because of the inherent consistency of automation and improvements in computer-aided engineering;
- Higher levels of reliability are resulting in lower field support costs with better customer service;
- Product delivery lead times are decreasing with the implementation of just-in-time concepts, process rationalization, and other automation projects.

Once unleashed, advanced manufacturing technologies will permanently change the basis of competition in an industry. This relationship of technology to market share can best be illustrated by the capital decay graph (Figure 1).

A technology explosion is accelerating the rate of change in manufacturing and process technology.

A study of the history of manufacturing shows a steady trend of substituting technology for human labor. What is different today is the worldwide explosion of technology which, during the last 30 years, has generated 90% of all current knowledge in engineering and the physical sciences.

The technology explosion is not supposed to abate in the foreseeable future. "There will be more technological change in the next 10 to 20

James A. Brimson is vice president for business development at Computer Aided Manufacturing—International (CAM-I), Arlington, Tex. He is responsible for the cost management systems (CMS) project whose goal is to bring together industrial companies, government agencies, and professional accounting firms to identify the cost management reforms necessary to support an automated factory. The article was submitted through Racine-Kenosha Chapter.

years than has happened in all history," predicts Bruce Merrifield, U.S. Assistant Secretary of Commerce. As a result of this technology explosion, manufacturers are faced with a constantly changing environment and a wide proliferation of technological alternatives, many of which are in varying degrees of "proof of concept."

Product life cycles are decreasing, and the rate of engineering changes is increasing.

The accelerating rate of change in technology is shortening dramatically the life cycles of products and manufacturing facilities. Traditionally, only about 5% of the product life cycle costs have been allocated to the conceptual and validation planning phases. The result has been to focus engineering design on product features while leaving many of the decisions on equipment configuration, operational planning, and organizational issues to be made on an ad hoc basis by manufacturing operations personnel. Today, many foreign competitors spend considerably more money and time in planning. This has often resulted in lower production costs, reduced time from the design to manufacture stage, higher quality, greater flexibility, and lower product life cycle cost. The relationship of life cycle costs is shown in Figure 2.

With shorter product life cycles, there is an increasing need to understand the total product cost over its entire life cycle to determine profitability. It should be the role of cost management systems to provide greater visibility of the impact of design considerations on manufacturing and support costs. Also, the impact of engineering changes on product/process cost should be understood in order to evaluate the need for engineering change.

Local Area Network (LAN) technology coupled with automated parts tracking and recognition technology are improving the availability of accurate data.

In a manufacturing environment with long lead times between processes, an informal, manual information system was sufficient. However, with the introduction of advanced manufacturing technologies has come an increase in the importance of and dependency on computerized information. Companies are realizing that manual data collection can seriously inhibit the success of factory automation management. Manually generated data have questionable reliability, they must be continuously reviewed and corrected, and they do not meet the timeliness needs of an automated process. This latter problem is particularly significant because typically as companies automate, they reduce the production cycle but do not adequately upgrade the timeliness of the information to support the new process. Firms which prosper in a computer-integrated manufacturing (CIM) environment will require a marriage of technical/ engineering competence with rigorous financial monitoring. A computerized cost accounting system will be a requirement for a CIM environment.

While technology is not only the source of the problem, because it forces companies to migrate to a computerized environment, it also is the source of the solution. LANs, automated parts tracking, and recognition technology permit the various components of automation to be linked together for control and communication purposes. Anticipated advancements in LAN technology over the next several years will decrease cost and complexity and increase reliability and flexibility. These improvements will accelerate the implementation of this technology. However, in spite of the technological breakthroughs, most of these data never leave the system and are unused for management purposes except for local process decisions. Thus, while the availability and accuracy of actual data have improved, they have not been integrated into the total manufacturing process.

Advanced manufacturing technologies have traditionally been implemented on an "islands of technology" basis, while future technologies will increasingly require an integrated approach with sig-

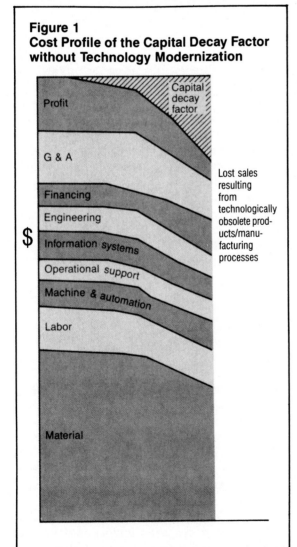

**Figure 1
Cost Profile of the Capital Decay Factor without Technology Modernization**

Profit

Capital decay factor

G & A

Financing

Engineering

$

Information systems

Operational support

Machine & automation

Labor

Material

Lost sales resulting from technologically obsolete products/manufacturing processes

nificant capital investments and long implementation cycles.

Under the traditional environment, manufacturing processes could be incrementally replaced by newer, more efficient processes. In the past, companies had the luxury of being able to gradually modernize their operations. This is no longer the case. Today, companies that develop integrated manufacturing systems must achieve a harmonious flow of materials, tools, parts, and information through the factory. In general, improvements will result from the coupling of a firm's computer and automated manufacturing systems. However, the difficulties of integration compound rapidly with the increased complexity of the interconnections of the components of manufacturing, e.g., physical connections, communication protocols, software, and data.

Also, companies are beginning to recognize that incorporating new technologies into a manufacturing facility will not by itself realize the promises of high technology. Most manufacturing facilities are a product of past unfocused manufacturing decisions. Often, top management is unaware that what may appear to be routine manufacturing decisions, based on incorrect cost information, frequently will limit a company's strategic options by burdening it with facilities, equipment, and personnel that results in a non-competitive posture that may take years to turn around. Thus, it is the role of cost management systems to provide strategic and tactical information.

Manufacturing factors of production are shifting from variable to fixed.

Automation leads to a higher percentage of fixed cost due to its inherent capital intensity. Labor, on the other hand, is largely a variable cost as reflected in the high rates of unemployment during recessionary times. Higher ratios of fixed costs (automation) to variable costs (labor) limit the ability of companies to respond to changes in the economy. Traditional labor-intensive industries have to cut costs during a recession by laying off workers—a luxury not available when managing robots and flexible manufacturing systems.

How Current Trends Affect Cost Management

As a result of these changes in the manufacturing environment, the following cost management issues have become more prominent.

Changing Cost Behavior Patterns. With automation, the behavior patterns of manufacturing cost will change. Some important changes are:

- Decreasing Direct Labor Component. The cost behavior patterns of manufacturing processes are shifting to a lower percentage of direct labor and to a higher percentage of other "indirect"

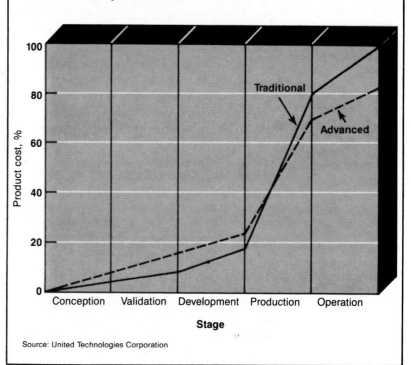

Figure 2
Product Life Cycle Costs

Source: United Technologies Corporation

costs. This trend has resulted in a significant decline in manufacturing processes where the operator controls the pace of the process. It is not uncommon to find that direct labor accounts for only 8%-12% of total cost at many manufacturers. This trend is even more pronounced when one considers current forecasts relating to the factory of the future. In many companies, however, manufacturing overhead continues to be distributed on the basis of direct labor despite the fact that there is no cause-and-effect relationship between labor and overhead.

- Increasing Equipment Component. A significant portion of total product cost is shifting to equipment-related costs as manufacturing facilities become increasingly automated. Coupled with this trend has been a decrease in the technological life of products and processes compared with their physical life.

- Increasing Information Component. With the introduction of advanced manufacturing technologies has come an increased dependency on computerized information. The impact of the information system on product cost is not widely understood in most manufacturing companies. Companies do not have a mechanism to evaluate the value added by information, data validation, maintenance, or the cost of poor decisions based on incorrect data.

Another impact is that many of the information flows that were originally manual must be automated to increase their timeliness. Much of the information that was processed in a batch mode must be processed real time.

The allocation problem is how to select and justify a particular allocation method. Any allocation method is arbitrary in the sense that a company must choose a single method among several potential options. Although choosing a theoretically justified allocation technique has always been a major problem facing manufacturing managers, today's changing cost behavior patterns increase the need for companies continually to reevaluate their basis of allocation.

Failure to change allocation techniques is a major problem for manufacturers. Many companies continue to cling to direct labor-based allocations despite the reality of automation. However, companies should not be trapped into the illusion that changing the basis of allocation (from direct labor to machine hours) will solve all their problems. Changing the allocation base does *nothing* to change the trend from direct to indirect costs.

Cost Classification. Manufacturers are faced with an increasing pool of indirect costs and a decreasing pool of direct costs. However, the determination of whether costs are direct or indirect is often a matter of definition. Clearly an environment with increasing indirect costs indicates the definition of indirect costs must be reviewed.

In a CIM environment, the economics of data collection will be improved as companies implement LANs and automated part tracking systems. With the increased availability and accuracy of shop-floor data, many costs which previously have been considered indirect can be evaluated and managed in a direct manner.

Depreciation Methods. Current depreciation methods based on fixed time recovery make the assumption that value added to the product is independent of individual products and actual utilization during the recovery period. An alternative, which is in accordance with GAAP but not widely used, is to depreciate equipment cost based on actual machine utilization rather than fixed time periods. An advantage of this approach is that it would better match automation expenses to changing economic conditions resulting in the lessening of the impact of economic cycles. Another approach might be to allocate cost on inventory velocity (the time a part is in process) to encourage companies to reduce factory throughput time.

Also, the shorter technological life will force a company to recover the cost of automation in a short time period or make the manufacturing process more flexible and responsive to changing requirements. Companies need visibility into the technological value in addition to the book value of the capital equipment. One step in this direction would be to use the technological life for de-

preciation calculations. Sound accounting requires the equipment life be based on the shorter of tax, technological, or physical life, whichever is less. However, most companies use tax allowable life even though it may be unrealistic.

Life Cycle Reporting. Decreased product life cycles have resulted in less latitude for management error because the cost recovery period is shorter. Current cost management systems are based on "period reporting" and do not provide life cycle reporting. Life cycle reporting would enable management to identify the impact of long-term decisions on product profitability.

Engineering Design Cost Impact. The primary determinants of life cycle costs occur during the engineering design phase, as illustrated in Figure 3. During this phase, companies need to understand the operational and support cost and not focus solely on development and production costs. It is the responsibility of the cost management system to provide this information.

Investment Justification. Many companies are currently struggling with the process of cost justification and benefits tracking of advanced manufacturing technologies. Organizations often religiously adhere to tough ranking methods where the likely costs are matched against the contribution the project is likely to yield. These methodologies often use data that are outside other cost management systems which are not currently providing the information necessary to support the decision-making process. Benefits have been elusive and cost estimates often unrealistic.

Product Costing. In today's environment, product cost information is distorted by burden rates which have become, in many companies, so high as to be almost unmanageable. The problem is made even more severe because many companies cling to a direct labor allocation methodology in spite of the fact that there is simply not enough direct labor to support the method. Some of the symptoms of invalid product cost include:

- The indirect costs far exceed the direct costs (typically direct labor or machine hours), and
- The relationship between the basis of allocation and the indirect costs has become obscure.

Verifiability. The integration of automated processes through LANs will result in fewer physical documents. This so called "paperless" environment will have a significant impact on internal control procedures.

Data Collection and CMS Standards. Management information software designed by one vendor is incompatible with software from other vendors. The solution to this growing "Tower of Babel" is the standard interface for cost management information and automated equipment.

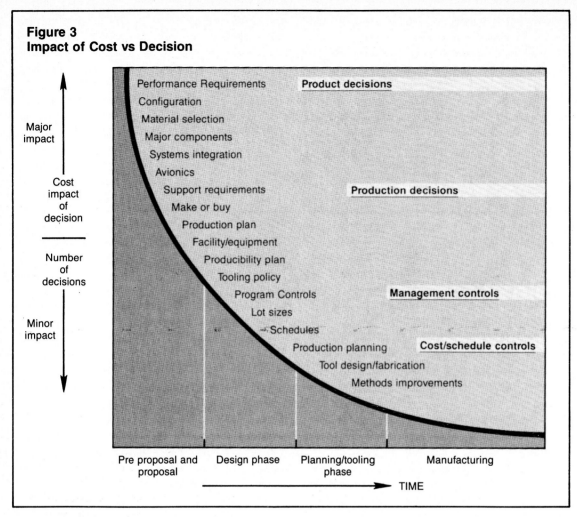

Figure 3
Impact of Cost vs Decision

Need for Strategic Measures. Most cost management systems are historical financial reporting-oriented and do not adequately measure operational performance. The strategic benefits of automation not only mean lower costs, but also improved quality, shortened production cycles, and a greater responsiveness to changing requirements. For example, improved quality opens new markets that demand precision products and gives the manufacturer an edge when competing for old markets.

Traditionally, operational performance measures have been used as an indication of the effectiveness of manufacturing operations. However, the performance measurements typically do not receive the same visibility, either internally within a company or externally as does financial information. It should be the role of the cost management accounting system to ensure that general goals such as "enhanced flexibility" have explicit operational meanings and are reported.

Need for Cost Driver Information. Most cost accounting systems are work order-oriented and do not adequately identify the impact of cost drivers on the manufacturing cost of individual manufacturing processes. Today, the direct labor orientation of most manufacturing managers results in

the attitude that responsibility and organizational structure are synonymous. While this approach is consistent with organizational objectives as expressed in the financial budgets, there is no assurance that the cost centers are organized consistently with manufacturing functions.

It is believed by many that the best way to control costs is to control cost drivers. Examples of cost drivers, as developed by Arthur Andersen in its *Accounting Futures Study,* include: engineering change orders, space utilization, forecast errors/master scheduling changes, inventory levels, product design and lack of interchangeable components, and multiple bills of material.

Future Challenge

Current cost management practices are inappropriate in a highly automated computer-integrated manufacturing environment. While an important first step in solving these problems is made by recognizing the need for change, the solutions to the problem are not as well developed. Change will not come easily. However, if experts from industry, accounting firms, accounting associations such as the NAA, and government agencies, share their views and experiences, I am confident that a solution will be found. □

Section 2

Changes: Factory Automation

Section 2 is the first of four sections that describe recent changes in the manufacturing environment. These changes are representative of the attributes that have come to characterize the new environment of the world-class manufacturer. Section 2 reviews the growth of factory automation and its influence upon future cost accounting systems.

The opening article, by David M. Dilts and Grant W. Russell, describes the "factory of the future" and discusses its financial and economic implications. The authors trace the evolution of factory automation from the standalone numerical control machines of the '50s through the introduction of robotics to the flexible manufacturing systems of the '80s. They illustrate and explain the flexible manufacturing system—an integrated collection of automated production processes, a material transport system, and a system-level controller that produces a flexible variety of products.

Dilts and Russell then proceed to cite the many benefits associated with the adoption of flexible manufacturing system technology, along with several disadvantages. They note that these benefits appear to address the major needs and solve the crucial problems of manufacturers who seek to protect themselves in world-class competition. They predict continued growth, limited only by the number of suppliers currently able to deliver this technology. Dilts and Russell close by discussing the profound effects that the new technology will have on cost accounting methods in the areas of product costing, control, and management decisions.

In an article written several years later, Dilts and Severin B. Grabski discuss the difficulties and benefits of integrating advanced manufacturing technologies (AMTs) and the accounting information system (AIS). They briefly explain many popular AMTs, citing four distinct groupings:

1. Design, such as computer-aided design, computer-aided engineering, computer-aided process planning, and simultaneous engineering;

2. Planning and control, such as material requirements planning, manufacturing resources planning, constraint management, and statistical process control;

3. Execution, such as numerical control, robotics, flexible manufacturing systems, and automated storage and retrieval systems;

4. Overarching, such as total quality control, just-in-time, focused factories, and computer-integrated manufacturing.

The authors review the fundamental differences between the data used by AMT systems and the AIS; the differences are highlighted in a table. Despite these substantive differences in measurement focus, control emphasis, timing, data volume, and flexibility, Dilts and Grabski argue for integration of the systems.

A second table contains examples of the types of manufacturing and accounting concerns that require exchange of information. The authors give case study examples, one in which a cooperative and collaborative effort is working and another in which it is not. Dilts and Grabski believe the benefits to date are just beginning and that the use of knowledge-based systems technology will aid in achieving total system integration.

The final article in this section, by Daniel P. Keegan, Robert G. Eiler, and Joseph A. Anania, discusses the development of an advanced cost management system that is an example of the kind of system needed in world-class organizations. The authors, consultants in a public accounting firm, detail the features of a system developed for the Electronic Systems Division of the U.S. Air Force for use by defense contractors. Some of the cost system features discussed include the focus on prospective costs and their cost drivers, accumulation of product costing on a part-by-part level, capturing cost at the operational process level, and separation of manufacturing-tracking from product cost-tracking functions.

The authors provide many useful visual aids, including a diagram of the cost buildup process, a listing of cost drivers, a partial description of the subsystems required, and an outline of the planning process for system installation. A final summarization reviews the objectives of the advanced cost management system.

Additional Readings from *Management Accounting*

Akers, Michael D. and Grover L. Porter, "Expert Systems for Management Accountants," March 1986, pp. 30-34.

Biggs, Joseph R. and Ellen J. Long, "Gaining the Competitive Edge with MRP/MRP II," May 1988, pp. 27-32.

Keys, David E., "Six Problems in Accounting for N/C Machines," November 1986, pp. 38-47.

Lammert, Thomas B. and Robert Ehrsam, "The Human Element: The Real Challenge in Modernizing Cost Systems," July 1987, pp. 32-37.

Mielcarz, Richard J. and Aida Shekib, "Telecommunications for the Factory Floor," April 1990, pp. 42-44.

Schwarzbach, Henry R., "The Impact of Automation on Accounting for Indirect Costs," December 1985, pp. 45-50.

Accounting
Get ready for the robots.
for the
Because they're coming.
Factory
They're overturning hallowed
of the Future
cost concepts in their wake.

By David M. Dilts and Grant W. Russell

Rapid growth in manufacturing automation is challenging the way North American manufacturing conducts its business. While most recognize that manufacturing automation is having a major impact upon marketing, finance, research and development, and, of course, production management, few realize there also will be a substantial impression upon management accounting.

Robotics, automated material handling, and computer-controlled machine tools are all part of this changing technolgy. The integration of this technology into a unified production system in order to manufacture economically viable medium-sized production volumes of a variety of parts is what is known as flexible automation.

Although much of flexible factory automation is still in the design stage, there are an adequate number of flexible manufacturing systems in operation to forecast with some accuracy the effect of this revolutionary technology upon the financial control aspects of the manufacturing sector. Currently, most documentation on flexible automation describes the physical and engineering aspects of the technology and not its financial and

economic implications. It is essential that management accountants be aware of this new technology because it is the first wave of the total reorganization of the manufacturing function of the firm. Often referred to as "the Factory of the Future," this new manufacturing technology will soon proliferate and it presents an urgent challenge to management accountants to understand and incorporate within their systems.

What Is FMS?

Automation is not new in the manufacturing environment. Numerical control machines have been extensively used since the 1950s. These machines, which are machine tools run by programs typically stored on punched tape, are standalone machines; each numerical control machine operates independently of all other machines in the production process. The introduction of robotics and computer-controlled materials handling systems into the manufacturing process permitted the linking of these standalone machines into a complete flexible manufacturing system (FMS). More precisely, an FMS consists of an integrated collection of automated production processes (which may consist of numerical control machines and robots), a material transport system (which typically consists of an automated transfer line and some use of robotics), and a system level controller (which usually consists of one or more computers) to manufacture efficiently a flexible variety of products. Figure 1 is a schematic.

The extent of the variety of products depends upon the particular FMS. The products, however, must share certain broad characteristics that allow them to be grouped within a particular family. These characteristics include size, type of material, type of operations to be performed, and required precision of finished goods. It is expected that with newer generations of FMS these constraints will become weakened. Nevertheless, the major strength of an FMS is its ability to manufacture a "family of products," as opposed to only a very narrow range of products. For example, at the General Electric plant in Erie, Pennsylvania, diesel engines of substantially different sizes can be manufactured on the same automated production line, without substantial retooling and setups.

Various types of material transport systems have been used in manufacturing since the 1920s. These transport systems have been used primarily for high volume, single-product, fixed-automation manufacturing. New developments in technology have permitted the application of automated transfer systems to lower volume and heterogeneous products. The most notable change in transfer systems has been the addition of pick-and-place robots. These robots, under central computer control, are able to manipulate a wide variety of raw materials and work-in-process. For example, pick-and-place robots are used to move items from the automated transfer cart to the appropriate machine fixture. When the process is complete, the product is retrieved from the machine and placed back on the transfer cart.

Coordinating this combination of equipment is the central computer controller. This controller performs tasks such as specifying the exact order of manufacturing, programming the appropriate machines to perform the manufacturing operation required, verifying the quality of the process, and gathering a wide range of system performance data. To provide this extensive degree of control requires several different levels of manufacturing computers and microcomputers arranged in a hierarchy. Figure 2 shows the flow of information in a company that has FMS technology in place. Such a hierarchy has only recently become economically feasible with the development of industrial microcomputers.

Most FMS installations have focused on the fabrication of precision metal parts and components that have high product diversity. For example, the Heavy Machinery Center at the Ingersoll-Rand plant in Roanoke, Virginia, is capable of handling 500 different machine tool parts, and of accommodating as many as 16 different part designs at any one time. Sperry Vicker has been using an FMS to produce hydraulic pump cover castings in 25 different sizes and shapes. Sunstrand Corp. eliminated 100 conventional metal working machines, replacing them with 10 computer-linked numerical control machines, and the new system can now process five times as many different part designs at twice the volume. In Japan, Fujitsu Fanuc Ltd. is one of the most advanced users of automation in the world, with an automated factory producing servomotors running for three shifts, of which two are almost completely unmanned. (A servomotor is the small motor used in robots.)

The characteristic common to all of these installations is that they are medium-volume, non-homogeneous production processes. Typically, volumes of 500 to 100,000 parts per year would be considered medium volumes, but, of course, this label would depend upon the manufacturing process being considered.

Factors Influencing FMS Growth

Over the past decade, North American manu-

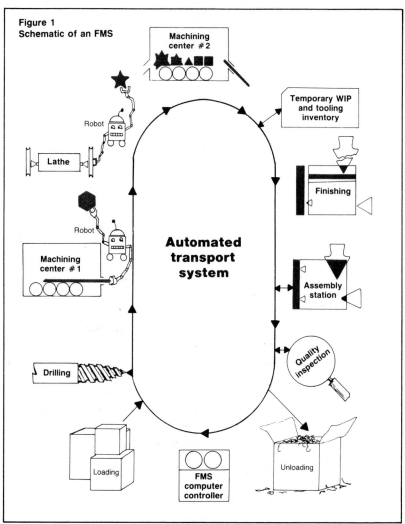

Figure 1
Schematic of an FMS

Machining center #2

Robot

Lathe

Robot

Machining center #1

Drilling

Loading

FMS computer controller

Unloading

Automated transport system

Temporary WIP and tooling inventory

Finishing

Assembly station

Quality inspection

David M. Dilts is an assistant professor of Operations Management and Management Information Systems at Michigan State University. He has a Ph.D. degree from the University of Oregon. This article was submitted through the Lansing-Jackson Chapter.

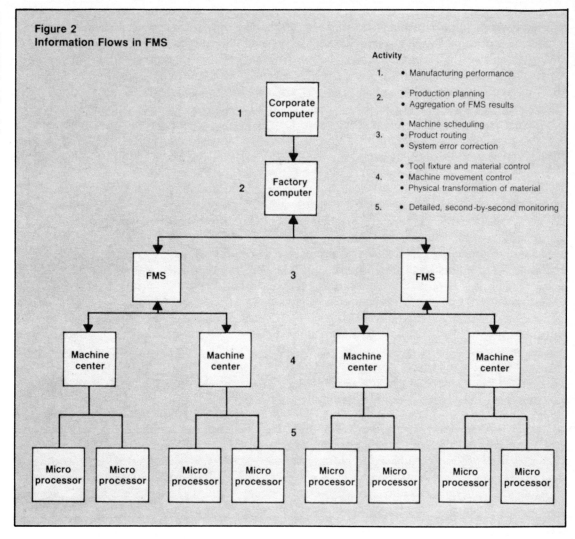

Figure 2
Information Flows in FMS

Activity

1. • Manufacturing performance

2. • Production planning
   • Aggregation of FMS results

3. • Machine scheduling
   • Product routing
   • System error correction

4. • Tool fixture and material control
   • Machine movement control
   • Physical transformation of material

5. • Detailed, second-by-second monitoring

facturers have experienced a number of economic traumas which have spurred them to rethink traditional manufacturing methods and technologies. Traditional manufacturing thought has separated production into two major categories, manual and fixed automation, and developed distinct technologies for each category. Table 1 provides a summary comparison of Manual Production, and Fixed, and Flexible Automation Production Systems.

These categories, however, have been blurred as manufacturers have sought out new ideas to protect themselves against economic adversities. Beginning with scarcity of raw materials such as petroleum, these shocks have included rapidly expanding competition from foreign competitors (Japan in particular), major declines and growth spurts in the national economy, increasing consumer quality awareness, and increasing governmental involvement in manufacturing through environmental protection and equal employment constraints. FMS technology is seen by many major corporations as a major contributor to the solution of these crucial problems because FMSs address the major needs of manufacturing

organizations in a volatile economy. For example, FMSs are noted for providing the following benefits:

1. Increased variety of output as compared to fixed automation without the low utilization typical of job shop systems.
2. Wider range of economically viable manufacturing volumes. If the cost-volume relationships for the three manufacturing methods of manual, fixed, and flexible automation are compared, you will discover that FMSs are the most cost-effective over the substantial middle range.
3. Increased product quality due to accuracy and repeatability of the manufacturing process.
4. Reduced machine setup times needed to initiate the manufacturing of a new product since the machines are more flexible and the computer controller can schedule the appropriate combination of products to reduce the number of tool changes required.
5. No learning curve effect due to reduction in direct labor and the consistency of the ma-

chine operations.

6. Reduced lead times to supply customer demands due to the reduction in setup times.
7. Reduced direct labor costs by using more capital equipment to replace labor.
8. Diminished work-in-process inventories resulting from reduced setup times and reduced lead times necessary to meet customer demands.
9. Increased machine utilization resulting from greater versatility of equipment and central computer scheduling of the process.
10. Lower physical space requirements for the total manufacturing plant because of reductions in inventory, reductions in the number of machines required, and the closer physical proximity possible with unmanned machines.
11. Reduction in capital cost of human environmental protection within the manufacturing setting; also, reduction in capital cost compared with fixed automation because of higher machine utilization.
12. Increased ability to sustain production when a single machine or group of machines breaks down, as the central computer schedules around it.
13. Quicker responses to changes in demand because changes in machine operations require only minor software or tooling changes.

While these factors make the acquisition of an

FMS seem very attractive, there are some disadvantages that must be looked at carefully:

1. FMSs have a capital cost in excess of that required for a manual system.
2. Worker resistance may be high due to fear of loss of employment.
3. There is an absence of expert knowledge in the field, particularly by supporting professions and occupations such as management accounting.
4. The lack of a communication standard for information flows between machines within the FMS.

Nevertheless, the rate of growth in FMS installations over the coming decade is expected to be high. This growth rate, however, is lower than what might be expected because of the absence of a large number of experienced manufacturers in the field. Current manufacturers include: General Electric, Cincinnati Milacrom, and Kearney & Trecker. General Motors recently has indicated that it will also become active in supplying this technology.

In addition to complete production facilities using FMSs, various degrees of application of FMS technology can be found. Although the Erie Locomotive Division of General Electric operates on the basis of FMS technology, the other divisions employ traditional manufacturing and assembly

Grant W. Russell, RIA, is an assistant professor of accounting at the University of Waterloo, Waterloo, Canada. He has an MBA degree from McMaster University.

Table 1
Comparison of Manual, Fixed Automation, and FMS

Factor	Manual	Fixed automation	FMS
Number of kinds of products	Many	Only one	Several
Viable volumes	Low	High range	Middle
Product quality	Varies	Tightly constrained	Consistent
Setup times	High (learning curve)	Very high	Short
Learning curve effect	Substantial	Depends on degree of automation	None
Lead times (per unit)	Usually high	Moderate	Moderate/low
Direct labor cost (per unit)	High	Low	Very low
Direct labor cost (in total)	High	High	Very low
Inventories	RM high WIP high	RM high WIP high	RM high WIP low
Machine utilization	Low	High	High
Space required	Extensive	Extensive	Moderate
Capital cost	Low	High	High
Sensitivity to breakdown	Low	High	Low
Responsiveness to changes in demand	High	Low	High

techniques. Moreover, FMS technology does not necessarily have to be applied to the total manufacturing facility. An FMS can be just one component of the entire manufacturing system. For example, in one plant in Japan, the FMS is one part of a manufacturing system that includes fabrication and assembly of finished products.

Cost Characteristics of FMS

Some of the characteristics that make an FMS attractive will have profound effects on the controllership and cost accounting functions. We will examine each of these characteristics and their ef-

fects on the areas of product costing, control, and management decisions. Much research remains to be done in determining how management should adapt to these changes in technology.

REDUCTION OF DIRECT LABOR COST

Management goals in manufacturing in recent years have focused upon decreasing the amount of direct labor as a component of total cost. Wage and benefit costs for direct labor have continued to climb, and the cost of providing suitable environment protection has escalated despite reductions in direct labor hours. In an FMS the direct labor cost is almost totally eliminated. The labor cost that remains in an FMS system primarily is made up of the cost of individuals performing initial machine, tool and raw material loading, but only for a single shift of a three-shift operation. The other two shifts, with respect to direct labor, are operated unattended; that is, there are no machine operators, loaders or quality control personnel on the shop floor.

As a result, there are a number of product costing consequences. First, absorption costing becomes the only meaningful costing approach. The All Fixed Company envisioned by Raymond Marple 30 years ago,[1] describing a hypothetical company which had only fixed costs, has become

more than just a classroom exercise. Basing a product cost on a variable cost basis means in essence costing the product only on materials cost, because the labor component associated with FMS is largely fixed.

Second, the use of direct labor hours or direct labor cost for purposes of overhead application in absorption costing situations is no longer reasonable. Historically, labor-based manufacturing systems collected data routinely on labor hours and labor costs, while machine hours and machine costs were collected only by engineers. There were several reasons for this. Labor information was used for payroll purposes. Labor standards were developed using this data, and compared against them. Labor costs were a major component of the product cost as well.

With an FMS, machine and product-centered data are routinely collected for use by the system in order for the system to be properly scheduled and maintained. Thus, the process of obtaining and using this already available data for accounting purposes is relatively simple. (See Figure 2 for an example of how machine information is collected with the Information System.) Also, with the major reduction or elimination of direct labor cost, this machine time and cost information becomes the only substantive and reasonable application base available for product costing.

There are also other more long-range implications to this reduction in direct labor. For example, learning curves (which rely upon human experiential learning) will no longer have any significance at the machine level. Once the system has learned the method to perform an operation, the FMS will repeat the task *identically* each time. (Learning curves again will become important when artifically intelligent FMS become available.) In the area of labor reporting, an FMS will not require time clocks, time cards, manual job tickets, and other source documents.

INDIRECT LABOR AND OVERHEAD

Coupled with the decline of direct labor costs is the increase of the factory burden or overhead. This increase, while taking many forms, will primarily involve the addition of highly paid professional and support staff. There are two primary functions of this support staff: monitoring and maintaining the FMS. Regardless of how automated an FMS becomes, it always requires supervision. Typically, the monitoring aspect of an FMS requires only the dispatching of mainte-

Machinist manually reprograms numerical controls on a boring mill in the FMS to temporarily isolate it from the system for maintenance. Production is automatically rescheduled by the executive computer to use the remaining stations.

nance personnel to correct come minor mishap. The maintenance support staff, however, is used primarily for pre-planned preventive maintenance. Although the FMS can perform control functions such as calculating and compensating for machine tool wear, the FMS cannot perform properly without sophisticated, routinely scheduled preventive maintenance. There are three principal reasons for this emphasis upon the maintenance function. A well-functioning system is necessary for guaranteeing that the system continues to produce a mix of products with consistent quality. Also, maintenance is required to minimize unscheduled machine downtime and to aid in the maximization of machine utilization. Finally, damage to complex machinery can result from the lack of proper servicing.

As the percentage of overhead to total product cost continues to climb in FMS and other manufacturing systems, the task of the management accountant in controlling this cost becomes more pressing. Breaking out machine cost separates out one major contributing factor from an otherwise amorphous cost category. Previous articles[2] have made suggestions concerning the recognition of the fourth cost of manufacturing (machine cost), but so far few (if any) implementations have been reported. Machine cost has been simply lumped together with general overhead.

CONTROL OF COSTS

One of the significant changes in the control process generated by FMS technology is the need to provide instantaneous feedback on the production process. The management accountant's normal variance analysis, done on a daily or weekly basis, is outmoded in an FMS. Inventory control also is drastically changed because Work-In-Process is directly under machine control. Thus, the controller does not need to be concerned with hoarding and the private inventories typical of manual systems, and because there is flexibility in the scheduling of machines, the WIP necessary for the continuous operation of the system is dramatically reduced. Finished goods inventories also become smaller, because the long-term handling of finished goods becomes more expensive than the short-term production of small quantities. In the past, many inventories were held simply because there was an economic production quantity. Thus the production of a few items meant the production of many, and a continuing investment in inventory.

Inherent in an FMS installation is a planned reduction in setup times. Because the primary purpose of an FMS is flexibility, this requires rapid and accurate machine setups. There have been several cases where the installation of an FMS has resulted in major reductions in setup time. For example, a setup at the General Electric locomotive plant which used to take 16 days is now completed in 16 hours. At another plant, setup time was reduced from 40 hours to eight minutes. These major reductions in setup time allow for: faster response to changing market conditions; reduced lead times necessary to meet demands; reduced economic production quantities; and, as a result, reduced finished goods inventory.

THE NEED FOR CONTROL
OVER THE PRODUCTION MIX

The installation of an FMS forces the adoption of a unique control variable. In order to achieve high utilization of the FMS, there must be sufficient diversity in the product mix to ensure that all machines are being used to maximize total system utilization. This product mix diversity is labelled "requisite variety" in the manufacturing literature. From an accounting perspective, mix variance has traditionally been concerned with the effect on contribution margin resulting from changes in sales mix from some predetermined standard mix. A production mix variance in an FMS environment is concerned with the proper mix of products to manufacture. Either too wide or too narrow a mix of products results in a reduc-

---

Table 2
Variance Calculations for Production Mix Variance

A production mix variance might be calculated by determining a cost of systems utilization. Because an inappropriate product mix will constrain the system and reduce the average utilization of all the machines, the appropriate variance might be:

$$\left(\frac{\text{Actual average utilization}}{\text{Standard average utilization}} - 1 \right) \times \text{total contribution margin}$$

The variance would then indicate the changes in contribution margin resulting from producing a variety of products which were nonstandard.

---

tion in total systems utilization. With too diverse a product mix an excessive amount of time is spent in setting up the machinery. Conversely, too narrow a product mix requires the high utilization of only certain of the machines within the FMS, resulting in the reduction of total system utilization. With a narrow product mix fixed automation is a more appropriate technology.

It should be noted that a production mix variance in an FMS environment is not a material mix nor a yield variance as conventionally defined. It is a new variance that will be required by management accountants in order to quantify and control the financial impact of deviations from the requisite variety of the system (See Table 2).

THE IMPACT ON QUALITY ASSURANCE COSTS

Traditionally, the majority of quality assurance

costs have been spent in verifying that the finished manufactured products conform to quality standards. In an FMS environment, the system ensures accurate conformance to finished product standards. One would assume that the cost of quality assurance would be reduced. In actuality, this does not occur. In a labor-intensive manufacturing environment, the machine operators can adapt to variations in incoming parts and raw materials quality. An FMS environment does not afford this latitude. Hence, the cost of quality assurance previously expended to verify the acceptability of finished products is now expended on verifying the acceptability of incoming raw materials.

In this new environment, the issues of spoilage

An FMS will not require time clocks, time cards, manual job tickets or other source documents.

---

and shrinkage become dramatically reduced. Because of the accuracy and repeatability of the system, the rates of spoilage and shrinkage are known with near certainty and the need to calculate materials mix variances is marginal.

Changes in the Capital Acquisition Decision

The decision to acquire an FMS is substantially different from the decision to acquire other manufacturing equipment. Some significant differences:

1. A more stable cash flow. Cash flows are a function of the salability of the products produced. An FMS has much greater ranges of products which can be manufactured than a fixed automation system. As a result, both cyclical and counter-cyclical products can be manufactured, and the portfolio of items to be sold can be diversified to provide a stable cash inflow.
2. A change in the priority of qualitative variables in the capital acquisition considerations. In an FMS, the qualitative variables of product quality, product flexibility, and rapid response time to changing market demands are critical.
3. A change in the determination of usable equipment life. Previously, equipment life was calculated on the functional life of the machine, that is, until the machine could no longer produce a

usable product. This life span concept is now replaced by a technological life span. In this situation, the appropriate life span for the acquisition decision is the time until the next technological breakthrough. This life span is dramatically shorter than the functional life span in today's rapidly changing technological environment.

4. A change in the focus of the capital acquisition. Again, because of the rapidly changing technological environment, the capital acquisition process is no longer used for evaluating new equipment within some firms. Increasingly, organizations in the forefront of manufacturing technology are using the procedures developed for capital acquisition to justify the retention of equipment rather than the acquisition of new equipment. The assumption underlying the change is that equipment should be replaced, unless it can be demonstrated that the retention will not result in foregone profits.

'Automate, Emigrate, or Evaporate'

North American manufacturing has a new tool to assist it in manufacturing. FMS technology provides a means of maintaining production within North America. Without automation, prospects for survival look dismal. As one major manufacturer has stated, the choices are three: "Automate, Emigrate or Evaporate."

Pressure on profit margins will continue as developing countries fight for market share by offering low-cost labor. Survivors in the manufacturing sector will have to process cost information in a manner that provides very accurate costs for competitive bidding, pricing, and management decisions. To provide accurate cost information, management accountants must do their part to understand the economic, financial, and control aspects of this new technology.

Management accountants must ensure that they continue to provide information from within the manufacturing process despite the technological impetus that could make manufacturing a black box. If controllers are not prepared to become actively involved in supplying management with financial expertise in the new manufacturing environment, the role of the controller will diminish dramatically as management turns to other professionals for the needed information. □

[1]Raymond P. Marple "Try This on Your Class, Professor," *The Accounting Review*, Vol. XXXI, No. 3, July 1956, pp.492-497.
[2]For example, see Henry R. Schwarzbach and Richard G. Vangermeersch, "Why We Should Account for the Fourth Cost of Manufacturing," *Management Accounting*, July 1983, pp. 24-30.

Advanced Manufacturing Technologies:
WHAT THEY CAN OFFER MANAGEMENT ACCOUNTANTS

The greatest benefit is better input for decisions.

BY DAVID M. DILTS
AND SEVERIN V.
GRABSKI, CMA

Advanced manufacturing technologies (AMTs) have become so prevalent in industry that accountants have begun to take note of all the data these systems provide. They have assumed that manufacturing and accounting systems can share the same data and information at all levels and that everyone can benefit from this sharing.

But this is not necessarily the case. Often it is difficult to use manufacturing data within the current accounting system, and the manufacturing and accounting functions do not always see the benefit of the sharing. The nature of advanced manufacturing technologies is one explanation.

AMTs can be divided into four types: design, planning and control, execution, and overarching (see Table 1). The design aspect concentrates on product design through computer-aided design (CAD). CAD becomes computer-aided engineering (CAE) when it is extended to include design evaluation and testing. CAE allows rapid testing of designs for various performance characteristics. It has shortened dramatically the time from initial to final product design. In more advanced systems, testing for the manufacturability of a design has been incorporated into the process through "design for manufacturability" or "simultaneous engineering." These procedures allow companies to design the product and the process by which to manufacture it simultaneously. The final step in the product design procedure is developing process plans that detail the exact steps required to produce the product for the manufacturing floor personnel.

With the product design and process plans completed, the next phase is to plan the inventory requirements and control incoming customer orders for the product.

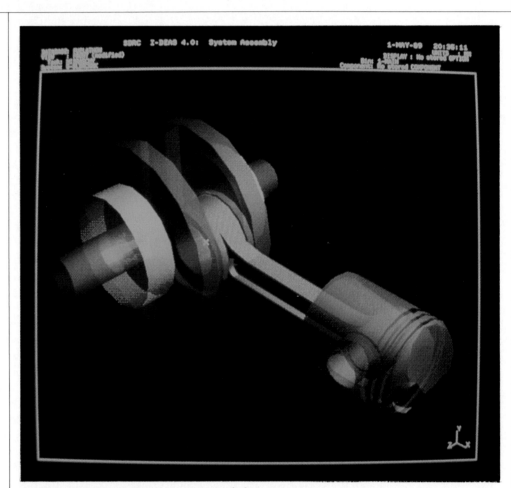

Testing a design is quick with computer-aided engineering.

This planning and control aspect of manufacturing has the closest links with accounting. In today's manufacturing environment, discrete manufacturing units typically are controlled by some form of material requirements planning (MRP) or manufacturing resources planning (MRP II). These methods "explode" a customer order into its component parts so inventory levels and expected delivery times can be predicted and controlled.

Two additional control techniques are constraint management and statistical process control (SPC). Constraint management controls the manufacturing process by identifying and managing bottlenecks (constraints) within the manufacturing system. SPC uses statistical analysis on the shop floor to identify and correct out-of-control production machines or processes quickly.

With the product design completed and orders for the product in hand, the third major area of advanced manufacturing technology is execution—converting raw material into finished product. The major technologies include machining processes (numerical control, computer numerical control, and direct numerical control machines), material movement, pick-and-place robots, (automated guided vehicles and automated storage and retrieval systems), and the blending of the two (flexible manufacturing systems, cellular manufacturing).

The final area of advanced manufacturing concerns those techniques that are global in context or content. They are called overarching technologies because of their total organization perspective and include group technology, computer-integrated manufacturing (CIM), total quality control (TQC), and focused factories. Just-in-time (JIT) manufacturing typifies such ideas. Beginning with product design and continuing to execution, manufacturing JIT methodically identifies and eliminates waste. It reduces machine setup times, accepts only perfect incoming raw material and zero deviation from standards, and calls for small lot sizes and value-added product design. The overarching techniques are so all-encompassing that they commonly are thought of as "philosophies" rather than procedures.

REQUIREMENT DIFFERENCES

The data needed by AMT systems differ fundamentally from the data used by traditional accounting and management information systems (AIS). Man-

ufacturing AIS are based on transaction-oriented data, data that can be aggregated and classified according to the traditional chart of accounts model. Unfortunately, the AMT data cannot be classified this way. Table 2 shows the differences in more detail.

The primary measurement basis also is radically different. Accounting is the only place where the primary measurement focus is on dollars and other financial measures. In the realm of AMTs, cost is considered, but it is not the driving force. Rather, the focus is on functionality, quality of the product that could be produced, the quantity of the product, the time to change production runs, or the ability to improve on-time delivery. These factors, which are critical in making the correct manufacturing decisions, may be obscured by a focus on dollars, particularly if the dollar figures are developed by a traditional cost accounting system.

The control emphasis also differs in AMTs and accounting systems. Accounting systems basically are feedback systems, and the expectation is that corrections will be made after the reporting period—a day, week, month, or year. Most AMT systems are designed to function in an opposite manner. Primarily they are preventive in nature, with on-line, real-time responses sometimes required. If a machine tool or robot is out of

---

TABLE 1/AMT TECHNOLOGIES

A. Design
- Computer-Aided Design (CAD)
- Computer-Aided Engineering (CAE)
- Computer-Aided Process Planning (CAPP)
- Design for Manufacturability and Assembly

B. Planning and Control
- Material Requirements Planning (MRP)
- Manufacturing Resources Planning (MRP II)
- Statistical Process Control (SPC)
- Constraint Management

C. Execution
- Numerical Control (NC, CNC, DNC)
- Robotics
- Automated Guided Vehicles (AGVs)
- Flexible Manufacturing System (FMS)
- Automated Storage & Retrieval System (ASRS)

D. Overarching
- Total Quality Control (TQC)
- Just-in-Time (JIT)
- Focused Factory
- Computer-Integrated Manufacturing (CIM)

TABLE 2/HOW AMTs AND ACCOUNTING USE DATA

	Design	Planning	Execution	Accounting
Primary measurement	Functionality	On-time delivery	Quantity, quality	Dollars
Primary control method	Preventive	Preventive	Preventive	Feedback
Timing of correction	On-line	Real-time	Subsecond response	End-of-period
Timing of information	On-line	On-line	On-Line, real-time	Batch
Quantity of data	Moderate	Moderate	Enormous	Moderate
Location of flexibility	At workstation	At planning system	At each process	At system level
Exception management	For each design	Expediting	SPC, machine	Variance analysis
Decision focus	Product	Plant level	Shop floor	Firm level floor
Hardware platform	Specialized workstation	Dedicated minicomputer	Dedicated minicomputer	Traditional mainframe

control, it needs to be stopped immediately, not at the end of a period or shift, or an entire shift's production may become scrap.

The direct use of manufacturing data by accounting brings another control consideration. Manufacturing data collection systems do not include any of the typical accounting control structures for external verification. Accountants should be reluctant to have these data commingled with "controlled data."

The volume of data generated by the two systems varies tremendously. As indicated in Table 3, the data requirements for one completely integrated system would be more than 309 billion characters. With subsecond response time comes subsecond data collection, and the sheer volume of raw data from even the simplest plant floor could quickly overwhelm the typical accounting information system.

The two systems also vary as to flexibility. The AMTs generally are very "fluid," changing to fit the need, while the typical accounting information system is static over time. There is little substantive difference between the cost system for a manufacturing concern at the turn of the century and now—the major difference is in the technology, not in the system. In addition, the accounting system tends to focus at the total system level. The focus of AMT systems, on the other hand, varies depending upon whether they are primarily design, execution, or planning systems. In design systems, changes are allowed at the individual engineering work-station level. In execution systems, changes are made at each processing point, and in planning systems, during the planning process. Accounting systems, however, are not as flexible. Changes to them generally must be approved at the top organizational level and can take months or years to be implemented.

The flexibility issue depends directly on the decision focus. The focal point of design tools is the product under design, a very narrow focus. The shop floor is the primary focal point for execution systems. Planning systems are aligned more closely to accounting systems, as their focus tends to be more global. Accounting systems are the most global because they must be able to provide data for organization-wide decisions. The level of detail and the amount of data used in design and execution AMTs would overwhelm a firm-wide system and obscure important details.

BENEFITS OF INTEGRATION

Given the control and data requirement differences between manufacturing and accounting information, it is natural to question whether accounting and manufacturing information systems should be integrated. This question could be addressed on several levels, from the highly detailed ("manually entering manufacturing computer data into the accounting system is wasteful") to the philosophical ("it is naturally good for systems to be integrated"). However, the most meaningful consideration for management accounting is the potential impact on decision making for both manufacturing managers and accountants.[1]

Table 4 summarizes some of the significant decisions that require exchange of information between accounting and manufacturing. Critical to manufacturing decision makers is the eventual cost impact of their

TABLE 3/DATA REQUIREMENTS FOR AMT	
Product planning and CAD	7 billion characters
Mfg. planning & purchasing	4 billion characters
Order management & MRP	44 billion characters
Shop floor reporting	127 billion characters
Machine level data	More than 127 billion characters
TOTAL	More than 309 billion characters

This was for only *one* strategic business unit.

Source: R.I. Benjamin, "Information Technology in the 1990s: A Long-Range Planning Scenario," *MIS Quarterly*, Vol. 6, No. 2, June 1982, pp. 11-31.

decisions. Designing a unique product for a customer, rescheduling an order, or choosing an alternate routing for a product has a direct impact on the profitability and performance evaluation of a manufacturing manager. These are decisions made every day, and manufacturing managers require better information in order to make more informed decisions.

Accounting also requires information from the manufacturing environment. Top management needs to be assured that AMT processes are under control and that the manufacturing side is making the most effective decisions. Consequently, the manufacturing data need to be integrated into the overall financial planning and decision-making data. The accounting and auditing functions need to be able, first, to verify that the data generated and collected by the manufacturing process are valid, and, second, to aid management in determining if the manufacturing function is under control. In order for both manufacturing and accounting to benefit from the union of their diverse databases, joint data collection and control methods must be developed. The controls and audit trails must be designed into the system rather than added as an afterthought.

In addition, the accounting function must begin to "sell" the joint benefits that would accrue to the manufacturing manager. The accountant and auditor traditionally have worn the "black hat" in the eyes of manufacturing. Accountants both rightly and wrongly have been accused of focusing only on dollar amounts, of using outmoded evaluation techniques, and of missing the important manufacturing issues such as quality.[2] Manufacturing managers must share some of the blame for not educating accountants as to the important factors.

TWO EXAMPLES

An example of well-conceived collaboration and cooperative effort on the part of top management, accounting, and manufacturing is the pilot project of a major manufacturer. The intent is to run three shifts in this facility, two manned and one unmanned, with robots. The plant operation information will be sent to a supervisory station on the second floor overlooking the shop floor. The system attendant loads the raw material and verifies its quality, the only quality check performed. The system will be able to track part and tool operations. If a machine breaks down and if a minor change is required, the system will attempt to reschedule around the cell or will prompt the supervisor for the revised production routing. The system also will track tool wear, and some pieces of equipment automatically will change the worn parts. On other pieces of equipment, the wear will be noted, and the maintenance staff or operator will be prompted to change the worn parts.

This system was formulated under the just-in-time concept. When parts are received from the supplier factory, they are placed manually in specially designed containers for passing through the system. In this way, each part can be tracked based on location in the container, machines used, and operations performed. Even though each container can hold 52 parts, the "batch size is one part," and every individual part is tracked.

A basic concept is that the data will be entered once into the system and then will be available to everyone. The managerial accounting reports are expected to use data from the AMT. The auditors were involved in the development of the system and did not have any major reservations about the adequacy of built-in controls; they were assured that the system outputs would be verifiable. The overhead rates for production use machine hours rather than direct labor hours as the basis for applying overhead because automated facilities have very little, if any, direct labor.

The various functional areas (accounting, industrial engineering, plant supervision) are cooperating in this facility, probably because of the "shared fate" mentality, the personnel themselves, and the fact that the project is "special." Even so, there appear to be some integration difficulties, mostly because of the differences between manufacturing and accounting data requirements.

We visited another facility that was touted as a "state-of-the-art" factory, also developed following the JIT concept. In this second facility the shop floor data generation and usage and the accounting and management information systems were completely independent. It was as if a wall had been built, with manufacturing on one side and accounting on the other. The two groups cooperated very little, and the facility was well behind production projections although it had been in operation for several years. The failure of accounting and manufacturing to communicate appeared to be a major factor.

FUTURE NEEDS

The pilot manufacturing facility is an excellent example of how manufacturing and accounting can integrate the execution and planning levels of AMTs with the accounting information system. This is an important step, but only the first step. Even the pilot facility did not combine all phases of AMT; the product design area was not included. This area also would benefit from better integration with the accounting information system so that the products could be costed out during the design stage. If this occurs, products that are technologically feasible but economically infeasible would be noticed during the design stage so that economically feasible components could be used. This would shorten the development effort, response time, and time to market for the firm.

A potential approach to the integration of the diverse data types and databases among the AMT types and the accounting information system would be to use knowledge-based systems technology. This procedure also could be done to verify the data generated by the AMTs prior to incorporating them into the accounting information system.

Much has been accomplished in the integration of accounting and manufacturing data, but the benefits attained so far are only the tip of the iceberg. Many more rewards await the organizations that complete the merging of the accounting and manufacturing information systems. ∎

TABLE 4/WHY INTEGRATE MANUFACTURING AND ACCOUNTING DATA?

Manufacturing Concerns:

In design:
How much does the designed product cost?
How much does an engineering change order cost?
Are there better materials that the product could be made from?
What would it cost to design a higher quality product?

In planning:
What is the cost to reschedule the plant?
What is the cost of adding short-term capacity?
What is the cost of a floating bottleneck process?
What is the cost if an order is delayed?

In execution:
What is the cost of operationg one machine over another?
What is the cost of shutting down part of or the entire production line?
What is the cost of preventive maintenance?
What is the cost of inspection?

Accounting Concerns:
· Is the new product or process design the best for the total organization?
· Is manufacturing under control?
· What key design, planning, and execution variables should be monitored to assure the proper use of resources?
· Are we spending too much on quality assurance?
· When should new technology be added?
· How should the managerial control information be integrated with the financial needs of the corporation?

David M. Dilts, CPIM, Ph.D., is associate professor of management sciences and is the director of the Center for Integrated Manufacturing at the University of Waterloo, Waterloo, Canada.
Severin V. Grabski, CMA, Ph.D., is associate professor of accounting at Michigan State University, East Lansing, Mich. He is a member of the Lansing-Jackson Chapter, through which this article was submitted.

[1]Dilts, D.M. and G.W. Russell, "Accounting for the Factory of the Future," MANAGEMENT ACCOUNTING™, Vol. 66, No. 10, April 1985, pp. 34-40.
[2]Kaplan, R., "Measuring Manufacturing Performance: A New Challenge for Managerial Accounting Research," *The Accounting Review*, Vol. 58, No. 4, October 1983, pp. 686-705.

Is this article of interest to you? If so, circle appropriate number on Reader Service Card.	**Yes** 72	**No** 73

An Advanced Cost Management System for

THE FACTORY OF THE FUTURE

U.S. Air Force sponsors project to develop conceptual design.

BY DANIEL P. KEEGAN,
ROBERT G. EILER,
AND JOSEPH V. ANANIA

Certificate of Merit, 1987-88.

During the last decade, much has been written about deficiencies in cost management systems. Unfortunately, most of the writings were prescriptive rather than descriptive. A recent project involving the U.S. Air Force, however, has succeeded in translating a cost system prescription into a cost system description. The result of the project was the development of an advanced cost management system (ACMS) that will assist companies with newly automated factory environments cope with cost system problems.

The Electronic Systems Division of the U.S. Air Force initiated a project to develop a conceptual design for an advanced cost management system suitable for the highly automated factories of defense contractors.* A major defense contractor completed this project for the USAF with technical assistance from Price Waterhouse and a broad-based industry advisory board.

The problems defense contractors face do not entirely differ from those of the commercial world. In the past, when many defense programs were sole-sourced to prime contractors, contracts were won and lost largely by the contractor's ability to deliver a technologically superior product. Cost management systems were required main-

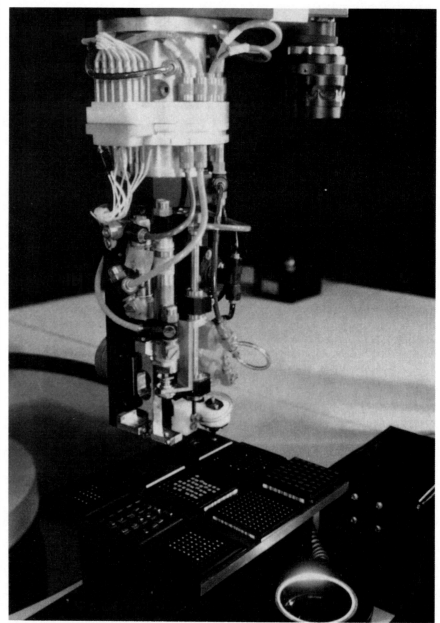

Surface mount component placement at a Westinghouse automated factory.

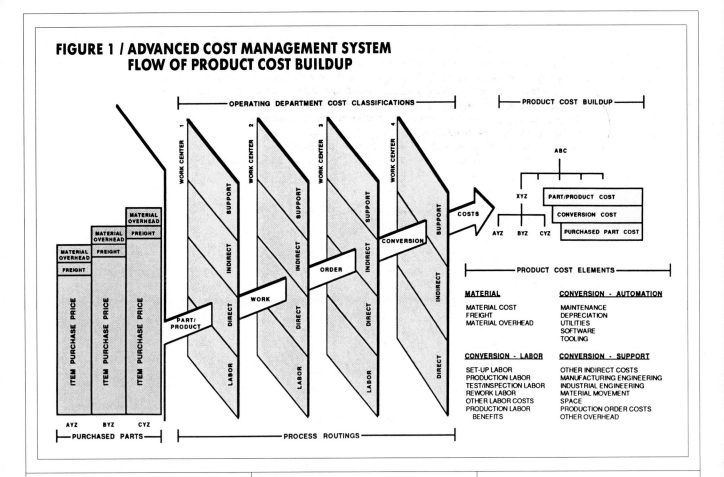

FIGURE 1 / ADVANCED COST MANAGEMENT SYSTEM FLOW OF PRODUCT COST BUILDUP

ly to provide cost visibility and control, and to allow end-item pricing.

In the past few years, however, market conditions in defense programs have changed radically. Defense systems are now being dual-sourced between multiple primes, and follow-up spare parts are being ordered directly from the prime's subcontractors. Cost competitiveness and product technology are equal drivers of a contractor's success. To compete in this arena, contractors must have accurate cost information, a problem compounded by the rapidly changing nature of modern production processes.

The conceptual design of an advanced cost management system as developed for the Department of Defense outlines a comprehensive and integrated cost management and performance measurement system. It addresses management questions about cost at many organizational levels. Certain principles included in the conceptual design depart from both current and historical cost accounting techniques. Whether those ideas represent "advanced" features is largely contextual.

Many businesses may have al-ready adopted these features or variations upon them; others may be still struggling to install a Spartan cost management system.

ACMS FEATURES

The following are features of the advanced cost management system. For some companies, these may be extremely advanced.

Prospective Costs. ACMS directs attention toward prospective future costs and the drivers that impact these costs. It provides current actual information for comparison against the plan and articulates historical information to assist in the development of the future plan. But overall, ACMS has been designed to *assist in decision making.* It is not a passive, historical system of data accumulation. It is very future-oriented.

Focus on Part Costs. The primary orientation of ACMS is to provide information on a part-by-part level for accumulation at the product-(or contract-) reporting level. The part-cost orientation of ACMS provides information concerning value added and value lost in the process, allowing for product cost control at the most detailed level.

Process Orientation. ACMS is directed toward capturing costs at the operational process, aggregating these amounts for part-costing and for contract-reporting purposes. Because data are collected at the process, or cell level, it is possible to pinpoint specific manufacturing steps that require attention, both as they relate to a particular part and to the process overall. Scrap, yield, rework, labor, machine utilization, and so forth will all be visible at the process level.

Separation of Manufacturing-Tracking from Product (or Contract) Cost-Tracking. ACMS is an integrated system. Data provided for production-order scheduling are also captured for cost management purposes. The same information provides the basis for contract-order monitoring. Each of these functions retains its own characteristics and is not compromised by the needs of another function. Thus, for example, management can establish a production-order tracking procedure that fits manufacturing needs with assurance that product-cost tracking also will meet accounting requirements.

Variance Identification. ACMS is a process-based system that requires predetermined estimates of actual results. Differences between the predetermined estimates and actual results are reported as variances—planning gaps. These differences, carefully classified by "causing" factors, reveal in detail the reasons for the variances. Variances computed by ACMS include those caused by yield, scrap, machine utilization, labor efficiency, labor utilization, set-up usage, lot size, order activity, spending, and volume.

Management Information Systems. An organization's data processing costs—operational and financial systems, mainframes, microcomputers, process controllers and networks—are so pervasive in today's environment (perhaps 2% - 4% of sales) that ACMS distributes them to every department in the company, often based on usage. This approach—similar to historical techniques for space and fringe-cost distribution—signals that management information systems is not a free resource. It is, in fact, a very expensive part of the manufacturing process.

Treatment of Automation Software. Within ACMS, the software needed for Computer-Aided Manufacturing, as well as the software required to control specific robotic devices, will be accumulated and distributed to product based on machine usage. Currently, such costs tend to be treated as overhead expense when incurred.

Manufacturing Order and Set-Up Costs. The costs of controlling manufacturing orders and setting up equipment are absorbed into product costs on a predetermined lot-size basis, thus showing the increased or decreased costs of larger or smaller manufacturing orders. By carefully segregating these costs, ACMS strives to quantify the effects of manufacturing control technologies such as "just-in-time."

Multiple Overhead Attachment Points. ACMS distributes indirect costs to product by more precise means. Certain costs attached themselves to purchased items, others are absorbed into the product manufacturing process level, still others are manufacturing order-related and additional costs are lodged at the plant or product level.

Elemental Cost-Visibility through the Cost Buildup Process. ACMS traces more than 20 different elements of product cost through the production chain (Figure 1). This classification makes it possible to determine the basis for costs throughout the manufacturing process, all the way to the end product. In addition, cost targets can be established to help manage cost reduction.

Activity Costs. In ACMS, most departments costs can be classified by functional activity to obtain an overall profile of the organization's cost patterns. Functional activity classification permits wide-ranging analysis of cost pools that can be identified with specific products or

FIGURE 2 / ADVANCED COST MANAGEMENT SYSTEM COST DRIVERS

DEPT: 150 - ACCOUNTS PAYABLE

	19XX	19XX	19XX	FORECAST 19XX
ANNUAL OPERATING PLAN ASSUMPTIONS				
A. SALES	XXX,XXX	XXX,XXX	XXX,XXX	XXX,XXX
B. DIRECT LABOR HOURS	X,XXX	X,XXX	X,XXX	X,XXX
C. MACHINE HOURS	X,XXX	X,XXX	X,XXX	X,XXX
D. INVENTORY TURNS	XX	XX	XX	XX
E. INFLATION RATE (%)	XX.XX	XX.XX	XX.XX	XX.XX
F. MANNING LEVELS				
• PRODUCTION	X,XXX	X,XXX	X,XXX	X,XXX
• SUPPORT	X,XXX	X,XXX	X,XXX	X,XXX
G. EXPENSE GROWTH RATE (%)	XX.XX	XX.XX	XX.XX	XX.XX
I. INVOICE PROCESSING				
A. INPUT TRANSACTIONS	XXX,XXX	XXX,XXX	XXX,XXX	
B. CHANGE TRANSACTIONS	XXX,XXX	XXX,XXX	XXX,XXX	
C. DELETE TRANSACTIONS	XXX,XXX	XXX,XXX	XXX,XXX	
D. INVOICE MICROFILM	XXX,XXX	XXX,XXX	XXX,XXX	
E. INQUIRY TRANSACTION	XXX,XXX	XXX,XXX	XXX,XXX	
II. THREE - WAY MATCHING				
A. NUMBER OF MATCH TRANSACTIONS	XXX,XXX	XXX,XXX	XXX,XXX	
B. MISSING PURCHASE ORDER REQUESTS	XXX,XXX	XXX,XXX	XXX,XXX	
C. MISSING ACCOUNT DISTRIBUTION REQUESTS	XXX,XXX	XXX,XXX	XXX,XXX	
D. AUTHORIZATION REQUESTS	XXX,XXX	XXX,XXX	XXX,XXX	
E. MISSING RECEIVING REPORT REQUESTS	XXX,XXX	XXX,XXX	XXX,XXX	
F. INVOICE APPROVAL REJECTIONS	XXX,XXX	XXX,XXX	XXX,XXX	

	19XX	19XX	19XX	FORECAST 19XX
III. CHECK PROCESSING				
A. AUTOMATED CHECKS	XXX,XXX	XXX,XXX	XXX,XXX	
B. MANUAL CHECKS	XXX,XXX	XXX,XXX	XXX,XXX	
C. INVOICES/CHECKS	XXX,XXX	XXX,XXX	XXX,XXX	
D. VOIDED CHECKS	XXX,XXX	XXX,XXX	XXX,XXX	
E. CANCELLED CHECKS	XXX,XXX	XXX,XXX	XXX,XXX	
F. RETURNED CHECKS FROM INTERNAL AUDITING	XXX,XXX	XXX,XXX	XXX,XXX	
G. CHECK PROCESSING RUNS	XXX,XXX	XXX,XXX	XXX,XXX	
IV. VENDOR MAINTENANCE				
A. NUMBER OF VENDORS	XXX,XXX	XXX,XXX	XXX,XXX	
B. INPUT TRANSACTIONS	XXX,XXX	XXX,XXX	XXX,XXX	
C. CHANGE TRANSACTIONS	XXX,XXX	XXX,XXX	XXX,XXX	
D. INQUIRY TRANSACTIONS	XXX,XXX	XXX,XXX	XXX,XXX	
E. DELETE TRANSACTIONS	XXX,XXX	XXX,XXX	XXX,XXX	
V. REPORT				
A. USER-REQUESTED REPORTS	XXX,XXX	XXX,XXX	XXX,XXX	
B. STANDARD REPORTS	XXX,XXX	XXX,XXX	XXX,XXX	
C. PAGES OF OUTPUT	XXX,XXX	XXX,XXX	XXX,XXX	
VI. PROCESSING STATISTICS				
A. INVOICE PAYMENT TIME CYCLE	XXX,XXX	XXX,XXX	XXX,XXX	
B. CHECK RUN BALANCING CYCLE	XXX,XXX	XXX,XXX	XXX,XXX	

PREDOMINATE DEPARTMENT COST DRIVER: INVOICES

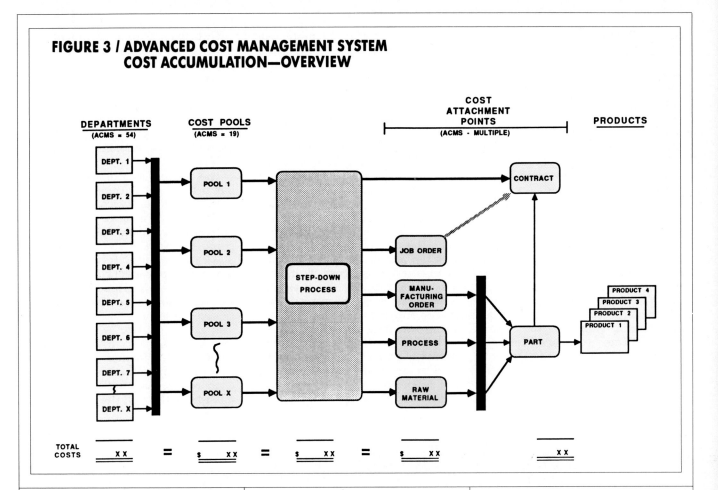

**FIGURE 3 / ADVANCED COST MANAGEMENT SYSTEM
COST ACCUMULATION—OVERVIEW**

contracts through the use of cost activity drivers.

Integrated Manufacturing Reporting. Reporting at the manufacturing process level and at the administration support level is based upon both flexible budgeting and full absorption concepts. This type of hybrid reporting assists in both short- and longer-term decision making.

Personal Time Template. When it is important to accurately correct personnel time, ACMS outlines a subsystem called the personal time template, which can facilitate such reporting.

FAILINGS OF TRADITIONAL COST ACCOUNTING

The traditional cost accounting model—developed for the efficient production of a few standardized products with a high direct labor content—does not meet the needs of a virtually unmanned, automated production environment. Accordingly, the ACMS advocates a new cost management model that computes product costs

as other than the sum of direct labor, material, and overhead (burden).

ACMS replaces the concept of labor and burden with that of conversion (the elements required to transform raw materials into finished product) by dividing product cost elements into four categories: material, conversion-labor, conversion-automation, and conversion-support. This classification dispenses with historical distinctions between direct and indirect costs that are unsuited to the realities of contemporary manufacturing.

As previously discussed, costs such as Computer-Aided Manufacturing (CAM) software development and maintenance—which traditional cost accounting would categorize as manufacturing overhead, applied on a direct labor-hour basis—are now directly associated with their cause and amortized on the basis of more appropriate cost determinants such as planned cost per piece. Similarly, the time assembly workers spend as a consequence of an automated process—which traditional cost accounting would classify as direct labor—is

identified in an advanced cost management system as aggregated *conversion-support* cost.

The ACMS acknowledges the changes in process technology that have altered the cost mix of operations. It also understands how control of the new manufacturing environment can be enhanced by a systematic relationship of costs to the structured activities that engender them. The system recognizes that advanced production technology has decreased certain activities. The ability to read bar codes, for example, has reduced the number of data entry operators; and computer-aided inspection has lowered the cost to process quality transactions.

The ACMS also recognizes that advanced production technology has dramatically increased other activities. Increased activities stem largely from transactions involving the exchange of service and information. These transactions are not tied directly to the product but rather to the dimensions of the product—such as design, quality, and on-time delivery—that automation is intended to improve.

PREDETERMINED ESTIMATES OF COST

The conceptual design of the ACMS incorporates a very strong planning orientation to create "a benchmark" for control. Government contracting exhibits a compelling need for accurate estimates, because contractual relationships are based upon cost information. Predetermined estimates are the "standards" used for product-costing purposes and as the basis for variance calculations.

Unfortunately, the term "standards" invokes images of industrial engineers hovering over operations with stop watches or tables of standard time factors. In fact, the ACMS does not require industrial engineering standards for minor costs. Rather, estimates derived from historical information or management judgment are sufficient. Such estimates, if closer to actual costs than industrial engi-

neering standards, are preferred. Standards may, thus, be described as "estimated actuals," or "benchmark costs," or "predetermined estimates."

The nature of information that constitutes a modern cost management system makes determining *actual* product costs extremely difficult. The classic example of the difficulties associated with actual product-cost tracking is a common situation: components are purchased at three different times and at three different prices. To determine the cost of an end-item that uses the purchased part, you must assume a flow of cost. Were the first items received the ones consumed first? Were the last items received more convenient in the stockroom and, therefore, issued early to fill manufacturing orders? Should each piece of inventory be tracked separately so that its exact cost is known? Are averaged costs sufficiently accurate?

Unless each item of inventory and its cost are identified, there is no assurance that the cost of the end-item, in fact, does reflect actual costs. Yet the effort required to keep track of specific purchase prices, even if automated, can be staggering. It is simpler to compute "actual" cost as standard costs plus variances.

The analogy continues throughout production. A component part is manufactured twice during the period. The first lot of 50 requires shop paperwork and a series of machine setups. The second order of 300 requires precisely the same amount of paperwork and setups, but a machine malfunction caused run times to be extended and additional direct costs to be incurred. The parts from Lot "A" have a different "actual cost" than the parts from Lot "B" (further distorted by overhead distributions). Should each unique part cost be tracked differently through the system?

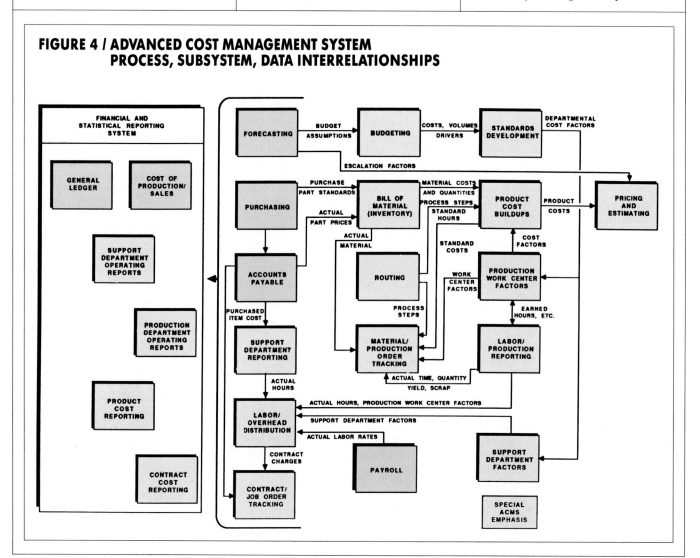

FIGURE 4 / ADVANCED COST MANAGEMENT SYSTEM PROCESS, SUBSYSTEM, DATA INTERRELATIONSHIPS

Most companies have long since concluded that they are not wealthy enough to afford an actual cost system—which is extremely expensive to maintain and does not really provide reliable information. It may provide approximations of actual costs for simple products, (or one-at-a-time very expensive products such as a ship) but this information is extremely difficult to obtain and very expensive to create.

Futhermore, actual cost information is not a particularly effective management tool. It is too erratic and does not yield useful insights.

In the preceding example of two manufacturing orders, it is of little value to know that the costs are different. It is of far greater value to know *why* the costs are different. And it is even more valuable to know why the costs are *different than planned*.

To solve the dilemma, a system

New products, new technologies, and new patterns of management require new control systems.

of predetermined costs should be developed and a general agreement established that small deviations from these predetermined costs can be monitored at summary levels and accommodated mechanistically without travail. That is not to say that a sloppy system is sufficient. In fact, much planning effort should go into establishing the predetermined estimates so that they

reflect "desired" cost patterns. This planning often will indicate areas where product cost can be reduced—even before the first item is made!

OVERHEAD DECOMPOSITION

Many companies have implemented programs for reducing direct labor. At the same time, these companies have experienced spiraling support costs. This shift necessitates a more focused effort to monitor and control support activities.

A cost-driver relationship establishes the conceptual link between costs and the occurrence of an activity that "creates" the cost. If the cost driver is reduced or eliminated, so are the related costs. An important consideration in this process is that the cost drivers will change through time: the validity of the relationship must be continually monitored. Also, costs do not always occur in a linear rate with their driver. For example, a disproportionate increase in support services investment may be required to support an increase in cost driver volume. Additionally, product and transaction complexity, in themselves, contribute substantially to the cost of operations. Complexity is a cost driver deserving particular attention.

Within the conceptual framework of an advanced cost management system, cost drivers include manufacturing engineering hours, materials purchased, manufacturing orders, move factors, utility units, maintenance work orders, machine hours, production cycle time, transaction counts, square feet, management information system usage, and staff headcount, among others. As can be recognized these drivers relate to *overall product costs*. But it may be necessary to determine separate sets of cost drivers that more fully explain the cost patterns of an individual support department. For example, the ACMS outlines the cost drivers within an accounts payable department as described in Figure 2. These cost drivers can serve as flexible budget determinants for the accounts payable department, while company-wide cost drivers relate to product cost (Figure 3).

FIGURE 5 / ADVANCED COST MANAGEMENT SYSTEM IMPLEMENTATION PLANNING PHASES

PHASE I	PHASE II	PHASE III	PHASE IV
APPLY ACMS CONCEPTS TO THE COMPANY	**ASSESS CURRENT SYSTEMS CAPABILITIES TO SUPPORT ACMS**	**TAILOR ACMS DESIGN TO MEET SPECIFIC COMPANY NEEDS**	**DEVELOP DETAILED IMPLEMENTATION PLAN**
Activities:	**Activities:**	**Activities:**	**Activities:**
■ Present ACMS concepts	■ Interview department managers to determine impact of ACMS on departmental operations	■ Determine company subsystem structure required to meet ACMS objectives	■ Evaluate implementation barriers
■ Identify future business changes which will impact cost management	■ Identify future systems requirements	■ Specifically define functions and features of ACMS subsystems	■ Assess departmental level procedure requirements
■ Determine preliminary advantages and disadvantages to the business of installing ACMS	■ Evaluate current 'in-house' systems status	■ Develop ACMS general design	■ Design detailed education/training program
		■ Identify and resolve major design issues	■ Design system integration requirements
		■ Identify potential alternatives	■ Determine implementation sequence and strategy
			■ Identify hardware/software requirements
			■ Develop detailed implementation plan
■ CHECKPOINT: Ensure understanding of ACMS concepts in view of business objectives	■ CHECKPOINT: Determine implementation feasibility	■ CHECKPOINT: Ensure consistency of general design to company objectives	■ CHECKPOINT: Approve implementation plan

The resulting conceptual framework provides detailed cost visibility:

- Within the support department,
- At the manufacturing-process level, and
- At the product-cost level.

Control reporting as outlined in an advanced cost management system relates these three dimensions of cost into an integrated whole. It, therefore, helps focus management attention on controlling support costs, similar to the unremitting pressure in the past to control labor costs.

EVALUATE EXISTING SYSTEMS

The ACMS described here has been designed to deal with the cost management issues of a large company. It is comprehensive and integrated. It affects, or is affected by, virtually every aspect of the organization.

Figure 4 presents a partial description of the subsystems required for an advanced cost management system. Despite the system's formidable appearance when described in depth, an advanced cost management system is—or can be—relatively straightforward in operation. Many of the subsystems that support the ACMS exist within most companies.

Part of implementation planning entails assessing how well a company's current systems support the ACMS's objectives. Requirements are documented, allowing the company to evaluate existing systems and determine the changes required to migrate to an advanced cost management system environment. In certain cases, existing systems have to be modified. In other cases they will have to be augmented, and, in a few cases, existing systems will have to be scrapped.

As was previously discussed, cost management information is a strategic corporate requirement. It is not surprising, therefore, that so many companies are revisiting the conceptual underpinnings of their existing systems, causing them to come of age.

Figure 5 presents a road map of the process required to *plan* the installation of the ACMS. Without such a road map, it is entirely possible that an organization will spend a great deal of time implementing only a small portion of a comprehensive cost management system. The proper architectural plan may allow management to achieve multifaceted cost management objectives with only a small incremental investment.

COST ACCOUNTING COMES OF AGE

The objectives of the ACMS are to:

- Initially serve as a guideline for cost estimation (during product development) and subsequently serve as the basis for updates to product cost information during the life of the product;
- Serve as a methodology for performing cost reconciliations between periods, based on major factors affecting the product cost (for example, material price, engineering changes, process changes, labor rates changes, labor productivity changes, spending changes, volume changes and the like);
- Support the tracking of product cost reductions through the product life cycle;
- Segregate and track various elements of support costs to provide a better basis for their control;
- Focus on prospective costs, with less emphasis on historical costs;
- Consider the materiality of cost elements. Control of high support and material acquisition costs should be a top priority;
- Support planning and variance analysis mechanisms;
- Carefully segregate the effect of volume and mix on expected and actual production costs;
- Differentiate between the level of cost detail needed by management for planning and that needed for budgeting, cost accumulation, reporting, and control;
- Provide exception-oriented reports that prompt action to various levels of management;
- Integrate data collection with the process controllers at the work-center level to automatically capture cost management data as a by-product of the production process; and
- Be able to monitor and report information necessary to measure the success of investment strategies.

In other words, advanced cost management is a strategic, closed-loop decision support system that relies on managerial estimates of future costs and monitors actual results against the organizational, departmental, and product plans.

In today's fast-changing world, with competitors looking for every opportunity to underprice in the market, cost management information is not a luxury, but a necessity. The United States Air Force, through its advanced cost management system project, has translated cost system prescription into cost system description.

Investments already are being made in the manufacturing technologies that will boost America's global competitiveness. The time to make the requisite changes to systems that support this investment is at hand. ∎

Daniel P. Keegan recently transferred to the New York office of Price Waterhouse where he serves as a Management Consulting Services partner responsible for engagements to Fortune companies. Mr. Keegan is a member of the Pittsburgh Chapter of NAA, through which this article was submitted.

Robert G. Eiler, CPA, is a management consulting services partner in the Cleveland office of Price Waterhouse. As partner of the Manufacturing and Cost Management Specialized Practice Unit, he coordinates the cost management practice throughout Price Waterhouse. Mr. Eiler is a member of the Indianapolis Chapter of NAA.

Joseph A. Anania, CPA, is an audit partner in the Pittsburgh office of Price Waterhouse. Mr. Anania specializes in manufacturing and inventory matters.

This article was adapted from material prepared by the authors and submitted to: The United States Air Force, Air Force Systems Command, Electronics Systems Division/TOM, Hanscom, AFB, Massachusetts 01731 (Contract # F19628-86-C0207).

Section 3

Changes: Technologies—JIT and Bar Code

Section 3 continues an examination of changes in the new manufacturing environment that have become characteristic of the world-class manufacturer. This section focuses on two technologies related to inventory management that have had a significant impact on cost management systems—the just-in-time (JIT) philosophy and methods, and bar coding techniques.

The lead article, by George Foster and Charles T. Horngren, introduces the just-in-time philosophy and methods and relates this approach to improvements apparent in product costing methods, cost control systems, and information systems costs. The article begins by reviewing four key aspects of the JIT philosophy: elimination of nonvalue-adding activities; commitment to a high level of quality; commitment to continuous improvement; and emphasis on simplification of all activities. The authors then conduct a two-part review of specific JIT operational techniques and their impact on cost management systems. First they examine JIT purchasing methods that can be adopted by retailers, wholesalers, distributors, and manufacturers alike and next, JIT production methods for adoption by manufacturing organizations only.

In their review, Foster and Horngren provide numerous documented applications of JIT methods. They summarize their findings in two figures, one citing five changes in cost accounting occurring in JIT purchasing applications and another citing five cost accounting changes in JIT production applications. Foster and Horngren are careful to point out that these changes vary among individual organizations. They conclude that although there is not a single blueprint for cost accounting that all organizations are adopting, one underlying commonality is movement toward simplification of cost accounting practices.

Robert D. McIlhattan, in the second article, analyzes the changes in cost management systems occurring as a result of implementation of JIT techniques. He relates numerous examples of organizations that have changed their cost management systems in response to the JIT philosophy. McIlhattan identifies four key areas where changes are taking place: the identification of cost drivers; the number of product cost elements; the application of product costs; and the nature of performance measures. He discusses each of these areas in turn and provides several tabular summaries highlighting the differences between the traditional and the JIT environment.

While McIlhattan notes that these cost management system enhancements vary across organizations, he points out that simplification was one of the primary objectives in every case. This simplification was achieved by focusing on only two or three true cost drivers, reducing the number of standard product cost elements, reducing the number of cost allocations, and establishing a few understandable key performance measures. McIlhattan concludes by identifying how change was initiated in these successful organizations, always beginning with change in the perceptions of both the accounting function and the management accountant.

The final article in this section, by Thomas Tyson and Arjan T. Sadhwani, discusses bar coding techniques and the impact this technology brings to the factory floor. Much of this work is an introduction to the concepts and definitions of bar coding. The authors first review popular bar code symbologies and the general types of bar code scanning equipment. They give a case study of an instruments plant that uses bar coding techniques; a sidebar provides a glossary of common bar coding terms.

Tyson and Sadhwani close by citing some of the cost management system improvements resulting from the application of bar coding techniques. They observe that data scanners and computers have simplified the traditional accounting functions of posting, transferring, and verifying data. This technique also reduces auditing costs associated with inventory counts and validations. The authors find that using bar coding in automated manufacturing settings provides opportunities to improve quality and reduce waste.

Additional Readings from *Management Accounting*

Barton, M. Frank, Surendra P. Agrawal, and L. Mason Rockwell, Jr., "Meeting the Challenge of Japanese Management Concepts," September 1988, pp. 49-53.

Calvasina, Richard V., Eugene J. Calvasina, and Gerald E. Calvasina, "Beware the New Accounting Myths," December 1989, pp. 41-45.

Robinson, Michael A. and John E. Timmerman, "How Vendor Analysis Supports JIT Manufacturing," December 1987, pp. 20-24.

Sadhwani, Arjan T. and M. H. Sarhan, "Electronic Systems Enhance JIT Operations," December 1987, pp. 25-30.

Sadhwani, Arjan T., M. H. Sarhan, and Dayal Kiringoda, "Just-In-Time: An Inventory System Whose Time Has Come," December 1985, pp. 36-44.

Sadhwani, Arjan T. and Thomas Tyson, "Does Your Firm Need Bar Coding?", April 1990, pp. 45-48.

Sauers, Dale G., "Analyzing Inventory Systems," May 1986, pp. 30-36.

Stec, Stanley F., "Manufacturing Control Through Bar Coding at Target Products," April 1988, p. 47.

Wagner, James, "Operating Rhythm," June 1986, pp. 36-39.

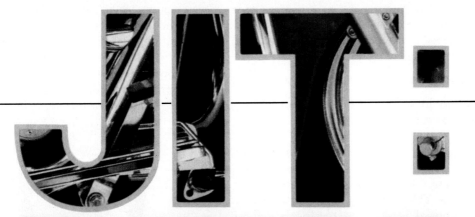

JIT:
COST ACCOUNTING AND COST MANAGEMENT ISSUES

There is not a single blueprint for cost accounting and cost management that all organizations are adopting as JIT is implemented.

By George Foster and Charles T. Horngren

Just-in-time (JIT) philosophy and methods are being adopted by many companies. As part of our research, we interviewed representatives from North American, European, and Japanese companies that have introduced JIT. Representatives from public accounting/consulting firms hired by companies implementing JIT also were interviewed.

What Is JIT?

JIT is a philosophy that focuses on undertaking activities immediately as needed or demanded. Four aspects pivotal to JIT are:

- The elimination of all activities that *do not add value* to a product or service. In the context of JIT, "not adding value" is a buzz-phrase loosely used to describe any activities or resources that are targets for reduction or elimination.
- A commitment to a high level of *quality*. Doing things right the first time is crucial if no time is allowed for rework.
- A commitment to *continuous improvement* in the efficiency of an activity.
- An emphasis on *simplification and increased visibility* to identify activities that do not add value.

The term JIT also is used to refer to operations management *methods* in functional areas such as purchasing and production. JIT purchasing can be adopted by retailers, wholesalers, distributors, and manufacturing organizations. JIT production only can be adopted by manufacturing organizations.

Choices in Cost Accounting

Cost or management accounting systems have two major purposes: product costing, and planning and control (hereafter referred to as control). Choices of product costing methods and detailed cost records should consider the following:

- Cost-benefit tests for designing and changing management accounting systems are paramount and pervasive. Elaborate systems are expensive in time and money. They are installed or changed only if managers believe collective operations will be sufficiently improved.
- Systems for product costing and control should be *tailored to the underlying operations* and not vice versa.
- Systems for *control* are common to all *product costing* systems. Examples include responsibility accounting, budgeting, and variance analysis.
- Management accounting systems are only one

George Foster is professor of Accounting at Stanford University. A member of the Peninsula-Palo Alto Chapter of the National Association of Accountants, Dr. Foster has research interests in how changing technology affects the design of cost accounting and cost management systems.

Charles T. Horngren is the Edmund W. Littlefield Professor of Accounting at Stanford University. He also is a member of the NAA, where he was on its Research Planning Committee for three years and was a member of the Board of Regents of the Institute of Certified Management Accountants.

source of information for executives. Other sources include personal observation and nonfinancial measures such as set-up times and the percentage of defective products.

Motivations for Change

The changes in cost accounting we are discussing have several motivations:

1. Develop more accurate *product cost* information. Uses include decisions on pricing, on the product mix, and in cost-based reimbursement contracts. The accounting system is the primary source of product cost information for management.
2. Better *control* of cost incurrence. JIT focuses on *reducing total costs for the firm as a whole,* not individual costs or departmental costs. Changes here may have several motivations.
   - Avoid or diminish dysfunctional decisions often associated with the existing cost accounting system, or
   - Change in the comparative advantage of accounting versus nonaccounting variables in cost control.
3. *Reduce the costs of the system.* A key aspect of JIT is the simplification of all activities. Simplification extends to the cost systems in the organization as well as to operational areas such as purchasing and production.

JIT Purchasing

JIT purchasing calls for goods to be delivered immediately before demand or use. Companies adopting JIT purchasing methods report a substantial increase in the number of individual deliveries, each containing a smaller number of units. The costs and time associated with purchasing activities have been reduced in one or more of the following ways:

Number of suppliers decreased and a reduction in the resources devoted to purchase negotiations. IBM at its Lexington, Kentucky plant cut the number of its suppliers from 640 to 32.

Long-term agreements signed with chosen suppliers that stipulate the price and acceptable quality levels. Negotiations do not occur for each purchase transaction. Some firms use an advanced delivery schedule (ADS) when purchasing goods. This schedule establishes the daily (or even hourly) delivery schedule for a time period such as a month. Clearly, firms using a schedule require a high degree of certainty regarding demand or production for the time period covered by the ADS. For example, several Toyota automobile plants freeze the production schedule at least one month in advance.

Companies frequently communicate details to vendors about quality and delivery specifications.

Some companies schedule "Vendor Day" programs several times a year to inform vendors of their requirements. These requirements can be stringent with stiff penalties for nonconformance. For example, Hewlett-Packard has contracts with some suppliers to its Boise plant that stipulate if a four-hour window is missed more than three times

At one of Motorola's semiconductor plants, all labor and overhead standards have been eliminated.

in a year, their contract would be up for renewal.

"Shop-ready" containers used. Activities associated with packaging and unpackaging are examples where "nonvalue added" costs often are incurred. Emphasis is placed on having "the correct" number of units in individual containers. In this way, all facets of material handling are diminished, often including the use of large material-handling equipment.

Minimal checking by purchasers of the quality and quantity of goods shipped. The cost of incoming quality inspection programs is reduced. For example, the number of quality inspectors may be dramatically lowered or even eliminated.

The goals set by firms switching to JIT purchasing are ambitious. For example, one company's objectives were: supplier productivity/price improvements (30%); total inventory and lead time reduction (90%); quality *without* inspection (100%); schedule performance (100%); and packing/unpacking costs (90%).[1]

How Cost Accounting Is Affected

Figure 1 links the motivations for changes in the cost accounting system to each of the five specific changes in cost accounting associated with JIT purchasing described below.

JIT purchasing can affect the cost accounting system in one or more of the following ways:

Increases the direct traceability of costs. In a traditional purchasing environment, many materials handling and warehouse costs are incurred for multipurpose facilities that service many different product lines. Companies typically classify the costs of operating such facilities as indirect costs. With JIT the materials handling facilities are often dedicated to a single retail area or a single production line. Such operating costs can be classified as direct costs of individual retail areas or production lines.

Changes the cost pools used to accumulate costs. In traditional purchasing environments, separate cost pools are sometimes used for purchasing, materials handling, quality inspection, and warehouse facilities. With JIT the warehouse facility will be eliminated and materials handling costs will be reduced. Consequently, the warehouse cost pool will be eliminated.

Changes the bases used to allocate indirect costs to production departments. If an organization previously collected purchasing, warehouse, and related costs in a single cost pool, the composition of this pool will change. This has implications for the choice of an allocation base. In a pure JIT setting, there will be no warehouse. Thus, warehouse space is unavailable as an allocation base. Allocation bases such as dollar value of materials or the number of deliveries may better capture the cause and effect relationship between purchasing/materials handling activities and indirect cost incurrence.

Reduces emphasis on individual purchase price variance information. In traditional purchasing environments, many organizations place great emphasis on purchase price variances. Favorable purchasing price variances can sometimes be achieved by buying larger quantities to take advantage of price discounts or by buying lower quality materials. In the JIT plant, the emphasis is on the total cost of operations, not just on purchase price. Factors such as quality and availability are given heightened emphasis, even if they are accompanied by higher purchase prices. Firms using JIT purchasing attempt to achieve price reductions by having long-term agreements with suppliers. Purchase price variances for each delivery have much less significance under JIT.

Reduces the frequency or detail of reporting of purchase deliveries in the internal accounting system. In a JIT purchasing environment, the number of deliveries of goods (raw materials, etc.) increase substantially. Organizations have sought to reduce the costs of processing information in the internal accounting system in one or more of the following ways:

1. Batching (summarizing) individual purchase

Backflush Costing

A backflush costing system focuses first on the output of an organization and then works backward when allocating costs between cost of goods sold and inventory.

Silicon Valley Computers (SVC), a hypothetical company, manufactures keyboards for personal computers and has a backflush costing system. The costing system has two trigger points for making entries in the internal accounting system: Purchase of raw materials and components, and the manufacture of a finished good unit.

For the month of April, there are no beginning inventories of raw materials, work-in-process, or finished goods. The standard material cost per keyboard unit in April is $19. For product costing purposes, SVC combines labor costs and indirect manufacturing costs into a single conversion cost category. The standard conversion cost per keyboard unit in April is $12. SVC has two inventory accounts: a combined Raw and WIP account and a finished goods account.

The following steps are followed by SVC in its backflush costing system:

1. Record the raw materials purchased in the reporting period. Assume that during April materials purchases were $1,950,000.

Inventory-Raw and WIP	$1,950,000	
Accounts Payable		$1,950,000

2. Determine the number of finished units manufactured during the reporting period. Assume that 100,000 keyboard units were manufactured in April.

3. Compute the standard cost of each finished unit. This step typically will use a bill of materials. For SVC, the standard cost per unit is $31 ($19 standard material cost + $12 standard conversion cost).

4. Record the cost of finished goods manufactured in the reporting period:

Inventory-Finished Goods	$3,100,000	
Inventory-Raw and WIP		$1,900,000
Conversion Cost		1,200,000

Assume that 99,000 units were sold during the month. The end of month inventory balance for April would be:

Inventory-Raw and WIP	$50,000	
Inventory-Finished Goods, 1,000		
units @ $31		31,000
		$81,000

The elimination of the work-in-process account considerably reduces the amount of detail in the internal accounting system. (There still may be tracking of units on the production line, but there is no "costs attach" tracking in the internal accounting system via work tickets.)

Variant No. 1

A variant of the above is a backflush cost system with the second trigger point for making entries at the sale rather than at the manu-

Backflush Costing (cont.)

facture of a finished good unit. The reasons are:

- To remove the incentive for managers to produce for inventory. (Under the "costs attach" assumption implicit in job, operation and process costing, period expenses can be reduced by producing units not sold and by increasing work-in-process.)
- To increase the focus of managers on a plant-wide goal (producing salable units) rather than an individual unit goal (such as increase labor efficiency at an individual production cell).

This variant has the same effect on net income as immediate expensing to the period of all conversion costs.

The summary accounting entry would be:

Cost of Goods Sold	$3,100,000	
Inventory-Raw and Wip		$1,900,000
Conversion Cost		1,200,000

Variant No. 2

The simplest version of a backflush product costing system has only one trigger point for making entries in the accounting system. Assume this trigger point is the manufacture of a finished good unit. For the example used previously, the summary entry would be:

Inventory-Finished Goods	$3,100,000	
Accounts Payable		$1,900,000
Conversion Cost		1,200,000

Figure 1
Motivations for Cost Accounting Changes With JIT Purchasing

More accurate product cost information.

- Changes in direct traceability of costs.
- Changes in cost pools.
- Changes in allocation bases.

Better control of cost incurrence.

- Reduced emphasis on individual purchasing price variance information and increased emphasis on total cost of operations (minimizes dysfunctional operating decisions often associated with existing cost accounting system).

Reduce the costs of the system.
- Reduction in the frequency or detail of reporting of purchase deliveries.

deliveries to avoid a separate transaction for each delivery. Where there is an advance delivery schedule (ADS), the transaction may relate to the period of the delivery schedule. Where there is no ADS, the individual deliveries may be batched on a weekly basis and only the aggregate of the deliveries recorded as a transaction.

2. Using an electronic transfer system where the initial purchase order (or delivery schedule) automatically sets up electronic data transfers at the delivery date and electronic funds transfers at the payment date.

An extreme case of reduction in detail is a "backflush" costing system that has a single trigger point for making accounting entries (see sidebar). Backflushing can be extended to the purchasing function so that the first time materials are recorded in the internal accounting system is when finished goods using those materials are completed.

JIT Production

In a JIT production environment, each component on a production line is produced immediately as needed by the next step in the production line. Key aspects include:

- The production line is run on a demand-pull basis, so that activity at each work station is authorized by the demand of downstream work stations. Therefore, work-in-process at each work station is held to a minimum.
- Emphasis is on reducing the production lead time (the time from the first stage of production to when the finished product first leaves the production line). Reduced lead time enables a firm to respond better to changes in demand. Another benefit is the reduction of manufacturing order changes.
- The production line is stopped if work-in-process is found defective. With JIT there are no buffer inventories at each work station to keep workers busy.
- Emphasis is on simplifying activities on the production line so that areas where nonvalue added activities occur are highly visible and can be eliminated. Firms adopting JIT production methods usually have restructured the layout of their plants. Much emphasis is placed on streamlining material handling between successive work stations.

Dramatic improvements in operating performance have been reported by firms adopting JIT production methods. A survey of five companies reported 83-92% reductions in production lead time, 70-89% reductions in work-in-progress, 75-94% reductions in changeover time, and 39-80% reductions in space required for production facilities.[2]

How Cost Accounting Is Affected

Figure 2 links the motivations for changes in the cost accounting system to each of the five specific changes in cost accounting associated with JIT production described below.

Companies adopting JIT production are making one or more of the following changes:

Increase in the direct traceability of some costs. Direct traceability of cost items has been increased by changes in the underlying production activities and by changes in the ability to trace

In the JIT plant, the emphasis is on the total cost of operations, not just on purchase price.

costs to specific production lines or areas.

The costs of many activities previously classified as indirect costs have been transferred to the direct cost category in JIT plants. For example, workers on the production line in JIT plants do plant maintenance and plant setups. Previously, such activities often were done by other workers classified as indirect labor.

Equipment suppliers to JIT plants are increasingly being asked to provide equipment that facilitates high speed changeover of tools by production workers, on-line monitoring of quality, and on-line packaging and labelling.

For those firms retaining direct labor as a separate cost category, these changes in the set of production activities increase the direct traceability of costs to individual product lines. These changes mean that indirect cost pools associated with activities such as plant maintenance and setup are likely to be eliminated (or at least combined with other cost pools because of the previous pools' diminished materiality).

Even if the underlying production activities are

unchanged, data may now be captured more economically. There is increased use of time clocks, minicomputers, and bar-coded identification codes for production workers (as well as materials, parts, and machines). This has made it more cost-effective to trace costs to specific production lines or areas. Improvements in databases relating to machine usage also are facilitating the development of cost functions that better capture cause and effect relationships at the plant floor level.

IBM is exploring how to increase the ratio of directly attributable product costs to total product costs at its plants using JIT (and in other plants as well). Controllers at plants where this ratio has been increased have reported improved sourcing decisions, cost reductions and improved competitiveness, and improved expense information to manage product cost.[3]

Elimination (or at least reduction) of cost pools for several activities classified as indirect. As we described, underlying production activities can be changed in JIT plants. Activities can be eliminated on the premise they do not add value. Prime targets for elimination are storage areas for WIP inventory and material handling facilities. Costs associated with these activities will decline in their magnitude.

Machines or work stations are located adjacent to each other so that materials and components can be moved by the workers themselves or on short conveyor belts. Increased emphasis also is given to the design and packaging of materials and components so as to reduce the need for large bulk containers that require fork-lift trucks. This likewise means that cost pools associated with these activities also are candidates for elimination.

Reduced emphasis on individual labor and overhead variances. In many traditional plants, much of the internal accounting effort is devoted to setting labor and overhead standards and in calculating and reporting variances from these standards. Firms using JIT methods report reduced emphasis on the use of labor and overhead variances.

Labor variances defined at the individual production cell level create incentives for workers in each production cell to ignore the effect of their actions on other production cells. At one of Motorola's seminconductor plants all labor and overhead standards have been eliminated. The benefits reported include reduced dysfunctional aspects associated with focusing on individual production cells (such as increasing work-in-process even if not currently demanded) and reduced administrative expenses.

Firms retaining variance analysis stress that a change in focus is appropriate in a JIT plant. The emphasis is on variance analysis *at the plant level* with the focus on "trends that may be occurring in the production process," rather than the absolute magnitude of individual variances. (The notion of continuous improvement that underlies a JIT philosophy means that standards will be revised at shorter intervals than in traditional plants.)

Reduction in the level of detailed information recorded on work tickets. There are several ways work tickets have become simplified:

1. Change in the production process so that there are fewer materials parts per finished product. This can be achieved by redesigning the product so that fewer parts are used or by increasing the percentage of components assembled elsewhere.[4]
2. Record only direct materials on work tickets and expense to the period all other costs.
3. Change from a job costing system to a process costing or backflush costing system.

Some firms have not changed their basic costing system, but they have reduced the number of individual cost centers. As an illustration, Omark Industries made the following changes at three of its product lines:[5]

Product Line	Pre-JIT Era	JIT Era
Chain Saws	18 cost centers	4 cost centers
Sprockets	5 cost centers	3 cost centers
Bars	4 cost centers	1 cost center

Reduction in the level of detailed information recorded about labor costs. JIT organizations have adapted to the declining materiality of labor costs in several different ways.

One way is to retain direct labor as a separate

direct-cost category, but reduce the number of individual labor classifications. An industrial machine manufacturer using JIT production methods reduced the number of labor classifications at one of its plants from 26 to 5 over a three-year period. This reduction is consistent with a JIT philosophy that emphasizes teams, not individuals. JIT plants train workers for many different activities. Such training increases flexibility regarding the assignment of workers to individual work cells. Plants with a high level of unionization have reported difficulty in negotiating these reductions in labor classifications with unions.

Some companies abandon labor as a separate direct cost category. The alternative treatments of labor costs are classification of labor costs as a part of an indirect manufacturing cost pool that is allocated to units of production, or classification of labor costs as a period cost that is immediately expended.

The Milwaukee plant of Harley-Davidson, the manufacturer of motorcycles, made changes in labor cost reporting. Although direct labor was less than 10% of the product cost, when direct labor was recorded as a separate cost category, the plant devoted 65% of its cost accounting efforts to the administrative work for these labor costs. This work included setting labor standards, correcting wrong entries associated with labor, and attempting to reconcile the labor reported on job tickets with the total labor time available. Harley-Davidson concluded that the effort did not meet a cost-benefit test. It now combines direct labor and overhead costs into a single conversion cost pool.[6]

Piecework payment plans are being eliminated in JIT plants. Therefore, labor costs may be recorded in far less detail. The elimination of piecework plans drastically reduces the transactions reported per worker. Piecework plans create incentives for workers to produce even though there is no demand for the finished good. In a JIT plant, management prefers workers to be idle rather than to produce for inventory.

Cost Management with JIT

Cost management in JIT plants includes three key activities that also may be applicable to plants not using JIT: Cost planning, cost reduction, and cost control.

Cost planning is started before production begins and in some cases before the production line is constructed. Plant engineers and product designers play important roles in cost planning. The aim is to design the product and the production line with a mix of cost, quality, deliverability, and flexibility that reflects top management's strategy.

Cost reduction takes place in both the pre-production and production stages. At several Japanese plants using JIT, cost reduction targets are

Figure 2
Motivations for Cost Accounting Changes With JIT Production

More accurate product cost information.

- Increase in direct traceability of some costs.
- Elimination (or at least reduction) of several activities classified as indirect.

Better control of cost incurrence.

- Reduced emphasis on individual labor and overhead variances (minimizes dysfunctional operating decisions often associated with existing cost accounting system).

Reduce the costs of the system.
- Reduction in level of detailed information recorded on work tickets.
- Reduction in the level of detailed information recorded about labor costs.

set for each product (e.g., a 25% cost reduction target for a product in its first year). Individual product line workers are required each year to submit a specific number of cost reduction ideas to be discussed by a cost reduction circle.

Cost control is undertaken when production starts. The sources of information include: personal observation by production line workers, financial performance measures such as inventory turnover ratios and variances based on standard costs for materials, labor, and overhead; and nonfinancial performance measures such as production lead-time, setup time, percent of product defects, and schedule attainment. The general trends in cost control activities at both the shop (production cell) level and the plant level that we have observed in JIT plants are: a declining role for financial measures, and an increasing role for personal observation and nonfinancial measures.

One reason for this trend is that production workers play a pivotal role in cost control activities. Worders directly observe nonfinancial variables on the plant floor, where they are intuitive and easy to comprehend.

The dramatic reductions in production lead times place a premium on the timeliness of data when controlling costs. Measurements taken on the plant floor are inevitably the most timely available. Also, increased recognition is given to early pinpointing and controlling of cost "drivers" (the underlying causes of costs). The focus is on before-the-fact rather than after-the-fact control. For example, workers are encouraged to reduce set-up times, minimize scrap, and minimize the number of reworked units.

Finally, the internal accounting system in JIT plants typically contains much less data about actual product costs at individual production cells that can be used in cost control activities. For instance, under the backflush costing method no tracking is made of product cost accumulation as products move through successive work cells. As a second example, those firms that have abolished standard costs for labor and overhead preclude themselves from using labor and overhead standard cost variances in cost control activities.

Inventory turnover and cost reduction target measures provide important financial information to companies using JIT production methods in their plants. An English consumer products company now computes separate inventory turnover ratios for each individual product line; and for raw materials and components, work-in-process, and finished goods. This company still records work-in-process via a process costing system. For companies using "extreme" backflush costing, cost measures of work-in-process will not be recorded in the internal accounting system.

Comparisons of actual product costs with target product costs play an important role in organizations that emphasize cost reduction activities. A Japanese automotive company using JIT has targets for the materials costs associated with individual product lines. Separate materials costs are accumulated for each variation in its product line to gain insight into how cost reduction ideas are leading to lower product costs.

Overview

There is not a single blueprint for cost accounting and cost management that all organizations are adopting as JIT is implemented. Considerable variation exists in the changes made in such areas as the cost pools used, the chosen allocation bases, the costing system adopted (job, operation, process, or backflush), and the types of performance measures used. However, there is an underlying commonality in the changes we observed, that is a movement towards simplification of cost accounting practices. This commonality is part of an overall theme of JIT: to simplify *all* activities.

Despite the fact that there are success stories, many companies reject JIT as inappropriate for their operations. Nevertheless, JIT reminds us that any significant change in underlying operations is likely to justify a corresponding change in the cost accounting and management systems.

If a company's accounting system is still creaking along on engines built 20 years ago, managers are probably not being served optimally in their attempts to cope with today's and tomorrow's manufacturing challenges. We consider the flurry of attention JIT is receiving as beneficial even if it only prods managers and accountants into making a zero-base review of their existing cost accounting and management systems regardless of whether the company is using a JIT philosophy in its purchasing or production activities. □

[1]T. Arenberg, "Vendor Support System—Partners in Profit," *Readings in Zero Inventory*, American Production and Inventory Control Society, 1984, p. 98. Further discussion of JIT purchasing is in C. Horngren and G. Foster, *Cost Accounting: A Managerial Emphasis* 6th ed., Prentice-Hall, 1987, Englewood Cliffs, N.J.. pp. 724-26.
[2]H. Johansson, "The Effect of Zero Inventories on Cost (Just-in-Time)," in *Cost Accounting for the '90s: The Challenge of Technological Change*, (Montvale, N.J.: National Association of Accountants, 1986), p. 145.
[3]R. Kelder, "CIM and Traditional Cost Accounting Practice," Presentation at AME Cost Accounting Conference, Chicago, November 1986.
[4]An example is the Hewlett-Packard personal computer. The HP15OB had 550 part numbers while the next model (HP15OC) had only 120 part numbers. See J. Patell, "Adapting A Cost Accounting System to Just-in-Time Manufacturing: The Hewlett-Packard Personal Office Computer Division," (Working Paper, Stanford University, 1986).
[5]G. Sanchez, "Manufacturing Accounting Cost Systems," Presentation at AME Cost Accounting Conference, Chicago, November 1986.
[6]R. D'Amore and W. Turk, "Just-in-Time Accounting at Harley-Davidson," Presentation at AME Cost Accounting Conference, Chicago, November 1986.
For further discussion of JIT and cost accounting see also:
R. Seglund and S. Ibarreche, "Just-in-Time: The Accounting Implications," MANAGEMENT ACCOUNTING, August 1984, pp. 43-45.
J. Heard, "JIT Accounting," *Readings in Zero Inventory*, American Production and Inventory Control Society, 1984, pp. 20-23.
W. Holbrook and R. Eiler, "Accounting Changes Required for Just-in-Time Production," American Production and Inventory Control Society, 1985 Conference Proceedings, pp. 747-49.
B. Neumann and P. Jaouen, "Kanban, Zips and Cost Accounting: A Case Study," *Journal of Accountancy*, August 1986, pp. 132-41.
B. Maskell, "Management Accounting and Just-in-Time," *Management Accounting* (UK), September 1986, pp. 32-34.
Also see C. Horngren and G. Foster, *Cost Accounting: A Managerial Emphasis* 6th ed., Prentice-Hall, Englewood Cliffs, N.J. 1987, pp. 588-93, 595, 727-30.

How Cost Management Systems Can Support

THE JIT

BY ROBERT D. McILHATTAN

The Just-in-Time philosophy is reshaping the physical nature of the production environment and changing both the behavioral patterns of production costs and how financial executives must measure and control these costs. Some of the changes that are being applied by financial executives to traditional cost management systems to make them better management tools consistent with the JIT philosophy need to be studied and, perhaps, emulated by others.

Each of the changes discussed have been put into practice by organizations that have had success with applying the JIT philosophies to their business and have realized that changes to their cost management systems were necessary in order to enable them to keep pace with the process changes that result when JIT is adopted.

The JIT philosophies are creating manufacturing environments that require a new, more innovative means of approaching cost management. Traditional methods and procedures for measuring and reporting production costs begin to erode in a JIT environment and require that changes be made to existing cost management systems. For example, the JIT philosophies will significantly impact:

■ Identification of cost drivers,
■ Number of product cost elements,
■ Application of product costs, and

■ Nature of performance measures.

A number of JIT organizations have enhanced their cost management systems to complement JIT methods. While specific solutions varied from one organization to another, common elements of how change was initiated existed in each of the organizations that successfully aligned their cost management systems and manufacturing processes.

IDENTIFICATION OF COST DRIVERS

Perhaps the greatest impact of JIT on an organization and the cost management system is that it focuses management's attention on *nonvalue*-added processes. A nonvalue process is defined as any activity or procedure that is performed within a company that does not add value to a product.

For example, assume that the lead time associated with manufacturing a salable product comprises the following general steps:

■ *Process Time* is the amount of time that a product is actually being worked on.
■ *Inspection Time* is the amount of time spent either assuring that the product is of high quality or actually spent reworking the product to an acceptable quality level.
■ *Move Time* is the time spent moving the product from one location to another.

Lybrand Gold Medal, 1986-87.

PHILOSOPHY

Traditional measures common in many cost accounting systems may encourage actions contrary to the spirit of JIT.

■ *Queue Time* is the amount of time the product waits before being processed, or moved, or inspected, or whatever.

■ *Storage Time* is the amount of time a product spends in stock before further processing or shipment.

Of these five steps, only process time actually adds value to the product. All other activities—Inspection time, move time, queue time and storage time—add cost but no value to the product and therefore are deemed as *nonvalue-added* processes within the JIT philosophy.

In many organizations, the amount of process time is much less than 10% of the total manufacturing lead time and cost (costs associated with longer lead times include shortages, obsolescence, and expediting) associated with manufacturing a salable item. Therefore, over 90% of the manufacturing lead time associated with a product adds cost, but no value to the product. It is this premise that leads to the JIT philosophy that reducing lead time will reduce total cost.

In order to assist in this process, financial executives in JIT environments have begun to identify the causes for the time and cost associated with the nonvalue added elements of manufacturing a process.

The key impact on traditional cost accounting is that cost management systems now need to identify the cause of costs—the "cost drivers," in addition to capturing the resultant costs. Harley Davidson, Omark Industries, Hewlett Packard, and other successful JIT users have undertaken studies to define the true "drivers" associated with increasing costs. See Table 1 for a list of cost "drivers."

In all cases, the organizations determined that there was a direct correlation between the number of transactions and the cost of produc-

Thomas P. Burnet (l.), CFO of NutraSweet, and author Robert D. McIlhattan discuss plant operations.

tion. In addition, Hewlett Packard determined that many of its costs were a direct function of: the number of vendors used, the number of engineering changes to the product, and the total number of part numbers it maintained.

In few cases there is a direct correlation between labor head count and total production costs.

By refocusing the cost management system to identify the true driving force behind nonvalue-added activities, the financial executives were able to assist the manufacturing managers in eliminating the product design and manufacturing process inefficiencies that were at the root of the product cost issues.

Product designs were simplified, reducing engineering changes and part numbers, which correspondingly reduced financial problems associated with excess stock, obsolescence, storages, rework, and other associated costs. Vendors were reduced, improving quality and delivery schedules; and reporting transactions were either eliminated completely (in the case of direct labor) or reduced to an obsolete minimum, thereby eliminating support costs for clerical activities associated with transaction process, error correction, waiting time, and moving time.

Through the identification of the costs associated with nonvalue-added activities, financial executives in each of these organizations have been able to help identify the true "drivers" of these activities and costs leading to their reduction or elimination.

NUMBER OF PRODUCT COST ELEMENTS

One of the other impacts that JIT is having on cost management systems is the reduction in the number of cost elements for a product. The philosophies of JIT, while applicable to virtually any industry or process, have had their greatest successes in the industries that, because of the nature of their products and processes, have adopted standard cost systems.

Most traditional standard cost systems maintain standard cost elements for material, direct labor, and manufacturing overhead. More sophisticated standard cost systems often maintained more than these elements. As managers' needs for better cost information increased, overhead costs were typically broken into more finite elements in order to better control production costs. Standard product cost elements associated with variable overhead, fixed overhead, set-up, material acquisition, energy, direct labor overhead, and others were added to cost systems in an effort to obtain better visibility and control over product-related costs.

However, as explained previously, one of the primary philosophies of JIT is to identify the cost drivers associated with production costs. Once identified, the concept of striving for continual improvement in the reduction of product cost through design and process improvements on a daily basis eliminates the need to define multiple cost elements.

Harley Davidson is an example of a JIT-dedicated organization that has reduced the number of standard cost elements associated with its products. It has converted from having five cost elements per part (direct material, direct labor, set-up, variable overhead, and fixed overhead) to just two (direct material and conversion cost). Similar changes have been made by many other JIT organizations including IBM and Caterpillar.

For these organizations, the JIT philosophies have helped them recognize that the issue is the elimination and prevention of costs, not simply the reporting of cost elements. The organizational acceptance and awareness that any cost, regardless of its nature, should be reduced, has focused attention that the design and process improvements necessary to implement JIT successfully will reduce cost through the enhancements themselves. The reduction of cost elements helps people focus on total product cost as opposed to individual elements. Additionally, the reduction of cost elements further reduces the support costs associated with their reporting, calculation, maintenance, and control.

It should be noted that while the number of product cost elements defined within the cost systems for JIT organizations declined, they all retained their standard cost systems. In fact, IBM is in the process of converting some facilities from a weighted average actual cost system to a standard cost system. The application of the standard cost system changed in that it was no longer used as widely to measure performance. Standard cost systems, however, are still important as a tool for valuing inventory and cost of sales and as a tool to estimate potential future costs associated with design and or process changes. Therefore, an additional impact of JIT is that standards are used to a much greater extent as a tool to prevent costs before they arise as opposed to report against once they have incurred. Again, fewer cost elements will suffice in order to meet their purpose.

APPLICATION OF PRODUCT COST

As stated, one of the key characteristics of JIT is the adoption of manufacturing cells dedicated to the production of single or similar products or major components. In addition to the primary objective of the reduction of

TABLE 1. POTENTIAL COST DRIVERS

Number of Labor Transactions	Number of Accessories
Number of Material Moves	Number of Vendors
Number of Total Part Numbers	Number of Units Scrapped
Number of Parts received in a Month	Number of Engineering Change Notices
Number of Part Numbers in an average product	Number of Process Changes
Number of Products	Number of Units Reworked
Average Number of Options	Number of Direct Labor Employees
Number of Schedule Changes	Number of New Parts Introduced

manufacturing lead time, manufacturing cells also change the nature of product costs and introduce alternative methods of applying production costs to specific products flowing through each cell.

The vast majority of traditional cost accounting systems in place today apply indirect manufacturing costs to products based upon either the direct labor hours or dollars charged to a specific product. A JIT environment challenges this practice in two significant areas:

1. The vehicle used to charge and collect labor hours (or dollars) to a specific product in most traditional environments is the factory work order. As individuals work on specific jobs, they charge their time to the factory work order that is associated with the item being manufactured. Costs are therefore accumulated as the factory work order travels through the product process. Within a JIT environment, there may be no factory work orders. Daily production schedules are provided for each cell and typically only finished items are reported by the cell over the course of the day. No detail reporting is performed (which again is consistent with the philosophy of reduction of transactions and lead time). Therefore, the total of all related costs are applied to the day's production, not individual jobs and tasks.

2. In a JIT environment, direct labor may not have a correlation to other manufacturing costs and, as previously stated, is usually included in the total conversion costs. Within a JIT environment, alternative methods of applying cost to a product may be more appropriate. For example, many JIT users apply total conversion cost based on velocity through a manufacturing cell. Velocity is based on the theoretical number of units that can be produced within a cell over a given period. Theoretical capacity is used because it is consistent with the JIT philosophy of continual improvement towards perfection with no allowance for inefficiency or downtime. Based on velocity, a cost per hour is computed for a given cell. Therefore, a day's production is costed

JIT requires careful planning.

WHAT IS JIT?

The most widely accepted definition of JIT is the constant and relentless pursuit for the elimination of waste, with waste being defined as anything that does not add value to a product—inspection, queue time, and stock. While this definition is true, it is too broad to gain a clear understanding of how JIT might impact today's cost management systems.

The JIT concept is built on the philosophy of lead time reduction from suppliers, through operations, and to customers. The common denominator for this concept is the pursuit of zero inventories, zero defects, flexibility, and zero schedule interruptions.

To accomplish these goals, JIT efforts usually include the following activities and/or attributes:

■ Setup reduction and introduction of continually smaller lot sizes. This is necessary to help ensure that products move continuously through the process, eliminating queue time and schedule interruptions.

■ Pursuit of improved product quality. Many JIT firms have adopted new quality awareness programs and/or implemented statistical process controls in order to "make it right the first time," and thus help eliminate product defects and the associated costs of scrap, rework, inspection, returns, and other inherent "costs of quality," i.e., production disruption.

■ Continual improvement in some specific element of the production process. An inherent maxim of JIT is that every person should attempt to improve in some dimension of JIT every day. Improvement can be made in many areas: defects, better product design, fewer stoppages in the schedule, more output, or other areas. Many JIT programs have worker involvement programs structured to help motivate and reward workers for making such improvements.

■ JIT firms generally adopt cellular manufacturing techniques. In order to reduce travel distances and inventory between machines, companies set up manufacturing cells that are dedicated to producing a product or major component start to finish without returning to the stockroom. This JIT feature, sometimes referred to as a "factory within a factory," also requires worker involvement and training, and instructing workers on how to move a product through a cell as efficiently as possible. ■

simply by multiplying the number of units produced by the cost associated with the hours required to produce that day's production. It does not matter whether the hours are direct labor, set-up, queue, or machine hours, the concept is that "time is money" and that the longer it takes to produce something, the more it will cost.

ing cells dedicated to singular or similar product production. However, many JIT organizations including Caterpillar, Harley Davidson, Omark, and IBM have begun to adopt new cost management methods of associating total production costs, including support function costs, directly to products in an effort to reduce allocations and increase cost information reliability

support costs could be associated to a product. Today, 75% of all support costs can be associated to a product without allocation.

Comments by controllers who have adopted direct charging concepts indicate the benefit of enhancing cost management systems to be more compatible with the philosophies of JIT and resultant process changes. Controllers have commented: "product manager's ownership of expense has improved;" "the accuracy of product cost is better;" "there is an increased visibility and awareness of expense items;" "it allows for flexibility in changing environment, improved sourcing decisions, and competitive analysis;" and "it allows for cost reductions and improves competitiveness."

TABLE 2. DIRECT VS. INDIRECT COSTS

	Traditional Environment	J-I-T Environment
Direct labor	Direct	Direct
Material handling	Indirect	Direct
Repairs and maintenance	Direct	Direct
Energy	Indirect	Direct
Operating supplies	Indirect	Direct
Supervision	Indirect	Direct
Production support services	Indirect	Largely direct
Building occupancy	Indirect	Indirect
Insurance and taxes	Indirect	Indirect
Depreciation	Indirect	Direct

It should be noted that other application methods do exist depending on the nature of the manufacturing cell process. These may include material usage, equipment costs, or more imaginative items identified as true cost drivers such as number of transactions, quality, or number of engineering change orders.

A second major impact of JIT on the area of applying product costs is the increase in the amount of production cost that can be directly applied to a product. This phenomenon is a function of the adoption of manufacturing cells and the dedication of those cells to singular or similar products (Table 2).

Within a JIT environment, a fundamental goal is the reduction of total product cost. In order for the cost management system to measure success in this area, allocations must be eliminated to the greatest extent possible. As most financial executives are well aware, the greater the degree of allocations, the less reliable (or accepted) the information is for decision-making purposes.

As illustrated in Table 2, JIT helps eliminate allocations through the implementation of manufactur-

and responsibility; i.e., for "ownership" of product costs.

For example, IBM has adopted a concept of directly charging costs to specific products as a result of their JIT enhancements. Costs are associated to products using one of three methods as follows:

1. Production floor expenses are charged directly to products as they flow through manufacturing cells.
2. Nonoccupancy related support costs, such as cost accountancy and data processing, are "billed" directly to the products utilizing their services. The billing rates are negotiated between support function managers and product managers before services are rendered and are based on the amount of support given to a specific product.
3. Occupancy-related costs are still allocated to products.

Through the adoption of its direct charging approach, IBM has significantly increased the amount of support costs that can be directly associated to a product without the need for allocations. Before this process was adopted, only 25% of

THE NATURE OF PERFORMANCE MEASURES

As organizations begin to adopt a company-wide commitment to total cost management, the performance measurements used to monitor improvement and motivate personnel begin to change. Traditional measures that are commonplace in many cost accounting systems are not appropriate within the JIT philosophy of cost management. In fact, in some cases they may encourage actions that are contrary to the spirit of JIT. Four such examples are:

- Direct labor efficiency,
- Direct labor utilization,
- Direct labor productivity, and
- Machine utilization.

These measurements are inappropriate for the following reasons:

1. They all promote building inventory beyond what is needed in the immediate time frame.
2. Emphasizing performance to standard gives priority to output, at the expense of quality. Relatively few companies even adjust results to reflect bad parts. Using standards for performance measurements can be somewhat limiting relative to continuous improvement. Once standards are attained, people usually feel they have "arrived."
3. Direct labor in the majority of

manufacturers accounts for only between 5%-15% of total product cost. Traditional cost managers have run with very tight direct labor control and relatively loose overhead control. Frequently, direct labor head count reductions have been more than offset by overhead increases.

4. Using machine utilization is similarly inappropriate because it encourages results in building inventory ahead of needs. Focusing on this measurement has frequently resulted in using expensive equipment and sometimes entire plants around-the-clock, thinking this would maximize ROI. The fact is that under this scenario virtually no time is allowed for preventative maintenance; equipment is run flat out until it breaks down. When it does break down, there is considerable disruption that ripples throughout manufacturing. This results in unnecessary costs and, in fact, reduction in ROI instead of its maximization.

Table 3 highlights some performance measures that may be appropriate for a cost management system that is consistent with the JIT philosophies.

Table 3 lists new JIT performance measures that may be appropriate for inclusion in a cost management system within a JIT environment. Specific performance measures are dependent on the unique business environment and process being managed. For example, Harley Davidson has adopted the following 10 measurements to assess its manufacturing effectiveness:

1. Schedule Attainment,
2. Manning Requirements,
3. Conversion Costs,
4. Overtime Requirements,*
5. Inventory Levels,
6. Material Cost Variance,
7. Scrap/Rework,
8. Manufacturing Cycle Time*
9. Quality Level, and
10. Productivity Improvements.

*Measures of Flexibility

Conversely, a different Fortune 100 company has adopted the seven measures and goals listed below for measuring its effectiveness in an integrated circuit facility.

While the measures are different for these two organizations, there are similarities. In both cases, non-financial indicators were used to measure performance as part of the cost management system. This is consistent with the identification of true cost drivers outlined earlier in this article and with the JIT focuses on quality and lead times.

Both measurement systems were proposed and maintained by the financial executives in these organizations. In each case, the financial executives took the initiative to propose more effective ways of monitoring performance and reducing overall cost and worked closely with manufacturing to refine these proposals and establish a "team approach to performance measurement."

Both performance measurement systems were simplified from their predecessor traditional systems. Simple, easy-to-understand measures were implemented so that everyone in the organization could understand their intent and interpret their results. Additionally, measurement results were posted in the factory so that everyone in the organization could be more

TABLE 3
PERFORMANCE MEASURES: TRADITIONAL VS. JIT

Traditional	JIT
• Direct Labor —Efficiency —Utilization —Productivity	• Total Head Count Productivity —Output - Total Head count (direct, indirect, administrative personnel)
• Machine Utilization	• Return on Net Assets
• Inventory Turnover or Months-on-Hand	• Days of Inventory
• Cost Variances	• Product Cost, especially relative to competitors' costs
• Individual Incentives	• Group Incentives
• Performance to Schedule	• Customer Service
• Promotion based on seniority	• Promotion based upon increased knowledge and capability
	• Ideas generated
	• Ideas implemented
	• Lead time by product/product family
	• Set-up reduction
	• Number of customer complaints
	• Response time to customer feedback
	• Machine availability
	• Cost of Quality

"The Spirit of Manufacturing Excellence," September, 1986.
Ernest C. Huge and Alan D. Anderson

TABLE 4

Measure	Goal
1. Unit cost—cell $/hr—theoretical units/hr	$1.00
2. Cycle Time = Through cell with no downtime	3 days
3. On time delivery	100%
4. Quality	0 defects
5. Linearity—Ability to meet daily schedule	0% deviation
6. Inventory turns	75
7. Scrap	0

aware and in tune to company improvements in these areas.

FOCUS ON SIMPLIFICATION

In each of the major areas of cost management outlined above, specific company solutions differ. The impact of true cost drivers within organizations will differ from one company to another; the number of product cost elements necessary to report and control costs properly may differ between companies. The ability to apply costs directly to product and the types of cost being applied to products will change based on organizational differences and products being manufactured; and, as we have seen, performance measurements differ between companies.

However, without exception, simplification was one of the primary objectives of every financial executive who enhanced his cost management system for JIT. The focus on the two or three true cost drivers within an organization, the reduction in standard product cost elements, the reduction of allocations and the establishment of fewer, easy-to-understand, key performance measures are all examples of simplification.

JIT strives for design and process simplification because with simplification comes better management. Better management allows for better quality, better service, and less cost. The same principles are true for cost management systems. Traditional cost accounting systems have a tendency to be very complex. Simplification of this process enables the cost accounting system to be used by everyone an organization, transforming the cost "accounting" system into a cost "management" system.

HOW TO INITIATE CHANGE

The management accountant can learn to think "just-in-time accounting." However, he must adjust to changing technology, new management philosophies, and the changing demands of information. Nothing is more discouraging than to hear financial people say "we can't accommodate that change because of our accounting system."

Each organization cited here had its own series of successes and failures before focusing on the cost management direction necessary to support JIT. As financial executives related their stories regarding the cost management changes they made, a set of common steps emerged as to how change occurred:

■ The perception of the accounting function needed to be changed. In each company the accounting function was perceived as a control function, a function that reported when things were bad. This perception (or reality) had to change from one of control of operations to cooperation with operations to reduce costs. The financial executives took the time and effort necessary to understand JIT and joined the op-

> *JIT focuses management's attention on nonvalue added processes.*

erating professionals in an effort to implement its philosophies.
■ The financial executives became an integral part of the manufacturing and engineering project teams. A cost manager sat in on all product design meetings, manufacturing engineering meetings, and production control and planning meetings on a regular basis. This accomplished the following: a) Accounting personnel learned the key elements of the engineering and manufacturing processes; b) Operating personnel became more aware of the implications of their actions on total cost, raising the total cost awareness throughout the company; and c) Perhaps, most important, it served as the basis for eliminating the communication barriers between accounting and operations. Each objective helped pave the way for obtaining the interfunctional cooperation necessary for the JIT philosophy to work in a company.
■ True cost drivers were identified.

Once accounting became more aware of operations and operating personnel became more aware of the cost implications of their actions, those processes or engineering issues that truly determined cost could be identified, segregated, and attacked.
■ Each company re-analyzed its application of costs to products and implemented a higher level of direct charging. The elimination of allocations gave a clearer picture of true product costs and raised the responsibility of costs to managers. Again, this is predicated on accounting's understanding of the engineering and production process.
■ Performance measures were altered to help motivate the entire operating group toward positive results. Individual performance measures were reduced to encourage a team concept. Personnel were trained and informed as to the meaning of performance measures.
■ All systems were simplified. Traditional accounting systems were redesigned to reflect principles of JIT. Information flows and reports were simplified to focus on the critical processes and measures.

The simplification increased awareness and allowed management to focus on only a few issues that greatly increased the benefits associated with their actions. As process changes took place, cost drivers, and performance measurements changed. Financial executives could change reports and information flows to reflect the new manufacturing process quickly and inexpensively.

Virtually any organization can enhance its cost systems to be more supportive of the JIT philosophy.. The first step is for the financial executive himself to adopt the primary JIT principle of continual improvement within the organization and cost management process. ■

Robert D. McIlhattan is the director of cost management for the Midwest Consulting Group of Ernst & Whinney, responsible for leading the cost management services for that region.

[1]Ernest C. Huge and Alan D. Anderson, "The Spirit of Manufacturing Excellence," Sept.1986.

BAR CODES

0 20248 000875

Speed Factory Floor Reporting

BY THOMAS TYSON AND
ARJAN T. SADHWANI

In less than 15 years, bar coding has moved from a supermarket oddity to a mainstay of shop floor efficiency and inventory control. As more companies reduce inventory stocks, automate production processes, and electronically interchange financial data, automatic identification techniques such as bar coding become absolutely essential.[1]

In automated manufacturing environments, production control personnel rely on accurate real-time information to make financially appropriate decisions. When a fully integrated bar code network is in place, accounting reports that once lagged production by days and weeks can now be prepared in a matter of minutes. Real-time management of these critical areas quickly identifies problems and inefficiencies that can be corrected before they become big problems.

Bar coding is frequently encountered in retail settings, but a growing number of industrial applications directly relate to management accounting. For example, production personnel might scan their bar-coded ID badges, work schedules, and menu of operations to assign labor costs to the products they assemble that day. In real-time environments, robotic equipment can electronically read bar-coded base components on a moving conveyor line and sequentially complete the progressive assembly tasks. In both examples, the related information is collected and immediately incorporated into cost

Bar coding has revolutionized data entry and collection procedures.

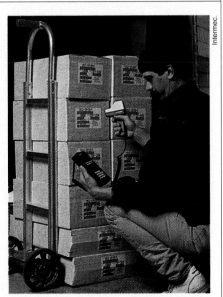

Worker uses bar code scanner to record inventory.

management reports.

As bar coding equipment costs continue to decline, application opportunities increase, and their interface with accounting procedures becomes more frequent. In many accounting applications, bar coding provides a logical bridge between data collection and information generated by the cost management

systems. To ensure full integration of these applications, accountants must thoroughly understand the concepts and components of bar code systems so that they can actively participate on development and implementation teams.

BAR CODE SYMBOLOGIES

The bar code is a symbol consisting of a specifically designed pattern of alternating parallel bars and spaces that are a binary representation of letters, numbers, and special characters. Bar code symbologies designate width, number, and separators of black and white bars for these characters. All symbologies encode a set of characters in repeated bar-space patterns to provide a self-checking attribute so that an ink spot or a torn bar code label does not result in an inaccurate read by the scanning device. Two of them, code 39 and interleaved 2 of 5, are widely used in industry. Table 1 compares the more common symbologies across several key factors.

Code 39 is an alphanumeric bar code that uses nine black and white bars for each character or symbol. It requires three bars to be wide and six to be narrow. This code can represent alphabetic, numeric, and six special characters and can be expanded to represent the 128 ASCII character set used in computer-based systems. The code has a strong self-checking feature that provides high data integrity and security. Code 39 is rapidly becoming the standard symbology for applications in manufacturing and inventory control.

Interleaved 2 of 5 encodes numeric characters exclusively. As its name suggests, each character contains a total of five bars, two of which must be wide. The character value of this bar code is determined by where the wide bars fall in the sequence. Thus, interleaved 2 of 5 modifies the usual meaning of a bar code by enabling both bars and spaces, rather than just bars to have meaning. Like code 39, it has a self-checking feature to guard against misreads. It is extensively used in the automotive industry and in warehousing, baggage handling, and photofinishing applications.

DATA SCANNERS

There are five general types of reading equipment: hand-held light pens, stationary fixed beam scanners, stationary moving beam scanners, hand-held lasers, and imaging array readers. All readers work on the principle of illuminating a bar code symbol and converting the reflected light pattern into an analog signal that is decoded and then digitally processed. The scanner's spot of light should approximate the width of the narrowest module, called the "X" dimension. Therefore, extremely dense bar codes require tightly focused laser light signals.

An important issue affecting the quality and reliability of scanning is print tolerance, or the degree that bars and spaces may vary from specifications. The use of check digits, a symbology's built-in structural requirements, high print tolerance, and a clean reading environment—all contribute to high scanning reliability.

Light pens are the least costly and most popular reading device. They are designed to emit light in wavelengths that correspond to the type of print media and inks used in the encoded symbols. Immediately after a symbol has been scanned, the operator is informed of an acceptable read by receiving the appropriate audio-visual feedback. Because of their portability and low cost, light pens are used in a number of accounting-related applications including labor tracking, tool check-out, cycle counting, document and asset tracking, materials management, and inventory control. In conjunction with a barcoded notepad of possible operator responses, nearly all manual or keyboard data entry tasks can be eliminated.

BAR CODING TERMS

ASCII	The code described in American National Standard Code using a coded character set consisting of 7-bit coded characters (8 bits including parity check), used for information interchange among data processing systems, communication systems, and associated equipment. The ASCII set consists of alphabet characters, numbers, and special characters.
Bar Code	A graphic (printed or photographically reproduced) bar.
Symbol	Code composed of parallel bars and spaces of various widths. A bar code symbol contains a leading quiet zone, start character, data character(s)(s) including a check digit (if any), stop character, and a trailing quiet zone.
Bar Length or Bar Height	The measurement of the long dimension of a bar.
Bar Width	The measurement of the thickness of a bar.
Bar Width Ratio	The ratio of the largest to the narrowest bar width within a bar code.
Bidirectional Bar Code Symbol	A bar code symbol format that permits reading in complementary (opposite) directions across bars and spaces.
Character	A letter, digit, or other special form that is used as part of the organization, control, or representation of data. A character is often in the form of a spatial arrangement of adjacent or connected strokes.
Check Digit	A calculated character included within a message, used for error detection.
Depth of Field	The difference between the minimum and maximum horizontal distance from the aperture of the bar code reader throughout which the bar can be read.
Discrete Bar Code Symbol	A bar code symbol in which the intercharacter gap is not part of the code and is allowed to vary dimensionally within wide tolerance limits.
First Read Rate	The number of successful reads of a bar code symbol on the first attempt, usually expressed as a percentage.
Intercharacter Gap	The space between the last element of one character and the first element of the adjacent character of a discrete bar code symbol.

Stationary fixed beam readers operate on the same principle as hand-held light pens except that the symbol rather than the scanning device must be moved physically. The advantage of their rela-

BAR CODING TERMS (cont.)

LOGMARS
A specification dictating the format for bar coding affixed to products sold to the U.S. government.

Message Code
A user-specific meaning ascribed to a bar coded message, including any message format restrictions or check digits.

Optical Throw
The horizontal distance from the aperture of a bar code reader to the leading vertical plane of the depth of field; the minimum distance a bar code symbol can be away from the scanner and still be successfully read.

Parity
A system for encoding characters as odd or even bar patterns to provide a self-checking feature in bar codes.

Print Contrast Signal (PCS)
A comparison between the reflectance of the bars and that of the spaces. PCS under a given set of illumination conditions is defined as:

$$PCS = \frac{\text{Space Reflectance - Bar Reflectance}}{\text{Space Reflectance}}$$

Quiet Zone
The area immediately preceding the start character and following the stop character, which contains no markings.

Reflectance
A measure of the amount of light reflected back from a surface.

Resolution
The ability of a bar code reader to read narrow bars in a bar code; optically reproducing fine detail.

Scanner
An optical and electronic device that scans bar code symbols and outputs the bar coded information in the form of electrical signals suitable for input to a computer system.

Scanning Range
The maximum distance at which a scanner can read a bar code symbol; equal to the sum of the optical throw plus the depth of field.

Self-Checking Bar Code
A bar code that uses a checking algorithm which can be applied against each character to guard against undetected errors.

Start and Stop Characters
Distinct characters used at the beginning and end of each bar code symbol that provide initial timing references and direction-of-read information to the coding logic.

Substrate
The supporting material upon which a bar code is printed.

---

scanning action, either by the symbol or the reading device. These are available in either stationary or hand-held models. They produce reliable reading performance by repeatedly passing an electronic beam of light over a stationary or moving symbol. Stationary readers are often found in automated conveyor applications such as stock sorting and inventory warehousing where consistent reader/symbol orientations can be maintained.

Hand-held lasers are used in similar applications as light pens, but differ in several ways. Laser light is more intense, provides greater reliability, and is far more tolerant of harsh reading environments. By employing a moving beam of light, laser readers significantly reduce operator frustrations that accompany repeated first-scan failures. Greater depth of field performance results in much faster read speeds and far easier access to symbols. Hand-held lasers are significantly more expensive than light pens, but newer models that integrate both reading and decoding intelligence allow for overall system cost reductions and may eventually replace light pens as the preferred hand-held reading device.

Imaging array readers envision all bar code characters at one time. They are used in stationary or hand-held applications that tolerate a limited depth of field performance. Low relative cost and slow reading speed make this device most appropriate for low volume point-of-sale applications. Table 2 compares the five types of reading devices across several key factors.

HOW DATA IS COLLECTED

Once data is captured, a variety of devices are available for transmitting data to a dedicated host computer or the firm's mainframe. An intelligent terminal can be hard-wired directly to the computer, tied initially to a transaction manager that preprocesses the data, or wedged to a keyboard and CRT. The decision among these on-line alternatives rests on the issues of visual verification, computer response time, or mainframe capability.

Another approach to data collection involves batch rather than on-line processing. Devices may be ei-

tive low cost must be weighed against their limited depth of field performance, that is, the distance from the light source to the encoded symbol. Fixed beam readers are most appropriate for in-line

verification applications such as tool check-out, package tracking, badge reading, and time and attendance recording.

Stationary moving beam readers eliminate the need for a physical

TABLE 1 / COMPARISON OF SYMBOLOGIES

Category	UPC	Code 39	Inter-leaved 2 of 5	Codabar
Primary Business Applications	Supermarket & retail	Industrial, commercial, health	Warehouse, industrial, automotive	Baggage handling, blood, library
Type of Character Set	Numeric	Alphanumeric & 6 symbols	Numeric	Numeric & 6 symbols
Highest Density	13.7 cpi[3]	9.4 cpi	17.8 cpi	10 cpi
Variable Length	No	Yes	No	Yes

[3] cpi = characters per inch

ther stationary or hand-held and can include alphanumeric keyboards, be fully programmable, contain time clocks, and provide for modem interface. Batch processing devices are frequently used in inventory control, document tracing, remote order entry, and manufacturing floor control. In one machine assembly application, for example, eight stationary models support an 80-person shop force and contain sufficient memory to accumulate a full shift's labor data.

The most expensive transmitting device adds a radio communication link between the reader and the host system for real-time processing capability. At present, communication costs limit these applications to high volume warehouse or robotic assembly operations. For example, forklift operators receive instructions on radio-linked portable terminals mounted on their forklifts to withdraw palletized stock and verify remaining quantities. They record completed transactions through bar-coded data entry which immediately updates supporting data files. Reduced search time, improved stock rotation, and leaner safety stocks are just a few of the resulting benefits.

IMPORTANCE OF PRINTERS

Printers and print media are key elements in the bar code network. Illegible labels can render a perfectly designed system inoperative. Adhesiveness, print contrast, label durability, and surface environment all affect the reliability of reading a bar code symbol. In harsh environments, symbols can rapidly become obscured and damaged. To solve this problem, some companies cover labels with a clear plastic laminate. Some symbologies also are more sensitive to ink spread, paper shrinkage and expansion, and other printing inaccuracies. Therefore, generous tolerances are required to allow for these and other inconsistencies.

Many types of printers are available in the marketplace. They range from an inexpensive general purpose dot matrix printer to more specialized laser models that produce high quality labels in large quantities at a reasonable cost. Most printers are software-driven and are able to produce labels of different sizes and on different print media. Some printers have intelligent graphic processing capabilities, allowing the users to design labels for several different applications. They can also produce labels in two or more symbologies in order to meet a variety of application needs.

BAR CODING AND MANAGEMENT ACCOUNTING

Ametek-Thermox Instruments Division's plant in Pittsburgh, Pennsylvania, uses bar code technology very effectively in its cost accounting applications and manufacturing information systems. Bar codes are used to collect data in purchasing and receiving, and to track time and attendance for payroll, shop floor control, and work-in-process accounting. Bar code data entry also assigns quality inspection times to jobs and maintains inventory control, including parts picking and cycle counting.

The company uses a simple menu-driven data collection system. Its software runs on PCs networked with a host computer that directs the data collection and assignment process. The system is

TABLE 2 / COMPARISON OF SCANNING METHODS

Type of Reader	Primary Accounting Application	Relative Cost	Human Operator Required	Processing Mode
Light Pens	Labor tracking Inventory control	Low	Yes	Batch
Stationary Fixed Beam	Inventory control	Medium	No	On-line
Stationary Moving Beam	Inventory control	High	No	On-line
Hand-held Laser	Same as light pen	High	Yes	Batch/ On-Line
Imaging Array	Low volume retail	Medium	Yes	On-line

interfaced with an IBM system 36 computer that runs MAPICS software for production scheduling and control operations. Ametek has enhanced the software with several modules that integrate it with job cost accounting routines. These enhanced modules reconcile the time applied on jobs with actual payroll hours. They generate accurate journal entries because all required data are captured and integrated with the requirements of the MAPICS software.

Microcomputers, with attached reading wands, are strategically placed on the shop floor, storeroom, receiving dock, and time and attendance area. Workers wand across their identification cards, work orders, and parts lists to capture the required data. Built-in clocks record the elapsed time whenever job start and stop codes are scanned. A bar code notepad of instructions guides the worker in initiating transactions or supplying passwords. The networking feature provides extensive real-time verification of the collected data. The error rate is extremely low because of the self-checking features of the symbology. The system has the capability to update the manufacturing information system database instantly or, if in a batch processing mode, at the end of the day.

The labor time information generated in various departments and operations is used to measure actual direct labor hours against established standards. Because paid hours are accurately reconciled with applied hours, the information is used to determine the productivity of operations performed in various departments. The system also produces accurate cost variance information by product code, product category, and even by individual employee.

Interviews with production managers, workers, and office personnel showed that all parties have benefited from the bar code technology. The integration and networking capability of bar coding allow the accounting staff to prepare reports that are both timely and accurate. Shop floor personnel record time and update records far more effortlessly and efficiently with bar coding. Furthermore, production management has much greater faith in the accounting numbers.

Actual costs are maintained as

The exceptional reliability of bar-coded transactions allows firms to reduce auditing expenditures significantly.

continual up-to-date running averages and are used to revise cost standards. Larry Mocniak, accounting manager at Ametek's Pittsburgh location, indicates that timely reports enable managers to focus on manufacturing bottlenecks and streamline the more critical processes.

There seems to be *no* negative aspects to bar code data collection at Ametek. In fact, with bar coding no longer can it be said that cost accounting information is too late, too aggregated, and too distorted for managers' planning and control decisions.

COST MANAGEMENT SYSTEMS IMPROVED

Many aspects of bar coding interface with a management accountant's responsibilities. With regard to basic accounting procedures, the ability of scan-

Teddy bear in a toy store gets the scanner once-over.

ners to automatically read and decode symbols with incomparable accuracy has revolutionized data entry and collection procedures. Furthermore, the traditional accounting functions of posting, transferring, and verifying have been effectively replaced by computer programs that unerringly relate a bar code identifier to the proper underlying transactions and accounts.

The exceptional reliability of bar-coded transactions allows firms to reduce auditing expenditures significantly, especially in regard to inventory cycle counts and work-in-process validations. However, the internal control responsibilities of accountants must encompass the bar code technology as well as traditional business data. As an example, accountants need to ensure that bar code labels are designed to minimize counterfeiting, reveal tampering, and to guarantee that the source of labels is traceable.

Fully integrated bar code systems now can assume nearly every aspect of an accountant's scorekeeping responsibilities. Specifically in automated manufacturing settings, bar coding and other automatic identification techniques provide many opportunities for cost management systems to provide information for improving quality and reducing waste. Management accountants must make certain that selected applications are designed to fully integrate with existing accounting procedures. They can best do so by familiarizing themselves with the concepts of bar coding technology and by participating as active members on bar code development and implementation teams. ■

Thomas Tyson, Ph.D., CMA, is assistant professor of accounting at Clarkson University at Potsdam, N.Y. Dr. Tyson is a member of the Northern New York Chapter of NAA.

Arjan T. Sadhwani, Ph.D., is professor of accounting and information systems at The University of Akron, Akron, Ohio. He is a past president of NAA's Akron Summit Chapter, through which this article was submitted.

[1]In addition to bar coding, other techniques include optical character recognition (OCR), machine vision, voice recognition, magnetic strip, radio frequency, and mark sense.

XEROX SCANS INVENTORY

Bar coding is an integral part of a sophisticated inventory control system at the Xerox Corporation copier assembly plant in Webster, New York. Within this site is a fully automated high-rise storehouse that handles over 1,000 transactions per day and deals with over 55,000 parts annually. The bar code network and system's unique software component integrate three separate material replenishment modules within the plant.

When parts are received at the dock, they are immediately assigned to uniform bar-coded pallets. If the parts are not immediately needed on the shop floor, they are routed to a fully automated high-rise storehouse by fixed bar code scanners that are mounted on a series of automated conveyor lines.

Timely scanning of bar-coded information is essential for Xerox's sophisticated MRP system that determines the quantity, frequency, and location of parts replenishment of all of its assembly lines and work stations. When warehoused parts are needed, pallets are automatically withdrawn from the high-rise and robotically delivered to material handlers. These handlers withdraw the required boxes, prepare a master replenishment ticket, and attach bar-coded routing tags to *every* box in the replenishment. Fixed scanners on another series of conveyors direct the boxes to appropriate assembly modules according to information encoded on the bar code label. At each module, designated handlers "detrash" the boxes and scan the label on the box to determine the total quantity and final destination of boxes in the replenishment.

In the automated assembly module, handlers place *all* boxed parts in uniform bar-coded tote bins which are then automatically routed to individual assembly work stations or assigned buffer areas. By scanning empty bins, the system is able to automatically replace needed parts at individual stations. In the console assembly module (CAM), handlers place part boxes in carts that are dedicated to particular assembly grid locations. Radio-directed drivers of forklifts transport these carts to the work-

in-process grids. They then physically place the part boxes in the more than 350 individual work stations flow lines.

Because the CAM line is not fully automated with regards to inventory replenishment, system design personnel felt compelled to introduce a scanning requirement to the assemblers' job functions. Before scanning, parts were brought by train from the high-rise to a central drop area and then transported to CAM assembly buffer locations. A team of expeditors would walk the floor to collect the type of parts needed by the assemblers. The ex-

At Xerox, Don Lattanzio works with CAM workstation operator, Barbara Barron, scanning for parts.

peditors would manually record and communicate this information to the material handling department which replenished individual stations. The system's weakness was its inability to acknowledge the receipt of parts at the individual work station. As a consequence, dispatchers and expeditors were never informed about parts' status and deficient inventory buildups often occurred. Under the new bar coding system, each assembler indicates his or her need for parts by scanning a menu of the location where the part is stored at the dedicated work station terminal. The system responds to the parts request by indicating the storage location and disposition of these

parts. Assemblers' requests are now communicated directly to material handlers who undertake the replenishment. The new system has significantly reduced the number of shop floor personnel involved in expediting and dispatching.

At Xerox, bar coding is looked upon as a naturally evolving productivity improving factor that enhances an MRP system and complements the philosophies of JIT and TQC. With the help of bar coding, records integrity has been improved, purchase lot sizes have been minimized, and parts can be accurately retraced to the date and source of supply if quality problems should develop. Bar coding has helped allow work station cycle counts to consistently reconcile to within 1% accuracy levels, a criterion that Xerox must fulfill in order to avoid complete physical inventories that used to require annual two-week plant shutdowns.

Xerox uses code 39 in all of its internal applications and is now examining how it can extend this coding requirement to its suppliers. By doing so, the need to create documents at the receiving dock can be eliminated and goods can move directly and automatically from incoming trucks to the high-rise storehouse. Fred Kull, the manager of the assembly facility's information system, cannot foresee Xerox operating without bar coding. In fact, he feels there is a lot more that could be done, especially in the area of production control and work-in-process accounting.

Mr. Kull indicates that while Xerox's accountants were not involved in the design, development, or implementation of the bar coding system, they did insist on the systems meeting strict control requirements regarding the transfer of parts from the storehouse to work-in-process.

Unlike their role in Ametek, accounting personnel are primarily concerned with inventory valuation, rather than with inventory planning or control. It appears that the level of interaction between accounting, manufacturing, and systems management determines the nature of accountants' participation in bar coding applications. □

Section 4

Changes: Quality Cost Measurement

Section 4 examines another change occurring in the new manufacturing environment—an emphasis on high-quality products and services and a resultant interest in quality cost measurement. This section focuses on defining and measuring the individual components of quality cost and incorporating their interrelationships into a total quality cost measurement system.

James T. Godfrey and William R. Pasewark stress the importance of focusing on total quality costs rather than on individual quality cost components. In their proposed model, they identify three primary components: defect control costs, which include prevention costs and appraisal costs; failure costs, which include rework costs, profits lost on defective unit sales, and customer return processing costs; and the opportunity cost of lost current and future sales. They emphasize that all these quality cost components need to be determined even though some are difficult to quantify or do not appear on the traditional income statement.

Godfrey and Pasewark provide several useful tables and graphs. One table summarizes the quality cost components in equation form. Several graphs and another table capture the idea of how individual quality cost components relate to one another. This second table illustrates how minimizing total quality cost differs from minimizing individual quality costs. The authors conclude that a comprehensive system of quality control requires identifying all the possible costs associated with defective units and understanding the relationships that exist among the different components of total quality cost.

The article by Dennis A. Loewe describes the total quality management system of Weyerhaeuser. This system is based upon its definition of quality as "providing customers with products and services that consistently meet their needs and expectations" and total quality management as "a process for continuous improvement to achieve full customer satisfaction." Much of the article describes the system in terms of its four components—leadership, customer needs, employee involvement, and processes.

In discussing leadership, Loewe cites 10 key paths where traditional management leadership style must change. Customer needs are met in a five-step "customer in" system attentive to customer requirements, complaints, and new product ideas. Employee involvement is enhanced by creating a blame-free environment and by an award program encouraging continuous improvement in providing quality service to customers. Process management involves standardization through measurable inputs, value-added activities, measurable outputs, and repeatable processes. After processes are standardized, continuous improvement through systematic and continuous elimination of waste becomes the goal. Loewe closes by reviewing the key role of management accountants in the total quality management area.

Thomas P. Edmonds, Bor-Yi Tsay, and Wen-Wei Lin describe an analytical program for evaluating quality costs, developed by a Taiwan-based international conglomerate, the Formosa Plastics Group (FPG). Prior to the main discussion, they review the four categories of quality cost cited in an NAA research report: prevention and appraisal costs, which are voluntary, and internal and external failure costs, which are involuntary. Examples of costs in each category are included in a table. The authors describe the FPG system at the local, division, and headquarter levels.

When analyzing products at the local level, the focus is on allocating resources to attain a reasonable level of quality assurance that minimizes total quality cost per unit. The authors show how trend analysis can help to determine the optimal point, which is often difficult to determine in practice. At the divisional level, the focus is on performance evaluation and planning, using ratio analysis and quality cost budgets.

At the headquarter level, the focus is on the competitive position of the firm within its industry. At this level comparisons should be made with competitors rather than among internal divisions, and a different group of quality ratios is used. The authors conclude that applying these techniques at all three levels helps managers compete in today's world-class manufacturing environment.

Additional Readings from *Management Accounting*

Clark, John, "Costing for Quality at Celanese," March 1985, pp. 42-46.

Clark, Ronald L. and James B. McLaughlin, "Controlling the Cost of Product Defects," August 1986, pp. 32-35.

Dietemann, Gerard J., "Measuring Productivity in a Service Company," February 1988, pp. 48-54.

Gass, Gerald L., Grover McMakin, and Roger Bentson, "White Collar Productivity," September 1987, pp. 33-38.

Morse, Wayne J. and Harold P. Roth, "Why Quality Costs Are Important," November 1987, pp. 42-43.

Smith, Gene L., "Improving Productivity in the Controller's Organization," January 1986, pp. 49-51.

Tyson, Thomas N., "Quality and Profitability: Have Controllers Made the Connection?" November 1987, pp. 38-42.

Woods, Michael D., "How We Changed Our Accounting," February 1989, pp. 42-45.

Controlling Quality Costs

A flaw in today's quality control cost systems is their focus on reducing individual, not the total quality costs of production.

BY JAMES T. GODFREY AND
WILLIAM R. PASEWARK

Despite programs to increase the quality of manufactured products, there is still the widespread belief that American manufacturers are losing a competitive edge to manufacturers that produce higher quality products abroad.

Corporate managers often are preoccupied with the goals of their individual departments, rather than the overall corporate goal of improving and maintaining product quality. Production areas tend to set goals in terms of numbers of units rather than quality of units. Expense center managers attempt to control the costs they are held directly responsible for. These costs rarely include long-term product quality considerations.

American systems of defective unit cost control often contain wishy-washy requirements and vague performance standards that are difficult for employees to interpret.[1] Companies that attempt to identify specific defective unit costs to be controlled often limit those costs to those that are readily quantifiable in dollars and appear on the income statement, thereby affecting current-year net income.

An effective system of quality cost control not only should consider the expenses traditionally emphasized on the income statement, but also should consider other aspects such as opportunity costs, long-term market considerations, and relationships among costs that affect total quality costs. Designing an effective quality cost control system should begin with the identification of all possible costs associat-

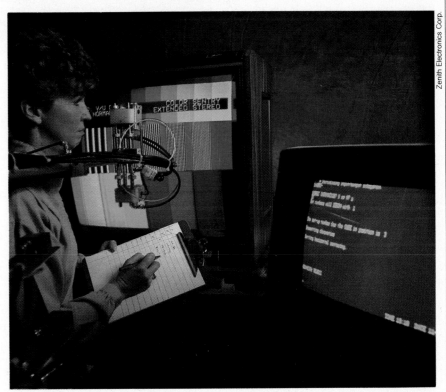

Zenith Data Systems personal computers must pass stringent quality-assurance tests at the company's final assembly plant in St. Joseph, Mich.

ed with defective units, and the determination of whether the cost easily is quantifiable and whether the cost appears on the income statement.

COMPONENTS OF TOTAL QUALITY COST

Total quality cost is composed of defect control costs, failure costs, and costs of lost sales. These costs are related so that a change in one type of cost can result in a change in another type. For example, larger defect control expenditures can result in lower product failure costs and costs of lost sales.

Defect Control Costs. Defect control costs are expenditures that prevent defective units from occurring during the production process or prevent defective units from being shipped to customers. Defect control costs are made up of prevention costs and appraisal costs. Defect Control Cost (Q) equals Prevention Cost (K) plus Appraisal Cost (A), or: $Q = K + A$

Prevention costs are investments in machinery, technology, and education programs designed to reduce the number of defective units during the production process. Specifically, prevention costs also include: ... administration of the quality function; design and planning of verification actions; preventive maintenance of equipment; review and updating of instructions, specifications, and procedures; surveys related to product warranty; and personnel training.[2]

Prevention costs, for the most part, are fixed and discretionary by management, although certain prevention costs may be considered necessary.

Appraisal costs are sometimes referred to as monitoring or inspecting costs. Expenditures for appraisal are designed to reduce the number of defective units released to customers. Appraisal costs include: appraisal of prototypes, new materials, methods, and processes; inspections performed by the company's quality department; equipment, supplies, samples, and premises necessary for the

Frequent discussions with employees can help ensure the success of a quality cost control system.

performance of inspections and tests; verifications by external laboratories or organizations; operators' self inspection; and evaluation of competitors' products.

These costs are fixed—although there is a possibility that some of them may be variable in terms of the number of units inspected or number of defective units—and are controllable by managers.

Failure Costs. Total failure costs consist of: rework cost, profit lost by selling units as defective, and the cost of processing customer returns. These costs vary with the number of defective units—as the number of defective units increases, failure cost increases.

Rework cost is the cost required to restore defective units to the quality standards required for "good" units. The number of defective units reworked depends on whether management determines that the defective unit can be restored.

On the other hand, management may decide not to restore the defective unit and attempt to sell the unit "as is." These units often are referred to as "seconds" or "irregulars" and may be sold for profit only if there is a market. Most certainly, the sale will occur at a reduced profit and even may be sold at a loss. The sale of a unit that has not been reworked results in an opportunity cost equal to the difference of the profit earned from a "good" unit and the profit from the

item sold as a second. We refer to this as lost profit because the product was sold as defective. (See Table of Formulas.)

If the number of units to be reworked (Y) can be expressed as a constant percentage of the total number of defective units (D), a direct or linear relationship exists between the number of defective units and both the cost of rework (R) and the opportunity cost due to selling a defective unit "as is" (Z) (Figure 1).

However, if the percentage of total defective units (D) reworked is not constant for different levels of D, the relationships depicted in Figure 1 become more complicated.

Defective units that are not discovered by appraisal, unfortunately, will be discovered by customers. Processing a customer return requires shipping and paperwork costs to supply the customer with a good product. If we assume a constant cost of processing a return, there exists a direct or linear relationship between the number of defective units discovered after appraisal (D_2) and the cost of customer returns (W) or the same type of relationship as in Figure 1.

The total costs of failure can be determined by combining the three components of failure cost. (Table of Formulas.)

Cost of Lost Sales. The most difficult quality cost to quantify is the cost of current and future sales that will be lost if defective units

FIGURE 1 / CERTAIN FAILURE COSTS AND DEFECTIVE UNITS

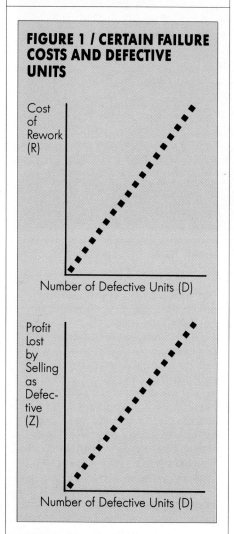

are received by customers. Customers may be discouraged to make future purchases either temporarily or indefinitely.

The difficulty in quantifying these costs, however, does not justify excluding them from decisions about defective unit costs. Customer surveys, product demand statistics, and other marketing resources are tools that can help in deriving estimates of these costs. It is particularly important to determine how these costs can change as the amount or percent of defective units produced changes. Some of the costs of customer surveys and

Quality cost components must be measured and analyzed.

use of marketing resources would qualify as defect control costs.

Calculating the Total Quality Cost. The total quality cost then can be determined by combining the three major components. (See Table of Formulas.)

TABLE OF FORMULAS

Calculating Cost Profits

Profit lost By Selling as Defective (Z) =
[Total Defective Units (D) − Number of Units Reworked (Y)]
× [Profit for Good Unit (p_1) − Profit for Defective Unit (p_2)]

or $Z = (D − Y)*(p_1 − p_2)$

Calculating Total Costs of Failure

Total Failure Cost (F) =
  Rework Cost (R)
+ Profit Foregone By Selling as Defective (Z)
+ Cost of Processing Customer Returns (W)

or $F = R + Z + W$

or in expanded form:
$F = (Y*r) + [(D − Y)*(p_1 − p_2)] + (D_2*w)$

where:
r = cost to rework an individual defective unit
D_2 = number of defective units returned by customers
w = cost of a single customer return

Calculating the Total Quality Cost

The total quality cost can be determined by combining the three major components:

Total Quality Cost (T) =

Defect Control Costs $\left\{ \begin{array}{l} \text{Prevention Cost (K)} \\ + \text{ Appraisal Cost (A)} \end{array} \right.$

Failure Costs $\left\{ \begin{array}{l} + \text{ Rework Cost (R)} \\ + \text{ Profit Foregone by Selling as Defective (Z)} \\ + \text{ Return Processing Cost (W)} \\ + \text{ Cost of Lost Sales (L)} \end{array} \right.$

or $T = K + A + R + Z + W + L$

In expanded form:
$T = K + A + (Y*r) + [(D − Y)*(p_1 − p_2)] + (D_2*w) + L$

MINIMIZING TOTAL QUALITY COSTS

A reasonable goal for businesses is to minimize total quality cost (T). Presumably, the cost accounting system at management's disposal should provide the relevant cost information to aid in accomplishing this goal.

An important aspect of the relevant cost information, in addition to measuring the individual quality costs, is to take into account any significant relationships among the different costs. A typical flaw of American quality control cost systems is that the systems are concerned with minimizing individual costs. For example, a company's goal may be to reduce the cost of processing the return of a defective unit by a customer. What the company also should consider is increasing appraisal expenditures so that the number of customer returns is reduced.

When a company examines its prevention costs, it should analyze the relationship between how much was spent on defective unit prevention (K) and how many defective units (D) were produced. Managers can assume that as the percentage of defective units approaches zero, the costs of preventing defective units must be increasing rapidly. For example, the increase in prevention costs required to reduce the percentage of defective units from 6% to 5% is likely to be smaller than the change in prevention costs required to go from 2% to 1% defective (Figure 2).

After determining how prevention cost relates to defective units, companies should consider how the level of defective units is related to failure costs. We suggested that certain failure costs are related to defective units (D) as illustrated in the Figure 1 graph. Given the cause-and-effect relationship between prevention cost and the number of defective units, and the cause-and-effect relationship between the number of defective units and failure costs, we can determine that indirect relationships exist between prevention cost and the other quality costs.

The same kind of indirect, cause-and-effect relationship can be assumed between defect control costs and the cost of lost sales. First, it is reasonable to assume a cause-and-effect relationship between defect control costs $(K+A)$ and the number of defective units discovered by customers (D_2). In addition, a cause-and-effect relationship between the number of defective units discovered by customers and the cost of lost sales (L) can be assumed. An indirect relationship, therefore, results between defect control costs and the cost of lost sales.

A company also may determine a relationship between the number of defective units detected by customers (D_2) and appraisal costs (A). The relationship is likely to be non-linear (which would be illustrated by a graph like Figure 2), because it is likely there will be diminishing returns from expenditures on appraisal.

TABLE 1 / QUALITY COST RELATIONSHIPS

| Defect Control Costs | | | Failure Costs | | | | Total Quality Costs (T) |
Prevention Cost (K)	Appraisal Cost (A)	Percent Defective	Rework Cost (R)	Cost of Not Reworking (Z)	Cost of Processing (W)	Cost of Lost Sales (L)	
$100	$100	5.00%	$50.0	$5.00	$10.0	$15.00	$280
120	80	3.50	35.0	3.50	7.0	10.50	256
140	65	2.25	22.5	2.25	4.5	6.75	241
160	55	1.25	12.5	1.25	2.5	3.75	235
180	50	.50	5.0	.50	1.0	1.50	238
200	45	0.00	0.0	0.00	0.0	0.00	245

FIGURE 2 / RELATIONSHIP BETWEEN THE NUMBER OF DEFECTIVE UNITS AND PREVENTION COSTS

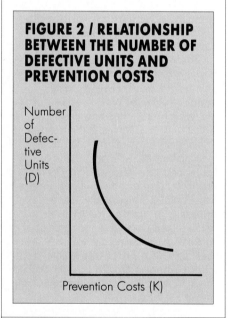

Number of Defective Units (D)

Prevention Costs (K)

Another potential relationship to consider is between prevention and appraisal costs. Decreases (increases) in prevention costs may result in increases (decreases) in required appraisal costs. It appears that a nonlinear relationship may be appropriate because it is likely that diminishing returns would occur as prevention costs are increased. That is, a minimum level of appraisal cost would always be required.

The amounts a company spends on prevention and appraisal can determine expenditures required for other components of total quality cost. It also should be clear that total quality costs (T) cannot be minimized by simply minimizing the individual costs that make up the total. For example, it would not always be in a company's best interest to minimize the costs of prevention and appraisal because of their effects on other components of quality costs. Likewise, it's not always in the company's best interest to increase how much it spends on prevention and appraisal when it tries to eliminate failure costs. In fact, the popular goal of zero defects may not be the strategy that minimizes total quality cost.

Table 1 illustrates how the different quality costs are related. In our illustration, we assume that the number of defective units reworked (Y) is a constant percent of total defective units. Second, we assume that the number of defective units discovered by the customers (D_2), is a constant percent of total defective units. In a more realistic setting, the number of units reworked (Y) could be a discretionary variable that depends on factors other than total defective units. The number of defective units discovered by customers (D_2) most likely would be related to appraisal cost (A) in addition to total defective units.

As shown in Table 1, there are six possible levels of costs and defective units. The maximum possible defective unit rate is five percent. This represents the base case for a minimum expenditure of $100 for prevention cost (K).

Total quality costs (T) are minimized at $235. To implement this outcome, management would select levels of prevention costs and appraisal costs of $160 and $55, respectively. With these quality control expenditures, a total defective unit rate of 1.25% is expected, which then leads to the failure costs and cost of lost sales.

We do not mean to suggest here that producing units with zero defects would never be a reasonable goal. We have simply used hypothetical data that reflect relationships often suggested as typical. However, different choices of numbers could clearly make any level of defectives, from zero to 100%, the optimal level. This suggests how important it is for a firm's accounting information system to analyze and measure the quality cost components and relationships among them.

American corporations are now experimenting with a variety of programs such as zero defects, failure cost control, and Japanese-style quality control techniques such as quality circles. Many of these methods are successful at reducing individual components of total quality cost. However, often they do not minimize the total quality costs of production.

Companies, unfortunately, do not have what we refer to as a comprehensive system of quality control because of their difficulty in determining certain components—especially cost of lost sales—and their need to understand the relationships that exist among the different components of total quality costs. ∎

James T. Godfrey, Ph.D., is professor of accounting, and William R. Pasewark, Ph.D., is an assistant professor of accounting, at J.M. Tull School of Accounting at the University of Georgia.

[1]P. Crosby, "The Management of Quality," *Research Management,* July 1982, pp. 10-12.
[2]A. Chauvel and Y. Andre, "Quality Cost: Better Prevent than Cure," *Quality Progress,* September 1985, pp. 29-32.

Quality Management at Weyerhaeuser

BY DENNIS A. LOEWE

Certificate of Merit, 1988-89.

Our definition of quality is providing customers with products and services that consistently meet their needs and expectations. The workable definition of total quality management is a process for continuous improvement to achieve full customer satisfaction. Together, these definitions form the basis for a management system to meet the future.

The components of total quality management—Leadership; Customer Needs; Employee Involvement; and Processes—provide a blueprint for constructing the new management system.

Note that these categories go beyond the usual elements of Japanese total quality control, such as JIT or quality circles.

Author Dennis Loewe meets with his financial services team at Weyerhaeuser.

Americans have difficulty understanding Japanese management because the subtler pieces are not tangible, nor are they easily communicated.

For example, when our company officers visited a plant in Japan and asked how the quality culture had been established, the Japanese manager was baffled. It had always been this way in his experience. Quality management had been introduced to Japan in the 1950s. Japanese managers with less than 30 years in the workforce had no cultural memory of the origins of quality management.

To compete globally, American managers must not only be able to assimilate the four components, they must be able to ingrain them in a culture that is wholly American.

LEADERSHIP

Leadership is the first of the four components. Traditional management styles must change in total quality management. There are 10 key paths in which we need to change direction (Figure 1).

Two of these directions merit some comment. A change from the status quo towards continuous improvement violates an old maxim: "If it ain't broke, don't fix it." To challenge our paradigms we're much better admonished that, "Standing still is moving backwards."

A move from "beat on suppliers" toward working with suppliers startles most American purchasing managers and their superiors. Yet, if we start from the premise that the reason we buy component goods or services is that they're integral to our business' success, a different scenario emerges. In fact, we're vitally interested in key suppliers enduring as a going concern. It makes much more sense to create a long-term partnership with a few quality suppliers and to help ensure their survival, than to put them on the edge of collapse with tough price negotiations.

Perhaps the single most important job of a new leader is to create a vision of where we want to be. Equally important is establishing where the organization is currently. Bridging

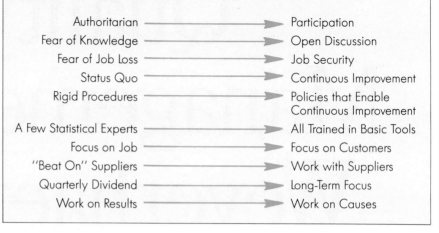

FIGURE 1 / PHILOSOPHY/MANAGEMENT STYLE

Authoritarian	Participation
Fear of Knowledge	Open Discussion
Fear of Job Loss	Job Security
Status Quo	Continuous Improvement
Rigid Procedures	Policies that Enable Continuous Improvement
A Few Statistical Experts	All Trained in Basic Tools
Focus on Job	Focus on Customers
"Beat On" Suppliers	Work with Suppliers
Quarterly Dividend	Long-Term Focus
Work on Results	Work on Causes

the two creates a series of steps that become actionable management tactical plans in a long-term strategy.

The vision statement should contain three or four broad areas of endeavor, each with multiple sub-parts that clarify the larger intent. For example, our vision states:

"We are an organization dedicated to full customer satisfaction;

...offering quality products and services;

...created by skilled, committed people;

...working in an excellent organizational setting;

...led by inspired leaders."

Determining where the organization is, is accomplished by diagnosis. As suggested by the vision statement, there are at least four components of diagnosis:

■ An employee survey to fix attitudes and beliefs at a point in time and to determine if employees are being treated in a supportive manner.
■ A customer survey to determine customers' perceptions of your products, services, and reputation at a point in time.
■ Benchmarking your operation against those perceived to be the best in your field.
■ Doing a value-added process flow check to ensure your efforts are designed to eliminate waste and deliver value to your customers.

To the extent an organization falls short of expectations in any of these areas, it is possible to design a series of tactical actions for continuous improvement. Annual recycling of the diagnosis will help keep the organization moving ahead and looking toward its future. Stated another way, if you don't know where you are, and you don't know where you're going, almost any path will get you there.

Managing cultural change is a process not a project. The characteristics of the transition state are low stability, high emotional stress, lots of undirected energy, control becomes a major issue, past patterns of behavior become highly valued, and conflict increases.

Overcoming the natural resistance to cultural change requires continuing support from the top of the organization. Cascading sponsorship is created as each level teaches and involves the next level. Management example and constant reinforcement aimed at the vision, will ensure that cultural change is accurate, supportable, and durable.

Successful change can be assessed by determining if resistance is overt or covert. Change is being successful if the challenges are overt, or out in the open. That gives management an opportunity to clarify and deal with the resistance. Change is not successful if the resistance is covert. When it goes underground, it can't be seen or dealt with. Covert resistance requires a tactic of backing away and re-establishing the fundamentals

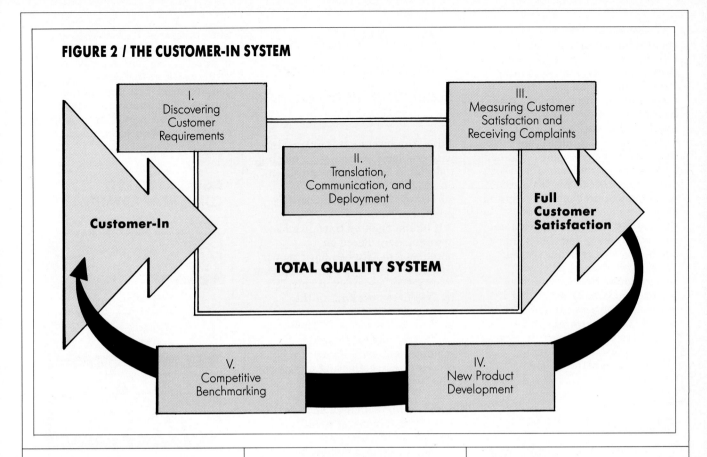

FIGURE 2 / THE CUSTOMER-IN SYSTEM

I. Discovering Customer Requirements

III. Measuring Customer Satisfaction and Receiving Complaints

II. Translation, Communication, and Deployment

Customer-In

Full Customer Satisfaction

TOTAL QUALITY SYSTEM

V. Competitive Benchmarking

IV. New Product Development

with particular emphasis on the vision.

CUSTOMER NEEDS

The customer-in system (Figure 2) comprises five parts, which are:

1. Discovering customer requirements;
2. Measuring customer satisfaction and receiving complaints;
3. Translation, communication, and deployment in the organization to satisfy customers;
4. New product or service development from customer input; and
5. Competitive benchmarking.

Together these five steps describe the total quality system.

Perhaps the most effective way to gain a competitive advantage is to pay attention in a systematic way to customer complaints about your products and services.

Figure 3 demonstrates survey results about customer complaints. If total actual complaints represent 100%, it's startling to discover that only 10% of the dissatisfied customers actually complain. Only 7% of the complaints reach the right people in time to be

Everyone accepts responsibility to examine his or her job and find ways to do it better.

addressed, and only 4% result in actual changes to correct the underlying problem. The 96% gap between total actual complaints and complaints that are fixed represents a tremendous competitive advantage over rivals that have no complaint tracking mechanism and, therefore, no real ability to respond to customers.

As accountants we spend a good deal of time focusing on cost but we may be neglecting the rest of the field. The Monitor Company of Cambridge, MA, points out that an obsession with cost can be overdone. Figure 4 displays two kinds of competitive advantage—low cost or differentiation. If our goal is to compete as the low cost producer of goods or services, we've defined a very narrow niche for ourselves. By definition, there can

be only one low cost producer. A much broader playing field can be created by differentiating ourselves from our competitors.

Personal experience tells us this is true. When shopping for clothing, we're often willing to pay more for the clothing in exchange for liberal exchange policies, courtesy of store personnel, and so on. The same is true in our choices of grocery stores, gasoline stations, and a host of other personal shopping choices. The concept is critical in understanding the value-added role of service, and more specifically, the role of management accountants in the success of the firm.

Primary activities, typically described as the manufacturing process, account for only a portion of the total delivered value to the customer. Support activities, including management accounting, are a source of major competitive advantage and differentiation that lies untapped, in a manner very similar to not measuring and using customer complaints. There are a number of anecdotal case studies of firms that add value through enlightened use of their support activities. Management accounting has the same potential.

Assume that a firm eliminated some error correction processes in the accounting department and freed up the use of an accountant's time. In most companies that accountant position would either be terminated or re-assigned to another area with analytical responsibilities. Couldn't we instead add value to our customer by sending this accountant to help our customer with his transaction or analytical problems? Assuming there are no legal or ethical constraints, wouldn't the customer receive value beyond the primary goods or services he purchased? What if we aligned all of our service forces toward customer orientation? Conversely, what if our competitors began doing it and we didn't? The leverage to be gained from deployment of support activities is a major source of competitive advantage for companies.

EMPLOYEE INVOLVEMENT

Employee involvement is a management process. It must be led by managers, taught by managers, and modeled by managers. Key to creating employee involvement is establishing a blame-free environment. In a blame-free environment, management directs attention to processes rather than focusing only on re-

Pay attention in a systematic way to customer complaints.

sults. The intent is to understand why problems occur, not on placing individual blame. By avoiding individual blame, managers encourage employees to identify problems

If blame must be fixed, it's more appropriately placed on management. Studies have shown that relative ability to fix problems in a system are affected only 15% by employees working *in* the system, and 85% by management working *on* the system. These studies merely confirm that management establishes the processes for conducting business (the "what"), and employees execute the processes (the "how").

Assuming management's goal is error-free delivery of products or services to its customers, employees must somehow be encouraged to point out process problems so that they can be managed. If managers point blame at individuals, the organization quickly learns to cover up problems and imbeds them in daily work where they can't be seen.

When management accepts responsibility for designing the

work processes, it also accepts responsibility for errors in the processes. The goal is to fix the process so that the same errors don't recur. In this environment, managers are supportive and responsible for providing resources to help employees eliminate the

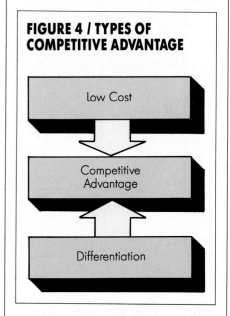

FIGURE 4 / TYPES OF COMPETITIVE ADVANTAGE

hassles in daily work. The organization begins to learn that surfacing errors and problems is not only safe, it helps them do their job and is expected and rewarded.

From management's perspective, waste is being eliminated from the system and employee activities are more directly focused on adding value to the customer.

Jan Carlson, president of Scandinavian Airlines, used this philosophy to turn around an ailing airline. The phrase used to communicate his philosophy was, "SAS has 50,000 moments of truth each day." What he was describing was the multiple encounters the flying public has each day with front-line employees of the airline: ticket agents, flight attendants, baggage handlers, and so on. Passengers (i.e., customers) don't deal with presidents and vice-presidents when they're traveling. The success of the airline is dependent upon how well management supports its passenger service through its employees on an individual transaction basis. To improve, or to even hold the line on service excellence, management must be

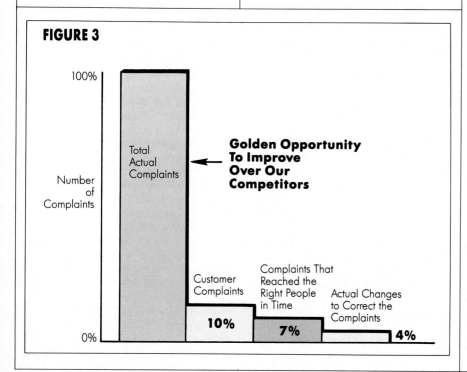

FIGURE 3

Loewe (at left): The key is to provide mechanisms to involve everyone.

kept informed of problems in the system to respond to them.

The key is to provide mechanisms to involve everyone—at all levels and in all functions. Everyone accepts responsibility to examine his or her job and to find ways to do it better. Everyone is a team member and is capable of contributing.

If an individual is not capable of task performance at a given skill level, the root of the problem can be traced either to ability or to willingness. If it's an ability problem, the answer may be in providing the necessary training to bring skill levels up to expectations. If training can't solve the ability problem, the individual needs to be re-positioned at a lower task level that better matches the individual's skills.

A lack of willingness to follow procedures prescribed by management suggests that the individual and the company are better served by helping the employee find a different firm where there is a better match to organizational philosophies.

It's also possible to encourage employees to help each other, and to receive management recognition in the process. A Star Award program has been developed in our Financial Services Department to support these behaviors.

The purpose of the Star Award program is to encourage continuous improvement in providing quality service to our customers. By recognizing all the

Employee involvement is a management process.

"little goods" that occur on a daily basis we encourage positive behaviors in others and, in the process, become more aware of caring for customers ourselves.

Each organization has many customers inside and outside the company. For many of us, our "customer" is the next person or process that relies upon the output from our job. "Customer" appreciation results from *never* passing on defects in our services, ensuring *quality* by doing things right the first time, and assisting the people we depend on to provide us with defect-free inputs.

STAR points are awarded on the following basis:

1-3 STAR Points -
     Quality Customer Service
4-6 STAR Points -
     Extra Effort
7-10 STAR Points -
     Above and Beyond.

Ranges are provided to recognize the varying levels of effort that are encountered in quality customer service. For example, the first range provides for the effort required to take down a complete

phone message so that the appropriate person can act upon and respond to the problem or question, rather than having the caller passed along to other individuals.

The second range provides for the individual who not only takes the complete message but offers to complete the necessary look-ups and respond to the customer without requiring the "proper contact" to take over and respond.

A third level of effort includes the first two steps but goes beyond and ensures that the customer is asking the right question and is getting the information he or she really wanted. Results in this category may be indicated by special thank-yous from customers, preservation of cash, cost reductions, or other objective measures. Also included in this category are highly creative or innovative ideas that result in improved quality customer services.

At the end of each year, a Star Awards celebration is conducted. It's held in a hotel ballroom, complete with a Dixieland Jazz Band or comparable upbeat theme. Employees shop for logo merchandise with their Star Award points. The festive atmosphere, with management in costumes, delivers a strong message about involvement and focusing on customer satisfaction.

PROCESSES, PROCESSES, PROCESSES

The foundation for an action-able quality management program is well-defined processes. Process management provides the "how" step against the theoretical basis. Quality of work is defined as the degree to which a process produces products or services that meet customer needs and expectations. The four components are shown graphically in:

■ Measurable inputs,
■ Value-added activities,
■ Measurable outputs, and
■ Repeatable processes.

Customers in this context are the next person in the process, and ultimately, the third party customer.

The purpose in rigorously

documenting processes is to develop a standard from which the process can be improved. If it's possible to measure the inputs, add value to the next "customer" in line, measure the output, and repeat the identical process, you've standardized it. Once a process has been standardized, we can seek to continuously improve it. H.J. Harrington in *The Improvement Process* states, "If you can't measure something, you can't understand it; if you can't understand it, you can't control it; if you can't control it, you can't improve it."

The goal of continuous improvement is the systematic and continuous elimination of waste. Waste includes people's time, materials, and capital not spent on activities that add value to the products or services required by the customer. Doing things right the first time adds nothing to the cost of your service—doing things *wrong* is what costs money.

Studies at IBM and ARMCO point out the significant financial leverage that can be obtained from elimination of waste.

IBM—"Between 15% and 40% of the revenue stream."
ARMCO—"Approximately 20% of sales."

Both of these examples refer to the manufacturing waste that can potentially be eliminated. Similar studies in their service sectors suggest the percentage of waste is closer to 50% of service activity.

In the accounting area, an example demonstrates how quickly the 50% range can be reached. An invoicing process, from mailing the invoice to applying the cash receipt to the customer's account, can take as few as three steps if error free to as many as 14 steps if corrective action is required. Doing it right the first time through process management eliminates more than three-and-one-half times the basic effort in this example of an invoicing process.

Bottom line financial performance can be very impressive when processes are managed to eliminate waste. Table 1 illustrates the point where only 20%, or the low-end, of the waste elimination potential, is attained.

TABLE 1 / WASTE ELIMINATION POTENTIAL

	Originally	Eliminate 20% of Waste	% Change
Sales	$500	$500	–0–
Costs	450	350	(20% of sales)
Net	$ 50	$150	200%

> *If blame must be fixed, it's more appropriately placed on management.*

A 200% net profit increase is achieved by elimination of waste equaling 20% of sales. At higher levels of waste reduction, more startling results can be achieved. Vince Lombardi may have said it best, "Perfection is not attainable, but if we chase perfection, we can catch excellence."

GOAL: CONTINUOUS IMPROVEMENT

Quality management is typically associated with manufacturing. But, achievements throughout every department can be obtained by breaking out of our paradigms about the manufacturing application of total quality management. By applying the same concepts to the service sector of a company's value chain the competitive advantage can be maximized.

In addition to the potential economic rewards to the company, there is a great deal of personal satisfaction to be gained by all employees. Managers have a template from which to manage. Armed with clear anchor points that determine the current state of the organization and where it needs to go to meet customer expectations, management can execute tactical plans for continuous improvement of delivery processes. For the first time there is a repeatable, teachable management process.

Employees are empowered by the system to manage how their job gets done. Elimination of process errors reduces the daily work hassle and enriches the quality of work life. Management is seen as a supportive partner, where the energies of the total organization are focused on satisfying the customer. Strength and purpose become the hallmarks of the organization.

Management accountants are uniquely positioned to capitalize on the concepts of total quality management. Their major strengths lie in a fundamental orientation to process management. The entire series of internal controls is built around a careful analysis of process flows and is already documented in most firms. Data capture, analysis, and reporting are fundamental to process measurement.

Management accountants are expected to help maximize returns to the firm. If these efforts are directed toward satisfying customers (the senior management and stockholders of the firm) by involving and leading people, a pro-active, value-added role can be enhanced for management accountants.

In the end, whether managing an accounting department, or helping to manage the firm, superior execution is the key to sustaining competitive advantage. With a model built around leadership, customer needs, employee involvement, and process management, management accountants can strongly position themselves to meet the future. ∎

Dennis Loewe is the financial services controller for Weyerhaeuser Co., Tacoma, WA. He is a member of Mt. Rainier Chapter, through which this article was submitted.

Analyzing Quality Costs

Formosa Plastics Group's techniques are relevant to U.S. firms.

BY THOMAS P. EDMONDS,
BOR-YI TSAY, AND
WEN-WEI LIN

Certificate of Merit, 1988-89.

Ford's slogan—"Quality is job one!"—epitomizes the American response to the invasion of foreign automobiles into U.S. markets. The trend toward liberal warranty policies by U.S. manufacturers in general also shows a broad-based recognition of the importance of quality products.

Unfortunately, quality does not result from the mere recognition of its importance. It requires the implementation and operation of a comprehensive quality control system. Indeed, today's managers have recognized this fact, and considerable progress has been made toward the effective management of quality programs.

Formosa Plastics Group (FPG) company, a Taiwan-based international conglomerate, developed an analytical program for the evaluation of quality costs. FPG's experiences in managing quality costs at the local, divisional, and headquarters levels and our analysis of its efforts are presented below.

Authors Dr. Edmonds (l.) and Mr. Lin discuss Formosa's techniques.

ANALYSIS AT THE PRODUCT LEVEL

Quality analysis begins with the identification of the components of total quality cost. The research report, *Measuring, Planning, and Controlling Quality Costs*, published by the National Association of Accountants, lists four distinct categories of quality cost: prevention cost, appraisal cost, internal failure cost, and external failure cost. The book includes a detailed list of examples of costs relating to each category. The list is shown in Table 1.

In general, prevention and appraisal costs are discretionary costs, incurred only to the extent management deems appropriate. Accordingly, they have been identified as *voluntary costs*.[1] In contrast, internal and external failure costs are involuntary costs. They are incurred when a product *fails* to comply with expected standards of quality and are therefore called *failure costs*.

Focusing on a Reasonable Level of Quality Assurance. Once the cost components are identified, managerial analysis centers on allocat-

ing resources so as to minimize total quality cost per unit. Total quality cost per unit is the sum of voluntary costs plus failure costs.

Implementing preventive and appraisal measures in the early stages of technological development can reduce both internal and external failures significantly. Under these circumstances, increased expenditures for voluntary costs are more than offset by savings on failure costs. Accordingly, increases in voluntary costs result in decreases in the amount of total quality cost per unit.

TABLE 1/COMPONENTS OF QUALITY COSTS

Voluntary Costs

Prevention Cost:

Training Cost:
Instructor Fees,
Training Equipment,
Tuition for External Training,
Trainee Wages and Salaries,
Planning and Execution:
Salaries,
Cost of Preventive Equipment,
Cost of Meetings,
Promotion Cost:
Awards,
Printing Cost,
Others.

Appraisal Cost:

Raw Materials Inspection,
Work-in-Process Inspection,
Finished Goods Inspection:
Inspector's Salaries,
Utility Cost,
Depreciation Expense,
External Inspection Fees.

Failure Costs

Internal Failure Cost:

Scrap,
Rework,
Loss Due to Downgrades,
Reinspection Cost,
Loss Due to Work Interruptions.

External Failure Cost:

Sales Returns and Allowances Due
to Quality Deficiency,
Warranty Cost,
Canceled Sales Orders Due to
Quality Deficiency.

In accordance with learning curve theory, however, this exchange process normally operates under the law of diminishing returns.[2] Each additional dollar spent on voluntary costs produces a smaller amount of failure cost savings. Eventually, the incremental savings on failure cost will decline to a point at which increases in voluntary costs cannot be offset fully by decreases in failure costs. The total quality cost, following the above process, will decrease to a minimum point and then increase afterwards. Figure 1 shows that voluntary costs increase and failure costs decrease as the level of assurance grows higher.

By analyzing these relationships managers can overcome the unrealistic expectation that the ideal state of quality control is absolute perfection, that is, 100% quality conformance. In reality, absolute quality conformance is seldom desirable. The reason is simple—it costs too much. Instead, managers should pursue a reasonable level of quality conformance. They should let the point of minimum quality cost determine the level of quality assurance, as depicted in Figure 1.

In other words, managers should curtail voluntary expenditures when total quality cost per unit reaches its minimum, even though 100% quality conformance has not

been achieved. While *zero defects* makes for a good slogan, it seldom, if ever, represents a practical operating strategy.

Minimizing Total Quality Cost Per Unit. In practice, it is hard to locate the optimal mix between voluntary and failure costs (the low point on the cost curve in Figure 1). Knowing exactly when to curtail

voluntary expenditures is a difficult practical problem. If voluntary costs are curtailed too early, the minimum point will remain unknown, and potential cost savings will be lost.

On the other hand, if management continues to incur voluntary costs until the total quality cost per unit increases, expenditures beyond the minimum point will have been wasted. A trial-and-error approach to locating the minimum total quality cost seems ineffective, yet it appears to be the method used by most businesses today. Indeed, the FPG manual fails to address this problem. As an alternative to the trial-and-error method, we suggest that managers consider the use of trend analysis.

Drawing the Total Quality Cost Curve. Figure 2 provides an example of trend analysis in a graphics format. The vertical axis shows cost per unit, and the horizontal axis shows time. The analyst would begin by projecting early period cost patterns for each of the four cost components into future periods. This phase can be accomplished by intuitive judgments on the part of knowledgeable managers, by indexing, or through the use of mathematical models such as regression.

The trends projected in Figure 2 imply a steady increase in volun-

---

FIGURE 1 / COST RELATIONSHIPS

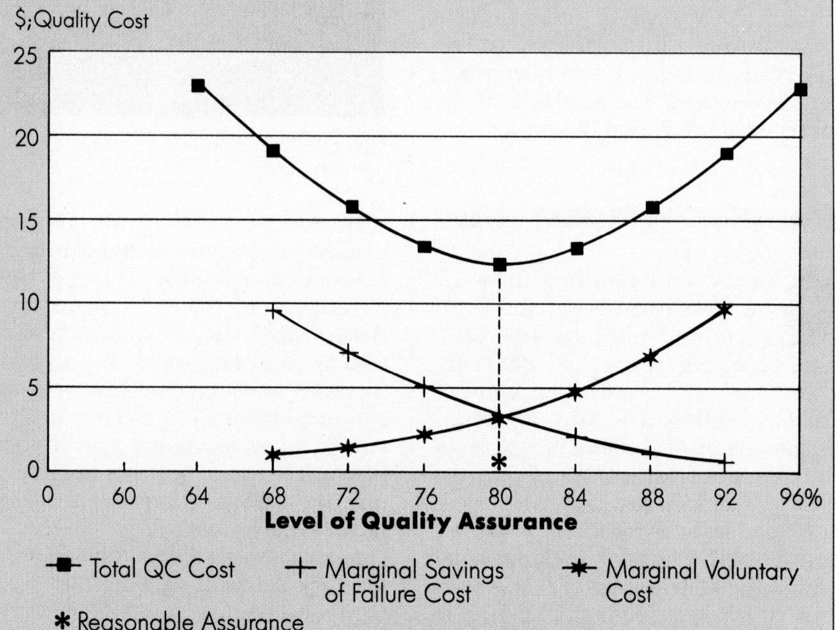

$;Quality Cost

Level of Quality Assurance

■ Total QC Cost   + Marginal Savings of Failure Cost   ✳ Marginal Voluntary Cost

✳ Reasonable Assurance

tary costs accompanied by a corresponding decrease in failure costs. This pattern suggests that as managers learn from their mistakes, they are able to reduce failure costs by expending funds to develop effective quality control procedures. The exact nature of these trends for each of the four components, of course, will vary among different firms and within firms, depending on the types of products that are being manufactured.

Once the projections for the cost components have been established, data points for the total per unit cost curve can be computed by adding the individual amounts for each component at several designated time intervals. The total cost curve then would be drawn through the data points, and the slope of the curve could be analyzed to determine when voluntary costs should be curtailed. A more conservative approach for drawing the total cost curve is to use actual rather than projected data. Managers simply can accumulate actual costs and plot them on a graph. The cost curve then could be drawn through the actual data points. Here, also, the direction of the slope would signal the appropriate time to eliminate further increases in voluntary costs.

Analyzing the Slope. The slope of the total quality cost function is a good barometer for controlling voluntary costs because it summarizes the rate of change between the quality cost components. To examine the usefulness of the slope as a control indicator, we will explore the total per-unit quality cost line at three different points along the horizontal time scale.

At Period 1 in Figure 2, the slope of the quality cost curve moves in a sharp downward direction, which indicates that the prospect of reducing total cost by increasing voluntary cost expenditures in the near future is bright. However, as expenditures for preventive and appraisal activities continue to rise, the rate of cost reduction declines and the slope of the curve flattens. Accordingly, the potential for further reduction in total quality cost becomes less.

At Period 4, the slope of the curve approaches zero as the cost function becomes horizontal. This means that one dollar spent on voluntary costs will result in an equal amount

of failure cost savings. At this point, managers will not be able to enjoy disproportionate failure cost reductions by increasing voluntary costs. Indeed, the amount of total quality cost will rise if the manager decides to increase voluntary costs further.

Additional voluntary cost expenditures after Period 4 will drive the slope of the quality cost curve in an upward direction. Not only does the curve change direction, but it also increases at an accelerating rate. In Period 8, the curve becomes symmetrical. Here the slope moves in a sharp upward direction. Accordingly, a dollar spent

on voluntary costs would result in considerably less than a dollar in failure cost savings.

The above analysis indicates that when trend projections produce slope estimates that approach zero, they are signaling that voluntary cost incurrence should be curtailed. A zero slope indicates that the minimum cost structure has been reached. Further expenditures on voluntary costs cannot be justified on the basis of cost minimization.

It is important to note that a quantitative approach, such as trend analysis, must be tempered by qualitative considerations. For example, managers may be re-

quired to incur voluntary quality costs beyond the zero slope point in order to meet standards set by their competitors. As with any analytic technique, trend analysis must be combined with sound judgment.

ANALYZING THE DIVISION

Each division within a company is likely to have several product lines, and the progress of quality controls on each product line may vary. Consequently, managers should no longer concentrate on the allocation between voluntary and fixed costs. Instead they should focus on performance eval-

uation and planning.

Ratio Analysis. The first step in the analysis of divisional performance is to aggregate quality costs by division. While the total number of dollars spent on quality by a division is interesting, some type of common size measure must be computed for the purpose of making comparisons between the divisions. One division may incur more quality cost than another division simply because it is larger. In such cases, a common denominator will be necessary in order to make a fair evaluation.

Finding the appropriate common denominator will depend on the

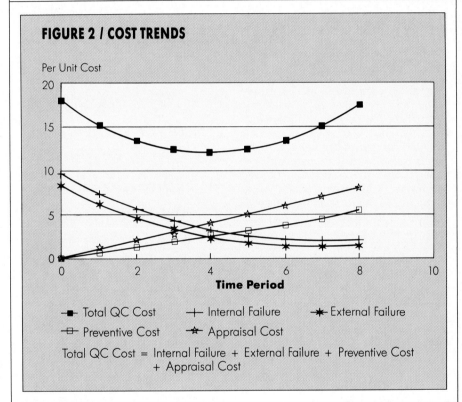

FIGURE 2 / COST TRENDS

Per Unit Cost

Time Period

- ■ Total QC Cost
- + Internal Failure
- ✳ External Failure
- ▫ Preventive Cost
- ✦ Appraisal Cost

Total QC Cost = Internal Failure + External Failure + Preventive Cost + Appraisal Cost

Author Tsay uses graphics program to simulate trend analysis.

structure of the division. If divisions are organized as profit centers, three logical denominators are sales revenue, cost of sales, and net income. On the other hand, if divisions are organized as cost centers, quality costs can be expressed in relation to total product costs, as a percent of some asset base associated with the division, or as a ratio to a measure of labor hours.

Three examples from the Formosa Plastics Group (FPG) corporate quality cost manual include:

1. Quality Cost per Dollar of Sales Revenue:
   Total Quality Cost ÷ Sales Revenue,
2. Quality Cost per Dollar of Product Cost:
   Total Quality Cost ÷ Total Manufacturing Cost,
3. Quality Cost in Relation to Direct Labor:
   Total Quality Cost ÷ Total Direct Labor Hours

These ratios represent only three examples of many possible combinations of logical indicators. While the direct labor hours ratio works well for FPG, other capital-intensive companies may find some form of asset measure more meaningful. The key to effective ratio analysis at the divisional level is to find a common denominator that results in meaningful comparisons for the particular company being analyzed.

100% quality conformance is seldom desirable—it sounds good but costs too much.

Fortunately, this task already has been accomplished by most companies. It is common practice to express various materials, labor, and overhead costs in relation to some common measure. That measure, whatever it may be, in all likelihood can be used to express quality costs in common-size terms. While most managers are accustomed to using ratio analysis for performance evaluation in general, they frequently fail to apply such techniques to quality costs. FPG's experience demonstrates that quality costs can and should be used in performance evaluation.

Quality Cost Budgets. In addition to performance evaluation, top executives can treat each department as a responsibility center for quality improvement. Targets for quality improvement can be stated specifically in an annual budget or longer-term budget. Some of the budgeted targets suggested by the FPG corporate manual include:

■ Total quality cost,

■ Total failure cost,
■ Total internal failure cost,
■ Total external failure cost,
■ Total voluntary cost,
■ Total prevention cost,
■ Total appraisal cost.

Generally, managers pay attention to total quality cost incurred by a division, but special circumstances may cause them to focus their attention on one or more of the other budget indicators. If a firm is operating in an industry with intensive competition as to product quality, managers may concentrate their attention on the external failure cost. For the control of manufacturing efficiency, managers can use internal failure cost as the primary focal point. If managers want to set targets positively toward control activities, the prevention and appraisal costs are good indicators for the budget targets.

Quality cost budgeting requires special consideration because of the longer time necessary to accomplish quality goals. Traditionally, budget techniques are oriented toward the evaluation of short-term cost containment goals. For example, the manager is held accountable for production quotas at some predetermined standard materials, labor, and overhead costs over some short-term period. Actual costs are compared with standard costs and favorable variances are rewarded, while unfavorable variances are punished. If this scheme were applied to the management of quality costs, the result could be disastrous, because the short-term minimization of quality costs can have several long-term negative consequences.

A manager who wants to hold down quality costs in the short run can do so by avoiding prevention and appraisal costs. Moreover, internal failure costs can be avoided by shipping substandard products to customers. These tactics ultimately will result in excessively high external failure costs and customer dissatisfaction. In extreme cases, an emphasis on short-term cost containment may lead to the demise of the product or even the enterprise itself. Thus, it is essential for management to establish a long-term evaluative strategy as to how it will include quality costs in the budgeting process.

The successful incorporation of quality costs into the budgeting process may even require a change in basic managerial philosophy. For example, the Asian management philosophy commonly referred to as Theory Z[3] lends itself to long-term performance evaluation more than the prevalent fast-track American approach. At a minimum, U.S. companies will have to adopt a selective strategy wherein certain budgetary items are given short-term emphasis while other items such as quality costs are analyzed more appropriately within a long-range context. Indeed, although FPG is Asia based, it has adopted a selective strategy rather than a strict long-term Theory Z approach. Perhaps East and West can learn collectively from each other's experiences.

HOW IS THE FIRM DOING?

Analysis at the headquarters level should focus on the competitive position of the firm within its industry. Some of the ratios used at this level of analysis are identical to those used to evaluate divisional performance, but the point of reference is totally different. Instead of asking, "How is the division performing in relation to other divisions?", the analyst is asking, "How is the firm doing in relation to its corporate competitors?"

The following ratios represent adaptations from FPG's corporate manual on quality costs. They include:

- The ratio of total quality cost to sales revenue as well as cost of goods sold,
- The ratio of external failure cost to sales revenue,
- The ratio of total failure cost to sales revenue,
- The ratio of voluntary cost to sales revenue,
- The ratio of total quality cost to direct labor hours,
- The ratio of total quality cost to plant assets.

The firm's ratio of *total quality cost to sales revenue* should be compared with similar ratios for its competitors. This comparison will reveal the relative burden of quality cost incurred by the firm. When price competition heats up,

> *The short-term minimization of quality costs can have long-term negative consequences.*

this indicator may signal excessive quality cost expenditures. If analysts are more interested in the comparison of cost structure than the burden of quality cost on revenues, the ratio of *total quality cost to cost of goods sold* can be used.

In a market characterized by fierce competition and high quality, it is useful to compare the ratio of *external failure cost to sales revenue* among competitors. This ratio is a good indicator of the current level of customer satisfaction. If the ratio is high in comparison to that of the company's competitors, it indicates that customers have suffered unduly from product failures. The logical result is customer dissatisfaction, which signals the need for stronger quality controls. If the ratio is low in comparison to the competitors', customers have suffered little and probably are satisfied with the existing level of product quality. Indeed, an extremely low ratio may be signaling excessive voluntary cost expenditures. Recall that unreasonably high quality standards purchased through excessive voluntary expenditures is not a cost-effective strategy.

The ratios of *total failure cost to sales revenue* and *voluntary costs to sales revenue* should be analyzed in conjunction with the ratio of *total quality cost to sales revenue*. When combinations of these ratios are viewed together with competitors' data, they can help diagnose quality control problems. A high ratio of *total quality cost to sales revenue* indicates the existence of a quality control problem but does not reveal the nature of the problem. Further analysis with additional ratios may provide the desired insight. For example, a high ratio of *total failure cost to sales revenue* accompanied by a low ratio of

voluntary cost to sales revenue suggests that the company has not undertaken enough control activities to reduce product failures. On the other hand, if both of the company's ratios of *total failure cost and voluntary cost to sales* are higher than the industry's average, it clearly suggests that the company's level of technology on quality controls lags behind the industry's. The solution in this situation is to enhance the level of technology rather than to reallocate the quality cost components.

For firms in labor-intensive industries, managers may evaluate the performance of their workers on quality controls by using the ratio of *total quality cost to total direct labor hours*. By comparing this ratio among different firms, managers can find out the competitive position of their labor force. Similarly, managers in capital-intensive industries can use the ratio of *total quality cost to plant assets* to measure the performance of their equipment on quality controls.

Applying the analytical techniques described here, on the three distinct levels of organizational structure, will help managers to compete in a world market that increasingly emphasizes product quality. ∎

Thomas P. Edmonds, Ph.D., is an associate professor of accounting at the University of Alabama at Birmingham. He is a member of the South Birmingham Chapter, through which this article was submitted.
Bor-Yi Tsay Ph.D., is an assistant professor of accounting at the University of Alabama at Birmingham.
Wen-Wei Lin is a graduate research assistant at the University of Alabama at Birmingham. He was a management analyst assigned to the Quality Control Development Team of the Formosa Plastics Group from 1985 through 1987.

1 Edgar W. Dawes, "Quality Costs-A Tool for Improving Profits," *Quality Progress*, September 1975, pp.12-13.
2 Ahmed BelKaoui, *The Learning Curve: a Management Accounting Tool*, Quorum Books, Westport, Conn., 1986.
3 William Ouchi, *Theory Z*, Addison-Wesley Publishing Co., Reading, Mass., 1981.

Section 5

Changes: Activity Accounting

The fourth and final change characteristic of the environment of the world-class manufacturer is a new emphasis in cost management on the activities that drive costs and consume resources. Section 5 focuses on activity accounting, examining the concepts and principles applied in its implementation and utilization.

In the lead article, H. Thomas Johnson calls for an extension of management accounting beyond traditional transaction-based cost information. His blueprint for world-class management accounting is built on activity-based information, or information about the activities that consume resources and deliver value in a business. Johnson cites two essential types of activity-based information: nonfinancial information concerning sources of competitive value, such as quality and flexibility, that indicates effectiveness in delivering value to the customer; and strategic cost information that assesses long-term profitability of the current mix of products and activities.

Johnson believes achieving world-class competitiveness requires managing activities, not costs. He outlines the steps to managing waste in operating activities: charting the flow of activities; identifying value in activities and eliminating those contributing no value; identifying causes of delay, excess, and unevenness in activities; and tracking indicators of waste. He also calls for activity-based chargeout and product costing systems that eliminate the distortions caused by traditional cost allocation methods. Johnson concludes that the combination of these nonfinancial and activity-based cost measures provides the management information needed in today's world-class competitive environment.

Michael R. Ostrenga introduces his public accounting firm's total cost management (TCM) philosophy of managing company resources and the activities that consume them. He uses examples from six applications, three in Fortune 500 firms and three in smaller companies, to explain these key TCM principles: process value analysis, the initial TCM building block that focuses on meeting customer requirements,

minimizing cost and cycle time, and improving quality; activity-based process costing and activity-based product costing; responsibility accounting; performance measurement, including effectiveness, efficiency, productivity, and utilization categories; and investment management.

Ostrenga summarizes the integration of these key principles in an illustration of a four-phase transition plan. He notes that while these six companies and their needs—from truer product costs and cost reduction to improved performance measures and product line profitability—differ and the perceived starting point in each application varies, the focal point does not. It shifts inevitably to the effect that activities and activity-consuming resources have on the business. Ostrenga contends that managing costs involves managing activities and the events or conditions that drive the activities; that reducing costs will not have a lasting effect unless the cause of the cost is removed.

In the final article, Michael O'Guin relates the success that a vertically integrated plumbing fixture manufacturer producing more than a billion products had in applying activity-based costing. He describes the old direct labor-based cost accounting system, with overhead that amounted to almost 60% of product cost, and the product costing distortions it created. He documents the development of the new system of 26 overhead cost pools that were accumulated into volume-driven and transaction-driven pools for allocation to products.

O'Guin includes tables that present a comparison of the system differences in product costs and product line profitability. The products most affected were the low-volume parts that had been severely undercosted by the old system. The new system revealed that the product lines once considered the most profitable actually were losing money. O'Guin relates how the cost information provided by the new system was used to sell unprofitable divisions and reduce the product line by 81%, improve the make-or-buy decision process, and estimate the impact of different manufacturing options.

Additional Readings from *Management Accounting*

Campi, John P., "Total Cost Management at Parker Hannifin," January 1989, pp. 51-53.

Roth, Harold P. and A. Faye Borthick, "Getting Closer to Real Product Costs," May 1989, pp. 28-33.

ACTIVITY-BASED INFORMATION:

A BLUEPRINT FOR WORLD-CLASS MANAGEMENT ACCOUNTING

BY H. THOMAS JOHNSON

For more than 60 years, managers have used cost information from transaction-based financial accounts to judge the impact of their decisions on company profits. Costs are used in budgets for planning and control, and they also are used to evaluate both the profitability of products and the effects on profit of resource allocation decisions. Relying on cost to evaluate the consequences of a manager's decisions succeeds if cost is the primary determinant of probability.

Today, however, we recognize that profitability no longer results

To be world-class competitors, companies should manage activities —not costs.

exclusively from controlling costs. New management methods make quality and flexibility as important as cost in determining profitability. These new methods, pioneered in Japan and adopted since 1980 by scores of American companies, prompt a need for new sources of

management accounting information.[1]

New management methods stress the need for focusing not only on cost, but also on quality and flexibility. New technologies of communication and information processing, by giving customers rapid access to the best products and services in the world, also make it imperative that businesses provide "world class" quality and cost, and be flexible enough to respond rapidly to changes in consumer demand. Profitability no longer results primarily from taking steps to control costs; it also hinges on maintaining world-class standards of customer value. To be

Photos by George Fenton, Anaheim, Calif.

Author Johnson (l.) and Paul Jackson, associate manager of Pacific Bell Billing & Report Center, Anaheim, Calif., watch as customer bills are printed out.

profitable in the global economy, businesses must know if their decisions will deliver value to the customer in excess of the cost of delivering that value.

Until now, cost information was deemed sufficient to enable businesses to manage profitability. Now, however, profitability encompasses more than just cost. Management accounting, therefore, must look beyond transaction-based cost information to know if decisions will deliver profit. It must develop new information to achieve this objective.

A NEW APPROACH

A new approach to management accounting must be built on "activity-based information." This information is about the work (or activity) that consumes resources and delivers value in a business. People consuming resources in work ultimately cause costs and achieve the value customers pay for.

Ideally, the way to achieve profitability is to manage activities. When managers attempt to achieve profits by managing costs, as has been done for decades, they implicitly use cost to measure activities indirectly. Initially, this practice was probably a matter of convenience and economy. Until the advent of electronic information processing it was very difficult, and costly, to gather information about activities.

Cost numbers always have been easily available. Moreover, cost information can substitute for direct information about activities when businesses use relatively simple processes and produce fairly homogeneous product lines. Before the end of World War II, homogeneity and simplicity characterized most, though not all, American businesses. Businesses trying to compete in today's global economy are neither simple nor homogeneous. In business today, cost and value cannot be assessed by transaction-based cost information. Achieving profitability requires activity-based information.[2]

Two types of activity-based information (see Figure 1) should form the backbone of world-class management accounting. One type is nonfinancial information about

Activity-based information focuses managers' attention on the underlying causes of cost and profit.

sources of competitive value (e.g., quality, flexibility, and cost) in a company's operating activities. This information indicates how effectively operating activities deliver value to the customer. The second type of activity-based information, strategic cost information, enables managers to assess the long-term profitability of a company's current mix of products and activities. Strategic cost information indicates if a company's activities are cost-effective in comparison to alternatives outside the company, and if the mix of products management has chosen to sell uses activities in the most profitable way.

These two uses of activity-based information resemble control and planning as defined in traditional management accounting. But activity-based information seldom comes from the transaction-based financial accounts that supply almost all information in traditional management accounting systems. It comprises any relevant information about activities across the entire chain of value—design, engineering, sourcing, production, distribution, marketing, and after-sale service. Activity-based information focuses managers' attention on underlying causes (drivers) of cost and profit

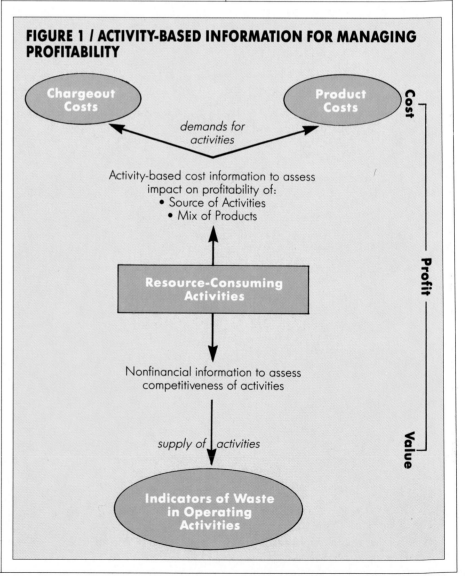

FIGURE 1 / ACTIVITY-BASED INFORMATION FOR MANAGING PROFITABILITY

unlike the distant, often distorted, financial echoes of those causes that appear in traditional cost and performance reports.

COMPETITIVE ACTIVITIES

Sources of customer value changed dramatically after 1970 causing business leaders to become concerned with value and competitiveness. Prior to the 1970s, companies competed chiefly on cost. Today's companies must compete on quality and flexibility, as well as cost.

Management accounting fails to help companies achieve world-class standards of quality, flexibility, and cost when it encourages them to manage costs. Accounting costs *per se* are not a source of competitive value. Only activities—work that consumes resources—have the power to add value. No activity adds customer value 100% of the time. Wasted effort, inevitable in human activity, detracts from the value all activities provide to customers. Thus, to achieve competitiveness, managers must monitor and remove wasted effort, i.e., nonvalue activities.[3] To do so, they must eliminate causes of delay, excess, and unevenness in all activities.

Cost accounts record results of nonvalue activity in categories such as scrap (a sign of excess), inventory (a sign of delay), and overtime for end-of-period production spurts (a sign of unevenness). But cost information about scrap, inventory, and overtime does not pinpoint activity that adds no value.

To achieve competitive operations that deliver value to customers, managers need information about sources of delay, excess, and unevenness that cause waste in operating activities. Eliminating delay, excess, and unevenness removes waste and makes activities more competitive. Let's look at a familiar example—managing setup costs.[4] This example will demonstrate the difference between managing operations with traditional cost information and managing operations with information about generators of waste.

The traditional way to manage setup cost is to produce in batch sizes that spread setup cost over as many units as possible, but not

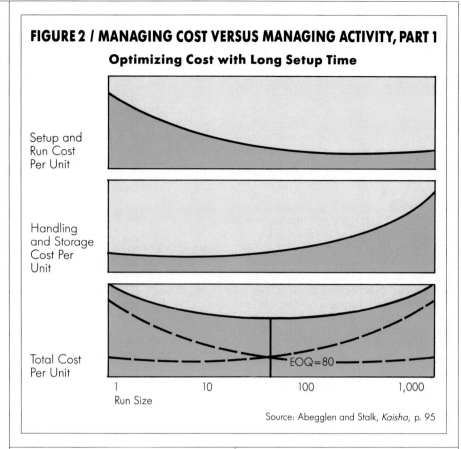

FIGURE 2 / MANAGING COST VERSUS MANAGING ACTIVITY, PART 1

Optimizing Cost with Long Setup Time

Setup and Run Cost Per Unit

Handling and Storage Cost Per Unit

Total Cost Per Unit

EOQ=80

Run Size: 1 — 10 — 100 — 1,000

Source: Abegglen and Stalk, *Kaisha*, p. 95

over so many units that the cost of storing output in excess of current consumption becomes prohibitive. The well-known EOQ paradigm, portrayed in Figure 2, calculates an "optimal" batch size that minimizes total unit cost of setup and storage. However, the paradigm takes for granted the activities (e.g., setting up and storing) whose costs we manage by optimizing batch sizes. This seems remarkable, because the resource-consuming activities that both setup cost and storage cost measure often add little value to customers. Setting-up entails delay and storing signifies excess.

As we know now, production people at Toyota over 30 years ago explored the implications of reducing waste in setup and storage activities. They began by working to reduce setup time. Reducing setup time causes EOQs to fall until, eventually, it is unnecessary ever to produce more than the amount needed for current consumption. (As shown in Figure 3, reducing setup time to a limit of zero produces an EOQ of one unit.) Producing to demand eliminates a need to store inventory, the activity that causes storage costs.

Thus, instead of managing setup cost, as we do with the EOQ paradigm, Toyota set out to curtail setup time—a source of delay that causes setup cost. In the process, it reduced setup cost. But it did much more as well. By reducing setup time it reduced economic batch sizes and eliminated a need for inventory. Reducing batch sizes and eliminating inventory removed major causes of defective output and improved quality. Moreover, by reducing economic batch sizes, Toyota reduced turnover time and became more flexible. In short, the company improved quality, flexibility, and cost simultaneously by managing waste in activities, not by managing cost.

Improving all determinants of competitiveness simultaneously by managing setup time runs counter to what occurs when we optimize batch sizes by managing setup and storage *costs*. Indeed, the EOQ paradigm suggests a trade-off among determinants of competitiveness. To see this trade-off, consider what happens if the marketing organization asks the factory to be more flexible (i.e., change models frequently) or to improve quality, once total per unit setup and storage cost is minimized by producing at the optimal batch size. Changing models more often means shortening run lengths, and shorter runs will raise total unit cost (see Figure 2). Thus, the factory can deliver increased flexibility only at greater cost. Likewise with quality. To improve quality when running large batches, one might stop a machine periodically and adjust its setting to eliminate out-of-tolerance pieces near the end of a run. But stopping a machine to reset it increases total unit cost. Thus, we can have higher quality, but only at greater cost.

Obviously, a company striving to achieve world-class standards of value should manage waste, not costs. The presence of nonvalue activity forces us to accept trade-offs among sources of competitiveness. By reducing waste in activities, companies can forestall the trade-offs among cost, quality, and flexibility that otherwise prevent them from becoming world-class competitors.

FOUR STEPS TO MANAGING OPERATING ACTIVITIES

There are four steps to managing waste in operating activities: chart the flow of activities throughout the organization; identify sources of customer value in every activity, and eliminate any activities that contribute no identifiable value to customers; identify causes of delay, excess, and unevenness in all activities; and track indicators of waste. The sidebar shows a partial list of causes for delay, excess, and unevenness in activities such as setting-up, storing, and moving. In the case of setup activity, these causes include poor training of setup personnel, conflicts in workers' assignments that interrupt setups, poorly designed machines, haphazard placement of setup tools, and more. Eliminating causes of delay, excess, and unevenness will reduce waste in activities. The presence of any nonvalue activity limits a company's ability to be as competitive as possible.

Identifying generators of delay, excess, and unevenness calls for the cooperation of everyone in an organization, from top to bottom. No activity should escape attention. Once you identify causes of waste,

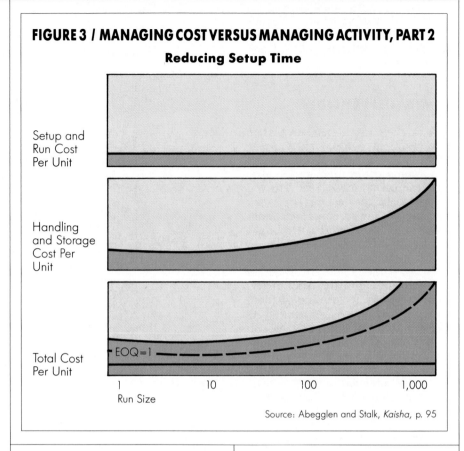

FIGURE 3 / MANAGING COST VERSUS MANAGING ACTIVITY, PART 2

Reducing Setup Time

Setup and Run Cost Per Unit

Handling and Storage Cost Per Unit

Total Cost Per Unit

EOQ=1

Run Size: 1 10 100 1,000

Source: Abegglen and Stalk, *Kaisha*, p. 95

the entire arsenal of new management methods associated with just-in-time, total quality control, and employee involvement is required to remove them.[5]

The serious attention paid to employee suggestions in Japanese companies indicates the importance Japanese managers place on this third step. Indeed, identifying generators of delay, excess, and unevenness is a task without end, and is the pathway to that inscrutable goal of Japanese management known as continuous improvement.

Managing waste in activities involves developing measures that track a company's success at eliminating generators of delay, excess, and unevenness. Here managers need a few broad indicators of waste, such as elapsed time. The elapsed time it takes to do something—make an assembly, make a product, run a process—is an all-encompassing index of competitiveness. Less time to do something means greater flexibility; it also means higher quality and lower cost in most cases.

Other indicators of waste are distance parts move, space occupied by production activities, number of part numbers per product, and, of

course, setup time. Indicators of waste help companies achieve the goal of continuous improvement by giving employees an incentive to continuously identify and remove generators of delay, excess, and unevenness. Continuously identifying and removing generators of delay, excess, and unevenness improves the indicators of a company's competitive position.

In contrast to traditional management accounting indicators of performance, the indicators of competitiveness referred to above—elapsed time, distance moved, space occupied, number of part numbers—are all *nonfinancial* measures of performance in operating activities. No financial numbers are used here to control operations. This conforms to the view of a leading authority on the new Japanese manufacturing techniques, Robert W. Hall, who says that "over time, financially oriented management should be weaned from thinking that detailed financial goals stimulate operating improvement." He argues that companies migrating toward JIT/TQC should abandon or deemphasize traditional factory measures such as budget variances, labor efficiency, and inventory turn. He goes on to say "the more confidence a management begins to have in JIT/TQC concepts, the fewer demands for this financial [information]. *It becomes obvious that any actions improving quality or reducing leadtimes will reduce operating costs* (emphasis added)."[6]

But managers should be aware that their success at eliminating nonvalue activity will not automatically reduce costs recorded in the financial accounts. Nonfinancial indicators of competitiveness such as elapsed time and space occupied can shrink without reducing book costs. The reason is clear. Expenditures do not stop automatically for resources made redundant by a campaign to reduce waste. Space or employees do not vanish just because a more competitive organization no longer needs them to get the job done. Consequently, not only must world-class operating managers develop systems to track waste reductions, they must have plans to use the excess resources productively or dispose of them.

Using nonfinancial indicators of performance to control operations does not eliminate financial cost information in businesses. Financial cost data is still compiled in budgets and other internal reports. But it is used for top-level planning, coordination, and allocation decisions—not to control operations.

World-class enterprises will not control operations by "rolling down" budgets into sub-units of an organization and then delegating to submanagers the task of achieving financial targets. Subordinate managers at the plant or department level will think in terms of nonfinancial indicators of competitiveness such as elapsed time, reject rates, and cycle time—not in terms of budgeted cost targets, net income, or return on investment. Having used budgets to plan and coordinate the allocation of resources among diverse sub-units of a complex organization, top managers may use imprest funds to control cash outlays subordinate managers are responsible for.[7]

COST-EFFECTIVE ACTIVITIES

A company may achieve world-class standards of competitiveness by removing generators of delay, excess, and

unevenness from operating activities and still not be as profitable as it should. Resources consumed in an activity can supply competitive value to customers, yet do so at a cost that exceeds the value supplied. This condition may reflect a need for the company to change its mix of activities, the mix of products its activities create, or both. Two additional types of activity-based information—chargeouts and product costs—reveal how profitably a company consumes resources in its activities. Managers can use this information to assess the scale and scope of a company's operating activities.

Activity-based chargeout information. In principle, all activities in an organization supply output to meet customers' demands. The "customer" in this sense is not only the final consumer of product or service, but also the next user of an activity's output. The goal of every activity in a business, mirroring the global goal of the business itself, should be to provide value to the customer at a reasonable cost. If any activity's output costs more

or provides less value than the output of an alternative activity, then the company is not as profitable as it could be. Managers need information to compare the competitiveness and cost of each activity's output with the next best alternative, whether that alternative be inside or outside the company.[8]

One type of information for this purpose is a "chargeout." Chargeouts resemble the price a company charges for output it sells to final consumers. However, a chargeout is the price an activity center charges for output it provides to its customers inside the company. A corporate accounting department, for instance, may prepare invoices for all customers the company sells to. A chargeout would be a price per invoice charged by the accounting department to any department that requests one. Chargeouts help allocate resources within a company in a manner similar to prices in competitive markets, although the comparison is not quite exact.

In one company that uses chargeouts extensively, chargeouts for

Author-consultant Johnson, who is doing field research for an NAA "Bold Step" study, gets behind-the-scenes look at Pacific Bell.

each activity are expected not only to recoup costs, but also to compare favorably with alternative market prices.[9] Users of each center's services know these charges for the coming year and are free to purchase each activity from the company or, if all parties agree a superior alternative exists, buy elsewhere. Similarly, activity centers are free to sell their output outside the company if they wish. Decisions to source or sell activities outside the company must consider all facets of competitiveness—quality and flexibility, as well as cost. In the long run, this company will liquidate and reallocate resources from an activity center that fails to satisfy customers efficiently, whether they be inside or outside the company. To do otherwise would diminish the company's long-term profitability.

Chargeout information gives users of activities, not suppliers, the ultimate say in decisions about long-term allocation of resources to activities. This gives activity managers incentive to keep their operations competitive by continuously identifying and cost-effectively eliminating generators of waste.

Chargeouts have a greater long-term impact on a company's competitiveness and profitability than do traditional methods for allocating activity center costs. Chargeouts to users, unlike cross-subsidized allocations based on company-wide denominators, do not reward intensive users of an ac-

tivity and penalize light users. Compare the chargeout for invoices that a selling division pays, for instance, with a charge that is allocated over all divisions' gross revenues. In the latter case, a division selling to thousands of small-volume retail customers—the division that likely causes the consumption of most of the invoicing center's resources—is charged relatively much less for the services received than is a division with a small number of high-volume industrial customers. Chargeouts mitigate

Pacific Bell manager Jackson describes company's operation to Mr. Johnson.

against the misuse of resources that usually is associated with such cross-subsidized allocations.

Chargeout information provides an especially powerful tool for managing corporate overhead ac-

tivities, a source of the fastest growing and least controlled costs in most companies during the 1980s. Its power lies in focusing managers' attention on the resource-consuming activities that ultimately cause costs, rather than on the recorded costs themselves. Traditional flexible budget information assigns responsibility for recorded overhead costs to activity centers that supply overhead services. Chargeout information puts responsibility for the scale of overhead activities on the shoulders of users who demand activities to provide value to final consumers. Chargeout information to price activities, together with operating information about causes of waste, help companies sustain profitability while giving competitive value to customers.

Activity-based product cost information. A company may achieve world-class standards of competitiveness in its operating activities and all its activities may be as cost-effective as any in the market yet, the mix of products or services it sells may not use the company's activities as profitably as possible. This occurs when the company uses traditional product cost accounting information to evaluate the costs and profit margins of its various products or services.

Traditional accounting systems efficiently and effectively cost products for one purpose and that is to value inventories for financial reporting. Traditional cost accounts do not distort total costs, inventory costs, or "bottom-line" net income figures. However, managers who use cost accounting information to judge an individual product's costs can make serious marketing errors.[10] This happens because the overaggregated averages that cost accounting systems use to distribute indirect costs to products *systematically* distort the costs of individual products.[11] The cause of this distortion is the practice of distributing overhead costs to products according to weights that vary directly with volume of output, such as direct labor hours, material dollars or machine hours. A product containing more direct labor hours (or material dollars or machine hours, etc.) than another product is assumed to incur proportionately more indirect cost. Volume-related weights reliably distribute overhead costs to products only if overhead varies directly with volume of output.

In recent decades, however, the chief cause for growth of overhead has been increased diversity, or scope, of output, not increased volume, or scale, of output. Thus, traditional cost accounting systems tend to overcost high volume products—not the ones that cause most growth in overhead—and they undercost the low volume products that are chiefly responsible for most overhead growth. When used to guide marketing strategies, this distorted cost information encourages managers to proliferate low-volume product lines. The result in many cases is declining profit margins and perceived difficulty competing with focused (usually foreign) competitors.

A business with diverse product lines and high indirect costs cannot abide the distortions in product cost and margin data that traditional product costing systems create. Fortunately, a solution is at hand. Known as activity-based costing systems, product costing systems are beginning to appear that do not distort by distributing indirect costs with overaggregated volume-sensitive averages.[12] In fact, they turn traditional product costing on its head. Traditional product costing assumes that products cause indirect costs by consuming the driver (e.g., direct labor hours) that is used to distribute indirect costs to products.

Activity-based costing, in contrast, assumes that resource-consuming activities cause costs; products incur costs by the activities they require for design, engineering, manufacture, sale, delivery, and service. Activity-based costing traces costs to products through activities—essentially the activities that operating managers control with nonfinancial indicators of waste. By linking activities to financial costs, activity-based product cost information complements, therefore, the nonfinancial information operating managers use to achieve competitiveness in operating activities.

The importance of having activity-based cost information to assess the profit consequences of product-mix decisions is highlighted in Figure 4. This figure is based on a case study of an actual manufacturing

company whose experience is typical of American businesses generally.[13] Disappointed by chronically declining profits and by difficulty competing with new Japanese competitors in the 1970s, the company concluded that its problems were caused in large part by making product mix decisions with distorted product cost information. The company always had relied on a traditional product costing system that distributed indirect costs to products with direct labor hours. In the early 1980s, it redesigned its product costing system along activity-based lines.

The two curves in Figure 4 show strikingly different views of its

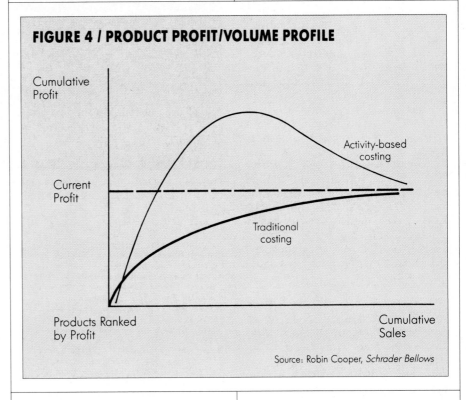

FIGURE 4 / PRODUCT PROFIT/VOLUME PROFILE

Cumulative Profit

Activity-based costing

Current Profit

Traditional costing

Products Ranked by Profit

Cumulative Sales

Source: Robin Cooper, *Schrader Bellows*

products' profits. Traditional cost information shows that all products make profit, some more and some less. Using this information over the years, the company's management had always pruned away products that lost money. The activity-based cost information reveals, however, that a very high percentage of the company's products actually generate losses in the long-run. Most surprising, and not evident in Figure 4, is the identity of products that generate profits and losses according to the two product costing systems. In general, those products identified as win-

ners by the traditional product costing system were found to be losers by the activity-based system and vice versa. The company's disappointing performance in the 1970s, in the face of new Japanese competition, resulted in no small way because distorted cost information caused management to proliferate its line with unprofitable products.[14]

MANAGE ACTIVITIES, NOT COSTS

Today's global economy calls for new management accounting information. Two types of activity-based management account-

ing information I have described enable a business to achieve profitability by creating competitive value for its customers that exceeds the cost of creating that value.[15] To be competitive, businesses need information that will make it possible for managers to identify and to eliminate generators of nonvalue activity. To be profitable, they need additional information to manage activity costs.

Traditional management accounting systems to control operations and to cost products do not serve managers well in today's competitive environment. Companies who control operations with costs and variances reported in flexible budgets will see their competitiveness and their profits shrink. Focusing operational control on financial costs does not assure competitiveness in the global economy. Today it is also necessary to achieve high quality and flexibility. Managers can achieve low cost, high quality, and flexibility simultaneously by focusing operational control on generators of nonvalue activity. Businesses become competitive and efficient by eliminating waste in operating activities, not by managing recorded costs.

World-class competitors will not necessarily see profits rise unless they also design activity-based chargeout and product cost systems. Activity-based costs eliminate distortions and cross-subsidies caused by traditional cost allocations. Activity-based cost information provides a clear view of how the mix of a company's diverse products, services, and activities contribute in the long run to the bottom line. Combined together, nonfinancial information to control operating activities and activity-based cost information can provide the management information that businesses need in today's competitive environment. Activity-based management accounting information is the key to continuous improvement of profitability, a journey without end. ∎

Prof. Johnson gets a rundown on the billing enclosing machine at Pacific Bell.

H. Thomas Johnson, CPA, Ph.D., is the Herbert Retzlaff Professor of Cost Management at Portland State University in Portland, Ore. Dr. Johnson is a member of the Mt. Rainier Chapter of NAA, through which this article was submitted. He thanks Robin Cooper, Elaine B. Johnson, and Robert S. Kaplan for comments on this article.

[1]H. Thomas Johnson and Robert S. Kaplan, "The Rise and Fall of Management Accounting," MANAGEMENT ACCOUNTING, January 1987, pp. 22-30.
[2]Activity-based information relates conceptually to the markets and hierarchies theory of Oliver Williamson and the value-chain concept of Michael Porter. Although not an influence on ideas in this paper, writings on management accounting by Gordon Shillinglaw and George Staubus also refer to "activity cost" information. Of the two, Shillinglaw in *Managerial Cost Accounting*, Richard D. Irwin, Inc., 1982, expresses ideas closer to those articulated in this article than does Staubus in *Activity Costing and Input-Output Accounting*, Richard D. Irwin, Inc., 1971.
[3]R.J. Schonberger, *Japanese Manufacturing*

Techniques: Nine Hidden Lessons in Simplicity, The Free Press, 1982, pp. 44-45. The origins of the nonvalue activity concept are hazy. General Electric Co. was an early advocate of the concept and contributed much to the articulation of nonvalue activity ideas in *CAM-I Cost Management Systems Conceptual Design Document, Phase I,* Computer Aided Manufacturing-International, Inc., Arlington, Tex., 1987.
[4]The setup example that follows is based on Richard J. Schonberger, *Japanese Manufacturing Techniques,* pp. 18-24, and James C. Abegglen and George Stalk, Jr., *Kaisha, The Japanese Corporation,* Basic Books, Inc., New York, 1985 pp. 93-96.
[5]For a concise up-to-date summary of these techniques see Ernest C. Huge (with Alan D. Anderson), *The Spirit of Manufacturing Excellence: An Executive's Guide to the New Mind Set,* Dow-Jones, Irwin/APICS, 1988.
[6] Robert W. Hall, "Measuring Progress: Management Essential," *Target,* Summer 1987, pp. 4-10. An excellent discussion of nonfinancial indicators of waste that is germane to JIT operations is in Richard J. Schonberger, *World Class Manufacturing Casebook: Implementing JIT and TQC,* The Free Press, 1987, pp. xi-xxiii.
[7]The budgeting procedures advocated here resemble those used by E.I. duPont de Nemours Powder Company from about 1903 to 1915. See H. Thomas Johnson and Robert S. Kaplan, *Relevance Lost: The Rise and Fall of Management Accounting,* Harvard Business School Press, 1987, ch 4.
[8]H. Thomas Johnson, "Organizational Design versus Strategic Information Procedures for Managing Corporate Overhead Cost: Weyerhaeuser Company, 1972-1986," in William J. Bruns and Robert S. Kaplan, eds.,

Accounting and Management: Field Study Perspectives, Boston: Harvard Business School Press, 1987, pp. 49-72. Also see Brandt Allen, "Make Information Services Pay Its Way," *Harvard Business Review,* January-February 1987, pp. 57-63.
[9]H. Thomas Johnson and Dennis A. Loewe, "How Weyerhaeuser Manages Corporate Overhead Costs," MANAGEMENT ACCOUNTING, August 1987, pp. 20-26.
[10]For more on the distinction between cost accounting and cost management information see H. Thomas Johnson, "The Decline of Cost Management: A Reinterpretation of 20th Century Cost Accounting History," *Journal of Cost Management,* Spring 1987, pp. 5-12.
[11]Robin Cooper and Robert S. Kaplan, "How Cost Accounting Systematically Distorts Product Costs," in Bruns and Kaplan, *Accounting and Management,* pp. 204-228. A condensed version of this chapter appeared in MANAGEMENT ACCOUNTING, April 1988, pp. 20-27.
[12]Robin Cooper, "The Two-Stage Procedure in Cost Accounting," *Journal of Cost Management,* Part 1, Summer 1987, pp. 43-51 and Part II, Fall 1987, pp. 39-45; R. Cooper and R.S. Kaplan, "How Cost Accounting Systematically Distorts;" H. Thomas Johnson and Robert S. Kaplan, "The Importance of Long-term Product Costs," *The McKinsey Quarterly,* Autumn 1987, pp. 36-48.
[13]Robin Cooper, *Schrader Bellows: A Strategic Cost Analysis,* Harvard Business School, Case Series 9-186-272, 1986.
[14]For additional insights, see Peter Drucker, "Managing for Business Effectiveness," *Harvard Business Review,* May-June 1963, pp. 59-62; also, Abegglen and Stalk, *Kaisha,* ch 4.
[15]Michael E. Porter, *Competitive Advantage: Creating and Sustaining Superior Performance,* The Free Press, New York, 1985, p. 3.

Activities: The Focal Point of Total Cost Management

Success depends on the firm's ability to manage activities.

BY MICHAEL R. OSTRENGA

Total cost management (TCM) is a business philosophy of managing all company resources and the activities that consume those resources. Managing costs in a TCM environment means focusing on activities and the events, circumstances, or conditions that cause or "drive" these cost-consuming activities.

It is important for management to understand that costs are not merely incurred, they are caused. When action is taken to reduce what causes the activities that consume resources, then a lasting reduction in costs will take place.

Based on our experience in applying the different principles of total cost management for several clients, we have verified that a central theme exists. That theme is "activities are the focal point of TCM."

This article is based on Ernst & Young's experience with large and small companies from discrete and process manufacturing. The large companies include an electronics manufacturer, a beverage processor, and a building supply company, all blue chip Fortune 500 companies. Companies with less than $50 million in revenue include a small sheet metal stamping company, a truck manufacturer, and a candy processor.

The specific project scope and business needs varied for each company and included:

■ Product costs that reflect the true resources consumed,

■ Process value analysis,
■ Cost reduction,
■ Improved performance measurements,
■ Responsibility accounting, and
■ Product line profitability.

Although the objectives for each company differed, when we analyzed their operations, the focus shifted inevitably to the effect activities and activity-consuming resources have on the economics of the business. In each case, although the *starting point* differed, the *focal point* didn't. It became apparent to us that activities were the focal point of total cost management.

The concepts discussed here are based on the application of TCM principles to the business needs of several of our client companies. I also will identify the role activity

Author Ostrenga presents process value analysis as an integrated foundation for activity-based costing.

management plays in the integration of these key TCM principles:

- Process value analysis,
- Activity-based process costing,
- Activity-based product costing,
- Responsibility accounting,
- Performance measurements, and
- Investment management.

PROCESS VALUE ANALYSIS

Process value analysis (PVA) is the initial building block of TCM and facilitates the development of performance measures, activity-based costing, responsibility accounting, and investment management. It focuses on meeting customer requirements, minimizing cost and cycle time, and improving the quality of output.

PVA relates activities to the events, circumstances, or conditions that create or "drive" the need for the activity and the resources consumed. These cost drivers are targeted for elimination/minimization if they relate to nonvalue added activities and optimization if they relate to value added.

PVA provides us with a better understanding of the cost relationship of processes and the underlying resource-consuming activities. As a result, our ability to manage resources and reduce the reliance on support costs is improved.

At one of our client companies, it became evident that the activity management and resultant cost reduction could be facilitated only by a reduction in the drivers or cause of resource commitment and not by the direct reduction in activities. This idea is a departure from much of the current literature that calls for the reduction of cost through activity management. Many articles fail to differentiate between activities and cost drivers and, whether it is intentional or not, obscure the need to reduce the driver of activities through process improvement to provide a meaningful and long-lasting cost reduction.

It's important to note, however, that a reduction in drivers, which results in a reduced dependency on activities, does not lower costs until the excess resources are reduced or redeployed into more productive areas.

The following project methodology enabled us to understand the client company's cost behavior and to position lasting improvements:

Process Definition

- Document the process flow,
- Identify the customer's internal and external requirements,
- Define the outputs of each process step,
- Determine process input requirements,
- Compare customer requirements with outputs/inputs, and
- Define the staffing levels (full-time equivalents) for each process.

Activity Analysis

- Define activities within each process,
- Identify activities as value added and nonvalue added using customer requirements,
- Determine cycle time of each activity,
- Calculate the cycle efficiency (value added time/total time) for each process, and
- Cumulate cycle efficiency along business value chain.

Driver Analysis

- Develop cause and effect—driver identification, and
- Perform a Pareto analysis on the drivers and the activities they control.

Opportunity Improvement Planning

- Develop perspective charts on value added/nonvalue added,
- Develop an opportunity improvement plan to eliminate/minimize nonvalue added and optimize value added, and
- Develop performance measures and improvement indicators to track opportunities.

ACTIVITY-BASED COSTING

There is a strong relationship between PVA and activity-based costing. Activities consume resources (cost) at a process level. Products consume activities in varying degrees based largely on their level of differentiation. Therefore, our ability to reduce nonvalue added activities and cost through process value analysis also reduces product costs because the activities consumed per given output as well as the cost per activity will be less. Furthermore, the cost drivers, uncovered by PVA, support the attachment of costs to the process and products.

According to activity-based costing theory, most support costs (nonmaterial costs) do not vary directly with labor volume but vary with product diversity and operation complexity. Thus, many existing product costs do not represent the true consumption of resources to produce them.

ACTIVITY-BASED PROCESS COSTING

Process control managers are responsible for and are held accountable for costs that are generated within their process area. These managers should have a cost management reporting system that provides them timely and accurate cost information to plan, control, and monitor the cost accounts for that process center.

Applying costs from outside the process or spreading costs from a corporate/plant level will not help the process manager correct a problem or know more about his process area. Yet, traditional cost information systems include allocated or noncontrollable costs in department reports that produce a "Pontius Pilate" syndrome among those responsible for managing a process. At the process level, managers should only see and be held accountable for controllable costs.

It's important to consider that the level of drivers identified in process value analysis may be at a lower level than the driver base used for activity-based costing. This occurs because the many different support costs at the process level could require an unmanageable number of cost pools and driver rates to show the same level of causal relationship. It may be appropriate to summarize costs into pools that have drivers that move in the same relative proportion. For example, setup, material handling to next sequence, and inspection all may be summarized into one pool having a common driver such as number of setups or number of work orders. This concept is called the surrogate driver method.[1]

One of our clients visualized controlling costs at the process level. The company was more interested in establishing better process costs that in turn could be related to process activities and controlled through responsibility accounting.

We demonstrated that, regardless of the traditional allocation of cost being used, the "economic" costs could be reduced through the focus on activities. These cost reductions would be realized at the process level. The effect of lower process costs would be verified by activity-based product costing, as product consumption of lower cost activities is shown.

This *process-cost* orientation is vital to the integration of PVA cost behavior identification to the realization of cost reduction through activity-based product costing. This concept has all but been lost in recent journals due to the activity-based costing emphasis on *product costs*.

Additionally, activity-based process costing provides a foundation for, and gives an organization important insights into, the interpretation of responsibility accounting.

ACTIVITY-BASED PRODUCT COSTING

Charging costs directly to products eliminates the need to allocate or assign costs. Costs that cannot be charged directly should be assigned to the product through activity-based costing.

In keeping with the philosophy that activities consume resources (process) and products consume activities, activity-based process costing becomes the precursor to product costing. Once the process costs are established, they become available for responsibility accounting and serve as the pool of costs to trace to products that consume the process activities.

Activity-based product costing methodology is similar to process costing. In process costing, financial accounts are associated with process activity pools through stage one drivers, and the costs in each process activity pool are summed and divided by stage two drivers or output measures to yield the activity-based costing rates. The costs within the pool represent those that are expected to move in the same direction and order of magnitude with a change in the "driver." The cost rates then are applied to products based on the identification of types and quantities of activities consumed by each product.

Our fieldwork has shown that activity-based product costing is sensitive to the ratio of overhead cost to total costs and the level at which product-focused processes enable direct charging.

One of our clients has a ratio of 80% material and 20% conversion cost at the plant level. With such a small amount of cost to reassign to products, the ability to demonstrate changes in product costs would seem to be limited. When we differentiated certain costs by product, however, significant cost changes were developed.

One significant area for improved costing was found in the assignment of storage costs. Because products and components had varying levels of volume and time in storage, the storage costs were segregated into transaction-related and storage-time related. The transaction-related costs were assigned to part numbers based on the number of times handled (received, issued, cycle counted), whereas, the costs related to storage time (depreciation, utilities, taxes) were assigned to part numbers based on the inventory turnover ratio.

This differentiation in storage costs proved enlightening from a product-cost perspective. It also pointed out the significance of cost and cycle-time relationships.

Other value-chain costs not typically considered product costs (research and development, marketing, accounting/finance, and so on) also were assigned to the product-cost level and added to the cost differentials.

Our focus was first to identify direct charge candidates, then to assign costs through driver rates, and finally to allocate any remaining costs. This method was followed in both the first and second stages of cost assignment. (See Figure 1.)

This company produced identical products in several plants. Thus, it gained a new product-cost perspective which in turn led to differentiated product plant costs and support for regional pricing decisions.

Another client had advanced to compact layouts with a product-focused process that eliminated resource contention for different product lines. In this environment, most support costs of the process were consumed by and were already being directly charged to the product. However, the significant cost of centralized purchasing, receiving, and material handling was still being allocated on an arbitrary labor-volume measure. Activity-

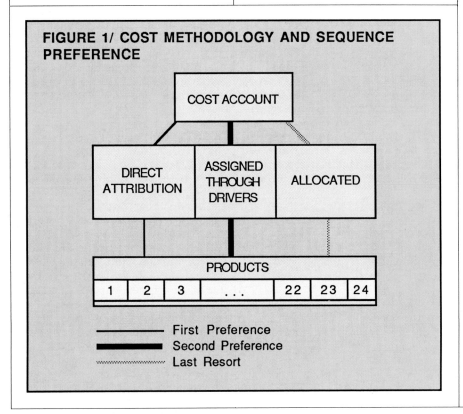

FIGURE 1/ COST METHODOLOGY AND SEQUENCE PREFERENCE

COST ACCOUNT

DIRECT ATTRIBUTION — ASSIGNED THROUGH DRIVERS — ALLOCATED

PRODUCTS

| 1 | 2 | 3 | ... | 22 | 23 | 24 |

——— First Preference
━━━ Second Preference
·········· Last Resort

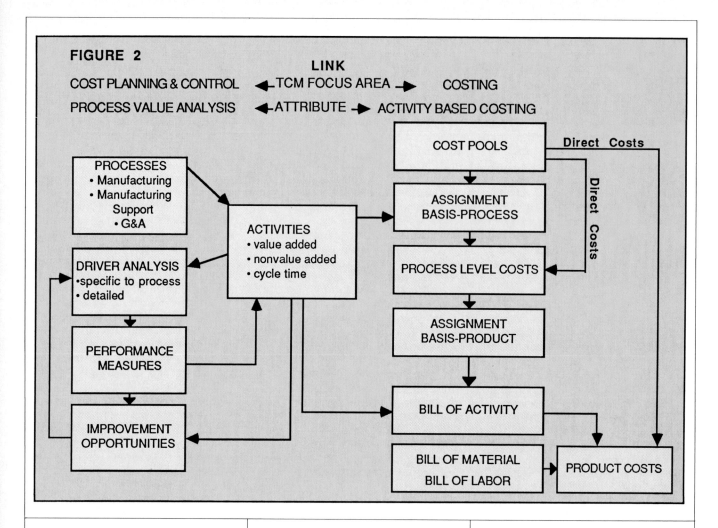

FIGURE 2

LINK

COST PLANNING & CONTROL ← TCM FOCUS AREA → COSTING

PROCESS VALUE ANALYSIS ← ATTRIBUTE → ACTIVITY BASED COSTING

based cost concepts were used to assign these additional "pervasive" support costs to product costs. The result was an improved cost and better insight into the material-acquisition cost related to raw material and components supporting each product.

Other situations, however, proved to have much more significant shifts in product costs where plant conversion costs were a higher percentage of total cost. Yet in all cases, the other value chain costs typically were allocated to products on sales, gross margin, or not associated with products at all. When applied through activity driver relationships, they have made a meaningful difference in the way costs were viewed.

In practice, a very powerful way to demonstrate the important connection between activity analysis and activity-based costing is to look at the value and nonvalue added costs concept (see Figure 2). To the degree we identify value added/nonvalue added costs in each process activity pool, separate costing

rates can be developed to preserve the value added/nonvalue added identification at the product level. Table 1 represents a typical cost profile using Ernst & Young's process value analysis/activity-based costing linkage methodology.

This new way of looking at product cost provoked one of our clients to comment, "If my product cost is X% or Y$ too high to be competitive, I now know how to trace it back to the process through my bill of activities." And, conversely, because cost is created at the process

level and absorbed at the product level, it is easy to see the effect of changes on driver rates. The added distinction of value added and nonvalue added at the process level as well as product level helps reinforce the mind-set of opportunity in minimizing or eliminating nonvalue added and optimizing value added costs.

RESPONSIBILITY ACCOUNTING

One of the foundations of cost management is the development of cost ownership through responsibility and accountability. Most companies fall victim to forcing costs incurred from manufacturing and administration support groups down to the department or process areas through inappropriate allocations. Typically, these allocations are on headcount or labor (salary) relationships. As we have discussed, not only do labor allocations distort the assignment of costs to products, but they also distort the cost of services

TABLE 1		
	VA	NVA
Material	$X	$X
Labor	X	X
Overhead	X	X
	$X	$X
Opportunity Cost		X
Other Value Chain Costs	X	X
TOTAL	$X	$X

provided by support groups.

A chargeout methodology designed to relate the service costs to the underlying driver creating the need for service allows for an equitable distribution of cost. Thus, chargeout development is integrated with activity analysis and activity-based process costing. Activity analysis identifies the appropriate driver base, and activity-based process costing develops the cost of the output (product or service).

Structuring cost assignment in this fashion consistently supports the causal relationship with cost incurred and the driver-user requirements.

We can draw a further analogy here. In activity-based costing we saw how activities consume resources and products consume activities. In responsibility accounting, support service activities consume resources, and users consume support services.

Responsibility accounting is effective only when a sense of ownership has been established. In order to ensure this sense of ownership, costs deemed to be noncontrollable at a given level should be excluded. It is important to recognize that noncontrollable costs at a certain level are controllable elsewhere in the organization. For instance, while the head of a department may have "influence" over the amount of space his area consumes, it is difficult to imagine this person having control over real estate taxes or building depreciation. Yet many companies force down an allocated cost and "impose" responsibility on a department's expense statement.

One of our clients sought a responsibility accounting solution to cost control. When we designed this concept, we realized it was important to introduce costs to the responsibility center in which they are controlled. For example, typical department costs such as material handling and inspection were found to be controlled at the demand source. In this case, the source was the manufacturing operation activities, and its driver was the number of work orders.

When we recognized this cost behavior, the decision was made to establish budgetary and expense statements with flexible parameters that are based on activities

Traditional cost information systems may produce a 'Pontius Pilate syndrome.'

and cost driver relationships. We also decided to charge the cost to the manufacturing operations department as a user of the service and reflect the chargeout to the material handling and inspection department cost statements.

Relating the cost to the drivers establishes the driver as the measure of planned activity. Cost targets will be determined by sensitivity analysis performed on the effect of cost change as the activity level deviates from plan. These flexible targets recognize that plans will change. They also demonstrate to operating management that they cannot attain their targets by performing in ways that are counterproductive to the organization.

For managers held accountable for cost improvement, this philosophy of responsibility accounting should improve their attitude toward cost management. Businesses with this culture in place can be transformed from an organization of employees to an organization of "cost managers."

PERFORMANCE
MEASUREMENT

Performance measurements traditionally have been financially oriented with an emphasis on short-term results. Short-term financial measures have been undermined by changes in technology, the advance of manufacturing process changes, and new ways to view the organization. Increased capital intensity and decreased touch labor costs have changed the way we must look at the business.

Traditional measures have become invalid measures of performance and often send misleading signals to management. Many of these measures are actually counterproductive because they modify behavior in such a way that leads to

increases in inventory, the creation of cost elsewhere in the value chain, increased levels of complexity, required resources, and quality problems.

Traditionally, companies produce significant amounts of data at higher levels of the organization. The amount of real relevant information for decision-making support should vary at different levels of management. Performance measurements should represent a mix of financial and nonfinancial operating measures consistent with the level of business responsibility. This structure will provide more meaningful information and a proactive support of the management of resources.

Our model suggests financial measures needed, for an overall reading of the firm's health must not be limited to any single measure such as ROI. Other considerations such as cash flow, earnings growth, capital employed, and so on round out the needs in financial measures.

As we view the middle management area, a pronounced increase in nonfinancial focus measures is required. These measures, although operational in nature, must still be integrated with the organization goals to ensure that management is moving toward the overall goals and does not suboptimize the organization while maximizing an individual area, department, or function.

Performance measures assist the cost reduction effort by focusing on the significant activity levels and measuring the drivers of activities. In concert with the continuous improvement philosophy, performance measures have baselines and targets established to measure the impact of change promoted through the operational improvements identified in process value analysis. The targeting of measures provides the necessary visibility to the status of nonvalue added elimination and value added optimization progress.

Performance measurements have a pervasive nature about them. As defined previously, total cost management is a business philosophy of managing resources and resource-consuming activities. Performance measurements position us for a better understanding of the economics of the business when activities and

An Overview of Total Cost Management

Total cost management has three major focus areas. These areas are cost planning and control, costing, and external regulations that must be supported by cost information. Each area consists of attributes that are critical to the overall focus area objective.

Cost Planning and Control. Cost planning provides operations management with prospective and historical cost and performance measurement information. The attributes of this focus area are process value analysis, responsibility accounting, performance measurements, and investment management.

Process value analysis is a cost reduction and process improvement methodology that focuses on identifying the resource-consuming activities within a process and the underlying "driver" of cost. The analysis is done at the process level (as opposed to product level), which represents the point of cost impact.

Responsibility accounting is the process by which actual cost information is reported against plans for those costs that are an individual's specific responsibility. These actual-to-plan comparisons are made at the level of cost impact (source)—not at the level of cost incurrence. For example, material handling costs are incurred at the support department level; however, the control and source of cost occur in the production department that demands the services.

Performance measurements measure the cost impact against a predetermined baseline. Measures are integrated vertically throughout the organization and horizontally along the value chain. Market, business, plant, and shop performance measurements should be consistent with the company's goals and critical success factors.

Investment management is the process by which management should relate investment decisions to strategic plans and operational goals while maintaining an acceptable return on investment. It uses the portfolio effect on the asset base and measures an estimate of improvements in quality, cycle time reduction, flexibility, and service through the elimination of waste (nonvalue added activities).

Costing. The second area of focus in total cost management is costing. Costing includes product valuation/profitability, pricing, product introductions, product discontinuances, and inventory valuation. Additionally, costing is necessary to support performance measurement and cost reduction opportunities through process value analysis. The costing focus area emphasizes the need to provide accurate and timely cost information in support of product and process costing.

Activity-based process costing and activity-based product costing are the two major attributes of costing. Activity-based process costing applies costs through a series of activity/driver bases. The process is made up of a series of activities directed at producing an output. Activity-based process costing is the precursor to activity-based product costing and helps facilitate performance measurements for responsibility accounting.

Activity-based product costing applies costs to products by developing cost pools within processes that represent costs that vary with a common activity/driver. An important distinction to note is that activities consume resources at the process level, while products consume activities. This allows us to integrate activity-based process and product costing by first costing the activity where incurred (process), and second, rolling up costed activities into products.

Activity-based product costing improves the tracing of costs to product where these costs typically were arbitrarily allocated in the past. Any costs that can be charged directly to products should be removed from the cost pools.

External Regulations. The regulatory focus area is directed toward providing the necessary financial and management reporting to meet the requirements of such external parties as the IRS and the SEC. Often, information required by these organizations differs significantly from information required for internal management purposes. (For example, allocations of overhead cost for financial purposes simply require a separation of costs deferred into inventory and those expensed through cost of sales). For internal management purposes, however, a much different distinction between causal relationships of cost and the effect of activities consumed by products for pricing, product introductions, discontinuances, and profitability measures is needed. ∎

resource patterns change. This was reinforced in our fieldwork.

Performance measurements provide an important building block in the process value analysis project. They set the baseline and measure the impact of changes in pursuit of continuous improvement. Performance measurements close the loop on activity-based process costing by relating the process cost to a measure of output producing "cost per" information.

Our client experience has shown that the comprehensiveness of measures can be demonstrated best by representing a balance between different categories such as:
- *Effectiveness.* Are we doing the right things—planned output/actual output?
- *Efficiency.* How well are we doing? What is the planned input per actual input?
- *Productivity.* How much output are we getting for a given input (or series of inputs)?
- *Utilization.* How are we using corporate resources such as inventory, asset turnover, etc.?

These measurement categories assist responsibility accounting programs by tying controllable cost measures to a more comprehensive view of managing resources.

INVESTMENT MANAGEMENT

Investment Management is a critical part of business strategy. Recognizing opportunities and earning an acceptable return is paramount for continued corporate health.

The investment strategy should be driven by specific product and process requirements as well as the company's strategy for dealing with technological change.

Investing and measuring return on individual assets is common but often shortsighted. The real value of an investment is the effect on the entire portfolio of assets. Consideration should be given to the synergy and integration of projects. The portfolio effect often proves that the total benefits outweigh the sum of the individual projects.

Typical cost and financial data such as ROI and ROA represent only one aspect of investment. Certain issues surrounding the use of ROI and ROA are subject to the accounting data. For instance, both the numerator and denominator of the equation is subject to certain accounting treatment on accruals, LIFO/FIFO inventory policy, and depreciation elections on assets. Consideration should be given to defining methodologies that demonstrate a better picture of the true *economics* of the business.

Improvements in quality, throughput, and other operational benefits are difficult to quantify but are real in terms of competitive posturing. These improvements should be included as estimates. It is better to make a fair representation than to ignore them altogether.

A company's cost management philosophy should provide visibility to cost reduction from new investment by focusing on the nonvalue added activities displaced and the improved efficiency of value added activities. All too often investment management focuses on the investment side of the equation and does little to follow the benefits. Our vision of cost management prescribes closing the loop by monitoring the change in activity-resource consumption through process value analysis. Figure 3 summarizes the role activities play in managing today's business through the principles of total cost management.

THE TRANSITION TO TCM

The first step to achieving total cost management is to assess the company's current environment, operations, philosophy, and organization. This assessment should identify the limitations of the current cost management system. It is important to have a sense of vision and a quest for continuous improvement through the management of resources in order to succeed.

We have developed a transition plan based on our experiences with clients (see Figure 4). Subsequent to the assesment, phase one begins with the process value analysis. The identification of cost behavior and activity/driver relationships through process value analysis then can be integrated with the performance measurements. Managers then can measure the impact of changes on activities and resources brought about through implementation of the operational improvement plan developed in process value analysis.

Phase two begins with the costing of activities at the process level where costs are incurred. Consequently, what efforts are made to reduce process costs will result in product cost savings when activity-based process and product costing are integrated.

Responsibility accounting can be built upon the phase one framework and the activity-based process costing work. Positioning responsibility accounting at this point takes full advantage of the understanding and differentiations of cost source (driver and demand source) and cost incurrence (expended activity resource). This will assist in placing the cost responsibility at the proper level of control in the value chain.

Phase two is completed with the incorporation of investment/asset management. The justification and tracking will be consistent with the operational improvement plan if the nonvalue added activities reduced or value added activities optimized are the focal point. Relating the investment of asset management to the responsibility area through established performance measures on the change in activities and the impact on process costs provides a solid basis on which to track the use of these resources after commitment.

Phase three produces a true picture of the total cost to provide products to the market. Using the insights gained in process value analysis and activity-based process costing, one can associate costs with products through:

■ Direct attribution,
■ Assignment through activities/

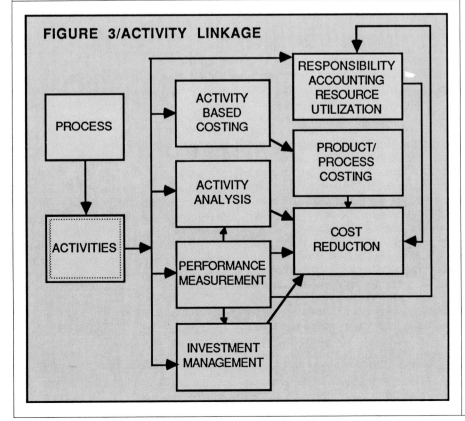

FIGURE 3/ACTIVITY LINKAGE

PROCESS

ACTIVITIES

ACTIVITY BASED COSTING

ACTIVITY ANALYSIS

PERFORMANCE MEASUREMENT

INVESTMENT MANAGEMENT

RESPONSIBILITY ACCOUNTING RESOURCE UTILIZATION

PRODUCT/ PROCESS COSTING

COST REDUCTION

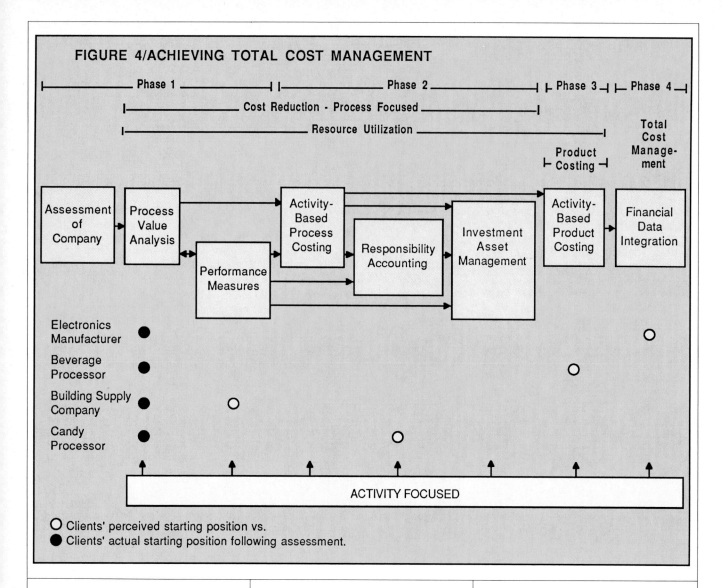

FIGURE 4/ACHIEVING TOTAL COST MANAGEMENT

drivers, and

■ Allocation — last resort for remaining costs.

The costs associated with products in this fashion will reflect the resource input more accurately to produce different products.

Phase four, financial data integration and the use of activity information for both managerial and financial reporting, is still on the horizon. The advanced stages of research and continued development in practical applications with off-line systems and models will help formulate the future needs for database definition and integration of total cost management into the financial data.

EQUATION FOR SUCCESS

Each total cost management principle positioned in this transition plan is strongly rooted in activity management.

Figure 4 illustrates the path to achieving total cost management.With most of our clients, the perceived starting position differed from the actual starting position after we assessed the needs of the company. While each project did not undertake a full PVA and performance measurement study, the work done in those areas was viewed as the critical foundation supporting the philosophy of managing company resources.

Many businesses still rely on managing by the summarized financial numbers.Yet the equation for success is a simple one: Cost is caused, cost is incurred. The only effective way to reduce cost is to manage resource-consuming activities through its driver relationships. Reducing cost alone won't have a lasting effect. If, however, the *cause* is removed, the savings are long term. Activities are at the focal point of our ability to create excellence in our businesses. It's vital to take a fresh perspective to help transform our businesses into an improved competitive position through total cost management and its focal point — activities. ■

Michael R. Ostrenga is a senior manager and director for Ernst & Young's Cost Management and Manufacturing Industry consulting services for Wisconsin. He is a member of NAA's Milwaukee Chapter, through which this article was submitted.

[1] Robin Cooper and Robert S. Kaplan, "How Cost Accounting Distorts Product Cost," MANAGEMENT ACCOUNTING®, April 1988.

Is this article of interest to you? If so, circle appropriate number on Reader Service Card.	**Yes** 58	**No** 59

FOCUS THE FACTORY WITH ACTIVITY-BASED COSTING

This plumbing company's profits were being drained by its low-volume product lines—its operations had to be recosted.

BY MICHAEL O'GUIN

Before our manufacturing strategy study was even started, we knew we faced a big challenge. Our client, a $100-million-a-year plumbing fixture manufacturer I'll call SuperFaucet, had a vertically integrated 720,000-square-foot factory encompassing everything from die casting, screw machines, pipe threading, chrome plating, stamping, polishing, and assembly. In addition, the client sold an enormous number of product permutations extending into the billions, including available functions, styles, finishes, and substitutions. These factors resulted in a large overhead structure that amounted to almost 60% of the cost of goods sold.

Recently the company began to lose money and decided to do a manufacturing study with the assistance of a consulting firm. The objective was to reduce costs and improve profitability.

The study team knew that the client could not be competitive in all of the diverse manufacturing processes it performed. But, we knew also the client's current labor and depreciation-based cost allocation system would not support accurate make/buy decision making. Therefore, the first phase of the study was a recosting of the client's manufacturing operations, primarily aimed at resolving make/buy questions.

COST SYSTEM FLAWED

SuperFaucet's cost accounting system allocated costs in a two-step process. Labor and

SuperFaucet's overhead amounted to almost 60% of the cost of goods sold.

expenses were accrued in a given department, and then all of the overhead department expenses were allocated to the direct labor (for example, manufacturing) departments. The overhead costs for production control, purchasing, manufacturing engineering, and supervision were allocated to each manufacturing department based on the standard direct labor hours earned last year. Tooling, utilities, and maintenance costs were allocated on annual depreciation dollars in each manufacturing department.

Unfortunately, although this procedure is the standard cost accounting practice, it provided a grossly distorted picture of the company's manufacturing process and its interrelationships. As an example, the screw machine department was allocated the

largest proportion of tooling overhead because it had the largest concentration of equipment depreciation, but screw machines required almost no tooling department support. The punch press department, on the other hand, consumed 40% of the tooling department's resources and was allocated just over 9% or $162,000.

Furthermore, allocating overhead on labor hours implies that a reduction in direct labor results in corresponding reductions in purchasing, receiving, and production control. Unfortunately this is not true. Automating a process or shortening a production run does not reduce the number of purchase orders placed, shipments received, or batches scheduled. This misrepresentation obscures true causes of these activities, confusing cost reduction efforts.

In addition, the cost absorption of products was flawed. Current cost systems are built around standard labor times. The standard time for each part is the sum of the theoretical times for each of the manufacturing operations (drilling a hole, tapping it, face milling a surface, and so on) required to produce that part. It may or may not include setup, but it certainly does not contain purchasing, receiving, inspection, or any of the overhead activities required. Those overhead costs are added to the part by applying an overhead rate for each standard hour of labor added.

When a buyer purchases a lot of material, a planner schedules a production run, or the machinist sets up a job. Processing may take 20 minutes or 20 hours, but the costs are the same. Currently, the costs of these activities are aggregated at the department level and spread across all of that department's parts based on earned labor hours. Therefore, a small batch of parts that requires the same activities but has fewer parts to amortize the costs across receives a standard cost that is irrespective of volume and is greatly understated. Because the cost system does not discriminate justly against low-volume parts, American factories are filled with one-of-a-kind parts that every plant manager knows are loss leaders.

REDISTRIBUTING THE COST

Using SuperFaucet's journal of accounts, we had a relatively accurate cost detail for each direct labor and overhead department. This left us with the major task of redistributing Super-Faucet's overhead.

The first step in the overhead distribution process was to interview each overhead department's manager or supervisor. For example, the maintenance supervisor was asked: "What causes your work or increases its frequency?" " How is your work recorded or tracked?" "Which direct labor departments consume most of your people's time?" After finding the most equitable and practical allocation method, the team would feed back to the interviewee a distribution of

how we perceived his department's cost should be distributed.

For example, we found that the tooling and maintenance departments recorded which departments they supported on their time cards. Therefore, we used the time card distribution to allocate tooling and maintenance costs.

The purchasing department's time was best related to purchase orders. Unfortunately, there were no purchase order data in SuperFaucet's computer system, but purchased parts did have unique part numbers. So we distributed the purchasing costs to each direct labor department on the quantity of purchased part issues from the warehouse to that department. In this way, the purchasing costs allocated to the faucet assembly department would be eliminated if that department was outsourced, as our faucet vendor would now buy those parts for assembly.

The work associated with the material departments of shop floor control, warehousing, receiving, and production control is not driven by volume of parts but by production lots. When a planner schedules a part number for manufacture, his work is the same for two parts or 2,000.

The same is true for the other material functions. The quantity of the work is proportioned to the number of times the parts are issued to the floor, pulled from the warehouse, received, or set up. It is not based on how many parts are in a batch or how many hours it will take to machine them. Therefore, we distributed all of these material departments' costs to each of the direct labor departments by the number of material issues to that department.

For most of the management and engineering departments, no quantitative measures of work existed, so we were forced to rely on management surveys. We asked the tool engineering manager, "Which direct labor departments do you spend a disproportionate amount of your time supporting?" Although, admittedly, this method is not exact, the objective of this recosting is to be approximately right and not precisely wrong. If one direct labor department stands out in a manager's mind as

particularly expensive, the recosting should reflect this relationship.

Overall, the redistribution increased the fabrication department's overhead and at the same time decreased the labor-intense assembly department's overhead. There were dramatic swings in some of the departments' overhead:

- Punch press went up to 20%,
- Screw machines went down by more than 15%,
- Autopolishing increased by $1 million, and
- Inner assembly decreased by $300,000.

COSTING PARTS

After we completed this procedure, we had a cost matrix. For each direct labor department, we had 26 overhead pools: tooling, indirect labor, utilities, maintenance, industrial engineering and so on. At this point, we decided to end our recosting and compare vendor prices for all of the parts in a given department to our total in-house costs.

We chose this approach for two reasons. First, at SuperFaucet, the savings were in overhead, and overhead would go away only if the work generating it went away. But eliminating only some punch press parts would cause its relative overhead to go up. Savings would be possible only if the entire department were outsourced. Second, we knew of no way to allocate overhead to piece parts accurately. Allocating overhead on direct labor hours—the standard practice—distorted true cause-and-effect relationships between part volume and cost. Fortunately, SuperFaucet's president demanded we be able to compare a vendor's piece-part price to SuperFaucet's in-house piece-part cost.

We based our next step on a MANAGEMENT ACCOUNTING® article by Robert Kaplan of Harvard Business School on the activity-based costing of products. Published in the April 1988 issue, the article discussed why activity-based costing should be used, which activities are driven by activities, and how powerful the effect of an activity-based approach could be. Using the article as a reference, we began to assemble an activity-based cost system.

Because we had 26 overhead allocations for each direct labor department, we decided to accumulate these allocations into two pools. One pool consisted of the overhead elements driven by volume, and the other pool consisted of elements driven by transactions. Our study found a significant number of overhead activities were generated every time a part was run through a production department: Planning scheduled the part, warehousing issued material, operators set up the machine, inspection examined the batch, and so on. So, a transaction was defined as a production run of a single part number. The team addressed every overhead department and debated whether it was volume or transaction driven.

We decided utilities, supplies, equipment depreciation, and maintanance were volume driven, while all of the material functions such as purchasing, receiving, warehousing, production control, and shop floor control were transaction driven. There was quite a debate about tooling. The fabrication of tooling originates with a particular number, which seems transaction driven, but for the past two years SuperFaucet had not fabricated any new tooling, only repaired worn tooling. Because the tool wear is volume driven, tooling was put into the volume pool.

Indirect labor costs—which are direct labor costs not charged to production work, such as setup, supervision, training, and material handling within a department—are driven by transactions. Another cost element was the difference between earned labor and actual labor costs. This is the "inefficiency" in a labor report. We believed the majority of this lost efficiency was directly related to production workers stopping one job and starting another. After learning a job, an operator's time was spent exclusively on that job, and if the standard was correct, the operator performed at standard.

For example, the aerospace industry has extremely short runs and, therefore, low worker efficiency. Operators spend most of their time just figuring out how to put together an assembly. When they do start to develop a rhythm, that assembly is finished and will not be seen again for months or years. At that time, the operators will get another chance to learn those same parts all over again. In the case of SuperFaucet, we firmly believed lost labor efficiency was a result of transactions.

Quality control was transaction driven because it inspected batches of parts—not each individual part. Scrap and rework were driven both by volume and transactions. The greater number of parts and the bigger the batches, the more scrap produced. But, the greater number of different parts produced, the less able a company is to get all of the bugs out of each part, tooling and process. So more transactions means more quality problems. Therefore, we split scrap and rework costs with 80% going into the volume pool and 20% going into the transaction pool.

The manufacturing management costs, we believed, were driven by transactions. The greater the variety of parts, the more management headaches and details to control. Manufacturing engineering was a product-support function and, therefore, driven by parts. On the other hand, industrial engineering was a process support function and, therefore, driven by volume.

At this point, we had two pools for each direct labor department: one for volume-driven activities and one for transactions. To distribute the cost to each product, we first needed to distribute the overhead to each product's component parts, so we created a database of all the component parts produced in 1987.

Using the company's mainframe, we exploded the year's sales into quantities of end products which we then multiplied by each product's bill of material. We then put these parts into each department by multiplying these components by their routings. This gave us a listing of all the year's component parts with quantitites by department. We could now allocate the overhead on this

TABLE 1 / STANDARD PART COST

Punch Press Part: 20-009-154-000

Transaction overhead calculation
MRP Code: C=2 transactions per year

Punch press transaction cost	$166.3 per transaction
$166.3 X 2	$332.6
Annual quantity	3,660
Transaction overhead cost	$332.6/3,660
Cost per part	$0.09087
Standard material cost	$0.19945
Standard labor cost	$0.00519
Volume overhead	$0.04205
Transaction overhead	$0.09087
Total standard cost	$0.33757

Zinc Die Cast Part: 55-004127-000

Transaction overhead calculation
MRP Code: A=13 transactions per year

Die cast transaction cost	$722.8 per transaction
$722.8 X 13	$9,396.4
Annual quantity	1,267,241
Transaction overhead cost	$9,396.4/1,267,241
Cost per part	$0.00741
Standard material cost	$0.04431
Standard labor cost	$0.00399
Volume overhead	$0.02351
Transaction overhead	$0.00741
Total standard cost	$0.07922

database.

We needed two measures on which to allocate the pools. We used earned labor dollars to allocate the volume overhead because it was readily available and showed how much production time or capacity a part took in a given department. For the transaction measure, we needed a measure that equated the number of production runs of each part.

The fabrication and finishing departments were supposed to run a batch of parts every four weeks for high-volume parts (A part) and every 13 weeks for medium-volume parts (B part) and twice a year for low-volume parts (C part). This production schedule from the MRP system was based on a part's annual usage times its dollar value. In the MRP system, each part was given an A, B, or C rating, which we used as our transaction count. A parts were given 13 transactions, B parts four, and C parts two. Eventually we invented D class parts that received one transaction because we knew the factory overruled MRP and made some parts only once a year. SuperFaucet's MRP classification was as follows:

- A Parts: More than $10,000 (annual usage x unit cost).
- B Parts: Between $1,000 and $9,000.
- C Parts: Between $500 and $1,000.
- D Parts: Less than $500.

In the assembly departments, SuperFaucet built to order and did not produce parts on a regular basis. Thus, we could not use the same method. Assemblies were produced whenever a customer order required it. Therefore, customer orders were the transactions for the assembly departments. We gave a part in the assembly departments a transaction for every different customer order that included that part.

On our component part databases, we totaled all the earned labor hours and transactions for each department in 1987. Dividing the transaction pool by the total number of transactions in the year, we calculated a transaction rate for each department. In the fabrication

departments, the transaction rate varied from a high of $772 per transaction in the die cast department to a low of $28 per transaction in power wash. Die cast's rate reflected the high cost of changing a die cast machine's setup. Power wash was nothing

more than dumping parts on a conveyor belt for cleaning.

For every department a part number passed through, the part number picked up a transaction cost. If a part was an A part, it picked up 13 transactions times the department's transaction rate. So

TABLE 2/ COMPARISON OF UNIT COST

Punch Press

Quantity	Traditional Costing (per PC)	Transaction Costing (per PC)	Percent change
3,732,260	$0.09106	$0.08705	-4.4 %
3,465,048	0.05417	0.05422	0.1
1,771,947	0.02461	0.02479	0.7
1,683,513	0.14196	0.13550	-4.6
762,869	0.04437	0.04492	1.2
405,589	0.02675	0.03096	15.7
360,960	0.05145	0.05418	5.3
203,513	0.03948	0.04904	24.2
170,406	0.02565	0.02846	11.0
118,312	0.01284	0.01805	40.6
96,662	0.02323	0.02906	25.1
51,219	0.07552	0.08522	12.8
13,872	0.02461	0.02739	11.3
7,247	0.01792	0.03905	117.9
3,098	0.02319	0.12815	452.6
22	0.02792	13.87500	49595.6

Screw Machines

Quantity	Old Cost (per PC)	New Cost (per PC)	Percent change
2,013,351	$0.13776	$0.11553	-16.1 %
1,115,148	0.17008	0.13959	-17.9
234,548	0.17727	0.15895	-10.3
169,798	0.13424	0.13432	0.1
118,395	0.16501	0.16962	2.8
92,758	0.19130	0.20372	6.5
49,119	0.14032	0.14182	1.1
37,014	0.17971	0.16538	-8.0
33,848	0.12253	0.13750	12.2
11,318	0.14660	0.17574	19.9
7,859	0.11739	0.17038	45.1
4,869	0.13335	0.22962	72.2
395	0.15033	0.85316	467.5
119	0.25410	5.10924	1910.7
26	0.26044	22.65385	8598.3

Die Casting

Quantity	Old Cost (per PC)	New Cost (per PC)	Percent change
3,265,809	$0.05110	$0.04844	-5.2 %
2,551,727	0.05946	0.06053	1.8
1,470,525	0.06918	0.07255	4.9
957,576	0.08362	0.08858	5.9
793,276	0.08362	0.08858	5.9
465,461	0.10213	0.11694	14.5
201,661	0.10382	0.14262	37.4
41,237	0.05071	0.07064	39.3
18,101	0.47044	0.60124	27.8
6,053	0.45966	1.21295	163.9
128	0.62267	23.07031	3605.1

TABLE 3/ COMPARISON OF TRADITIONAL AND TRANSACTION COST SYSTEMS

	Commercial Division				Residential Division		
	Old	Transaction	Change		Old	Transaction	Change
Units	27,879,000				9,100,000		
Sales	$72,563	$72,563			$17,712	$17,712	
Cost	$70,342	$66,408	-6%		$18,320	$21,522	+17%
Profits	$ 2,221	$ 6,155	+177%		($ 608)	($3,811)	+527%
ROS	3.1%	8.5%			-3.4%	-21.5%	

	Product Line A				Spare Parts		
	Old	Transaction	Change		Old	Transaction	Change
Units	6,074,000				16,641,000		
Sales	$64,489	$64,489			$2,489	$2,489	
Cost	$62,626	$55,867	-11%		$2,025	$3,586	+76%
Profits	$ 1,863	$ 8,622	+363%		($464)	($ 1,076)	-332%
ROS	2.9%	13.4%			18.7%	-43.2%	

	Product Line N				Product Line B		
	Old	Transaction	Change		Old	Transaction	Change
Units	42,000				15,000		
Sales	$8,464	$8,464			$ 367	$367	
Cost	$8,258	$9,113	+10%		$ 295	$375	+27%
Profits	$ 207	($ 649)	-414%		$ 73	($ 8)	-111%
ROS	2.4%	-7.7%			19.7%	-2.2%	

punch press part 10-13440-2 received $2,158 (13 transactions times $166 per transaction) of fixed transaction overhead. This $2,158 then was allocated to the 1,771,947 10-3440-21's produced in 1987, adding $.001218 to each part's cost. A similar punch press part, 10-12778-3, had $166 allocated to its 22 parts, increasing its part cost by $7.5454. Overall, this new cost system now revealed that a part's manufacturing cost was inversely proportional to volume (see Tables 1 and 2).

An equally dramatic discovery was that product lines once thought to be the most profitable were actually losing money. The old standard cost system did not reflect a low-volume product's higher cost, but marketing intuitively knew it had a higher cost so low-volume products were priced at a premium. This resulted in the low-volume products reporting the highest profitability. Conversely, the high-volume products received more than their fair share of overhead and had their profitability understated (see Table 3).

As these results unfolded,

SuperFaucet's president requested the team to undertake a marketing survey to find out if all of the company's product offerings were necessary. The survey found that customers valued short product delivery lead times much more than a broad product line.

Unfortunately, SuperFaucet's broad product line inadvertently led to poor customer service because manufacturing could not support so many product permutations. As a result, SuperFaucet's management directed the team to incorporate different product line configurations into the different facility configurations under consideration. The different product line configurations would reflect the decreased sales of product line reductions and the subsequent overhead reductions.

The results of the product line reduction analysis were staggering. Vast improvements in profitability could be made by eliminating low-volume product lines and their accompanying costs.

The analysis predicted that by selling the residential faucet

division and reducing commercial sales by just 3%, profitability would improve from $2 million to $11 million per year (see Table 4). The product line reduction cut the number of product combinations by 81%. The number of parts manufactured in the screw machine department was slashed from 551 to 105, an 81% reduction. Punch press was cut from 1,250 part numbers to 341 with only a 17% decrease in volume.

Without these part number reductions, outsourcing of any of the fabrication departments would have been impossible. No vendor would have been willing to produce so many different parts.

TO MAKE OR BUY

The study team next addressed SuperFaucet's vertical integration. Given the size and complexity of SuperFaucet's operation, we knew it could not possibly be competitive in all the process technologies under its roof. Super-Faucet had access to small die casting houses and screw machine shops that did not have its huge overhead structure, were equipped with the latest equipment, and possessed a well-trained focused work force. The company firmly believed, however, that no vendor was cheaper than in-house production.

In the past, purchasing always would try to buy from multiple sources. If a vendor failed to deliver, the company (and purchasing) would not be in trouble. Unfortunately, this also meant that smaller quantities were being requested from the vendors than were being produced in-house. Also, SuperFaucet would buy only five of the 15 quoted parts (SuperFaucet "cherry picked" the vendor's quotes), so the vendors padded their quotes to make a profit on each part. SuperFaucet compared vendors' quotes to the in-house variable cost, not SuperFaucet's full cost. Because SuperFaucet knew if 10,000 parts were bought from the outside, very little overhead would be eliminated, no tooling men would be laid off, no equipment would be excessed, and so on.

No one ever complained that the make/buy analysis was flawed because the production manager wanted to keep his headcount up, the operations vice president wanted to keep his direct-to-indirect ratio high, and purchasing wanted to use multiple sources so it could switch vendors to keep reporting large price savings. Altogether this amounted to a lot of vertical integration and not much competitiveness.

To solve these problems, the team used our new cost database, which included all of a given department's fixed and variable costs. We had vendors quote the entire department's volume and not just a few parts. We approached the outsourcing from the standpoint that in the long run no costs are fixed. If SuperFaucet got out of the punch press business, eventually all the punch press department's floor space would be used up and all of the equipment sold.

The vendor quotes eventually were found to be from 8% to 44% lower, depending on the process. The vendor quotes took more than one attempt because we first had to reduce the number of vendors. We could not manage five vendors quoting on more than 100 parts—

there were too many questions to answer. Vendors had to be convinced we were serious about single sourcing the work and were not going to "cherry pick" the bids.

MANUFACTURING OPTIONS

We estimated the impact of different manufacturing options using the cost database and actual data from similar case studies. We estimated savings in indirect labor, material handling, scrap, rework, maintenance, floor space, and so on from JIT and then applied them to the affected departments. The company considered establishing a Maquilladora in Mexico with lower labor and fringe costs but higher coordination and overhead costs. We calculated long-term costs and benefits of relocating the facility.

In the end, SuperFaucet's manufacturing strategy was to select one of the facility and product combinations. The consulting team stayed on to implement it. We then validated our results by profiling the proposed scenario and converting our cost database into

departmental headcounts.

THE FOCUSED FACTORY

SuperFaucet's employees—from the cost accountants to the production manager—were supportive of our new cost system. They all knew the residential business was losing money. It was clear that the low-volume parts were expensive, but now there was proof. The only department that was not happy was sales because it was losing many unique products.

SuperFaucet's controller was given the job of installing an on-line, activity-based system patterned after the prototype. But we intended to do some things differently. We were going to have three overhead pools and not two.

We also analyzed an automation project and found allocating volume overhead on labor distorted our analysis. If we automated the punch press line, labor would be eliminated. If we eliminated direct labor, our system told us there would be substantial savings in overhead costs. We knew this was false. So, we recalculated the savings using machine hours as our volume basis, and we computed more realistic results. Therefore, our new system will have a machine-time overhead pool for distributing maintenance, tooling, utilities, depreciation, scrap, and industrial engineering. We will have a labor volume overhead for fringe benefits, supervision, departmental supplies, and janitorial services.

Activity costing justifies the focused factory, which is critical to making U.S. companies competitive. SuperFaucet succeeded by implementing both product-line reductions and manufacturing configuration changes. Without activity costing, we never could have convinced the client of this dependency. ■

Michael O'Guin is the president of Activity Costing Systems, Hunting Beach, Calif. Previously, he worked for the international management consulting firm, A.T. Kearney.

TABLE 4/ SUPERFAUCET'S MANUFACTURING OPTIONS

Product Options	As-is Facility	Partial Outsource & Offload, JIT Assembly	Complete Outsource & Offload, JIT Assembly	Partial Outsource & Offload, JIT Assembly, Relocate Facility
No changes				
Sales	$100	$100	$100	$100
Return on sales	2%	10%	14%	15%
Minor product reductions				
Sales	$76	$76	$76	$76
Return on sales	2%	10%	13%	15%
Major product reductions				
Sales	$73	$73	$73	$73
Return on sales	2%	10%	12%	15%
Sell residential division, minor commercial reductions				
Sales	$71	$71	$71	$71
Return on sales	6%	13%	15%	18%
Sell residential division, major commercial reductions				
Sales	$69	$69	$69	$69
Return on sales	11%	18%	20%	23%

Section 6

Implications: Product Costing

Section 6 begins a final sequence that examines the influence of the new manufacturing environment on future cost accounting systems. The three management accounting areas of product costing, performance measurement, and investment management each are examined in turn. Section 6 looks at product costing in the world-class manufacturing environment.

Robert A. Howell and Stephen R. Soucy see cost accounting in the world-class environment as dramatically different from classical cost accounting. They stress that one cost accounting system can no longer serve all of management's needs. After a brief review of the trends occurring in the world-class environment, Howell and Soucy outline the specific future management informational needs in each of three areas: cost management and control; product cost determination; and inventory valuation. They review the reasons why the classical cost accounting model, a single system with inventory valuation as the primary objective, is no longer adequate.

The authors recommend a single database with multiple systems that maximize the effectiveness and benefit of each purpose. They say two primary systems will develop, one with a longer-term orientation for product costing and another for cost control, and that inventory valuation will be a minor concern. Howell and Soucy group the product cost system changes that are likely to occur according to the three basic distinctions of job order versus process costing, actual versus standard costing, and full versus variable costing. They foresee a complete reversal in current patterns, with the future focus on individual products, actual costs, and different layers of cost variability.

Robin Cooper and Robert S. Kaplan discuss the shortcomings of traditional cost accounting and offer specific suggestions for comprehensive product cost systems in the world-class setting. Their observations are based on field research of companies making inappropriate product-related decisions, three of which are cited in the article. They found two common characteristics in the cost accounting systems of full-line pro-

ducers that were causing systematically distorted product costs: Few had a cost accounting system capable of reporting variable product costs (failure of marginal costing), and most used direct labor hours to assign costs from cost centers to products and/or assumed that costs increased in direct proportion to production volume (failure of fixed cost allocations).

Cooper and Kaplan do not believe that adoption of marginal costing is the solution for product costing in the contemporary manufacturing environment, providing as evidence a detailed example of how costs vary with complexity and diversity, as well as with volume. They cite changing cost allocations from a direct labor to a transactions basis and identifying long-term variable costs (support department costs that are unrelated to short-term volume changes) as the two fundamental changes that must occur.

In the final article, Kaplan discusses a cost system design process leading to a more effective integrated management information system. His process is summarized in a diagram illustrating four stages: poor data quality, common only in small or new enterprises; focus on external reporting, the extent of most present systems; innovation—managerial relevance, a critical developmental stage; and integrated cost systems, the final step. Kaplan reviews the inadequacies of current stage two systems prior to explaining the key third stage. Stage three temporarily maintains the existing company-wide external reporting system while developing local, customized operational control systems focusing on short-run process efficiencies and activity-based cost systems focusing on product and process decisions.

While noting that many financial executives do not want multiple cost systems and that bypassing stage three may be possible, Kaplan offers arguments to support his position of initial independent experimentation with new operational control and activity-based cost systems. In the final stage, he recommends integrating information between operational control and activity-based cost systems and replacing the external reporting system with one deriving its information from the new systems. He advocates this approach rather than the present philosophy that primarily satisfies external reporting, concluding that this design process also results in lower development costs, greater flexibility in system modification, and more opportunities for organizational learning and acceptance.

Additional Readings from *Management Accounting*

Barton, Thomas L. and Robert J. Fox, "Evolution at American Transtech," April 1988, pp. 49-52.

Brunton, Nancy M., "Evaluation of Overhead Allocations," July 1988, pp. 22-26.

Campbell, Robert J., "Pricing Strategy in the Automotive Glass Industry," July 1989, pp. 26-34.

Cardullo, J. Patrick and Richard A. Moellenberndt, "The Cost Allocation Problem in a Telecommunications Company," September 1987, pp. 39-44.

Fox, Robert J. and Thomas L. Barton, "Management Control at American Transtech," September 1986, pp. 37-47.

Frank, Gary B., Steven A. Fisher, and Allen R. Wilkie, "Linking Cost to Price and Profit," June 1989, pp. 22-26.

Hakala, Gregory, "Measuring Costs with Machine Hours," October 1985, pp. 57-61.

Johnson, H. Thomas and Dennis A. Loewe, "How Weyerhaeuser Manages Corporate Overhead Costs," August 1987, pp. 20-26.

Wright, Michael A. and John W. Jonez, "Material Burdening: Management Accounting Can Support Competitive Strategy," August 1987, pp. 27-31.

COST ACCOUNTING IN THE NEW MANUFACTURING ENVIRONMENT

> *No longer can one cost accounting system serve all of management's needs.*

BY ROBERT A. HOWELL
AND STEPHEN R. SOUCY

The manufacturing operations of a number of U.S. businesses are in the midst of significant change as their managements strive to become truly world-class manufacturers in order to compete in the ever demanding global marketplace. Customers are insisting upon significantly higher quality, greater reliability, faster

Editor's Note:
"Cost Accounting in the New Manufacturing Environment," the second in a series of five articles, addresses the important changes taking place in manufacturing.

delivery, and more product variety. Domestic and foreign competitors are putting increased pressure on these manufacturers to compete or disappear. Obviously, to compete successfully on a continuing basis, U.S. manufacturers must be able to do so profitably. That does not necessarily mean lowest cost, but it does mean being able to make money and achieve a satisfactory return on invested capital.

U.S. manufacturers are respond-

A contact insertion machine in the World Contactor Assembly Facility.

Allen-Bradley Co. photos

ing to these heightened requirements and are creating a new manufacturing environment through higher quality, lower inventories, product-oriented flow lines, automation, product line organization, and the effective use of information technology. In turn, the cost accounting system must evolve in order to be compatible with the new manufacturing environment.

Cost accounting systems are used for cost management and control, product cost determination, and inventory valuation. The classical model of cost accounting has inventory valuation as its primary driver of financial information. The model, through the use of standard costs, functional overhead cost pools, and full cost construction methods, often based on labor allocation methods, focuses on establishing an "accepted" value for inventory rather than cost control or product cost determination. We believe the classical cost accounting model—still being taught by accounting faculty and used by many companies—is seriously deficient for the new manufacturing environment. It encourages inappropriate behavior and fails to provide information that management needs to make sound decisions and be truly competitive.

IMPACT OF TRENDS

The trend toward higher quality is driving world class manufacturers to more tightly control all aspects of their manufacturing operation. It is therefore critical to know how much the cost of quality or, more appropriately, nonquality represents. Cost accounting systems need to be modified to accumulate and separate all nonquality costs such as scrap, rework, product warranty, field service, and other costs so that this information is available to management.

Efforts to reduce inventories are forcing manufacturers to identify the root causes of inventories and make the necessary modifications to their manufacturing processes to eliminate them. A manufacturing environment with little or no inventories operates quite differently from one where inventories are maintained to provide a protective cushion against unforeseen events

Cost accounting systems must evolve in order to be compatible with the new manufacturing environment.

and changes in operations.

Also, as inventory is reduced through the greater understanding

and modification of the production process, management is likely to realize that current product cost data does not reflect the relative resource usage of different products. With this knowledge, operating and accounting managers will no longer continue to drive product and process cost data with current inventory valuation techniques. Ultimately, the successful elimination of inventory makes the inventory valuation issue irrelevant allowing cost accountants to focus on valuing inventory solely for managerial purposes.

Many manufacturers are rearranging their factories into product oriented flow lines and away from functional groupings of equipment.

A proximity sensor senses the presence of a contactor cover (yellow).

At the same time, they are pulling together the various stages in the manufacturing process to minimize the amount of material handling and work-in-process inventory required between stages. But the flow lines of today's manufacturing plant also have a high degree of manufacturing flexibility in order that a variety of products may be produced across them. Emphasis also is being placed on production throughput and cycle time to minimize the length of time that a unit is in process.

This shift from functional organizations to product lines changes the definition of a homogenous cost center. While the product line orientation will allow direct identification of many overhead costs to the product line, minimizing the need for allocations, the heightened flexibility of the assembly lines increases the problem of cost assignment to the products flowing across a given line.

One of the most dramatic evidences of the new manufacturing environment is the level of automation many companies have implemented. The automated equipment is intended to reduce labor cost. It also contributes to the objectives of high quality, product reliability, fast and flexible manufacturing, and lower inventories.

The shift from labor to equipment changes both the proportion and characteristics of the manufacturing costs. Labor decreases, overhead increases. Variable costs drop, fixed costs and break-even points rise. The assignment of cost to products similarly changes. The heightened investment in fixed assets also raises the issue of the assignment of capital charges to specific product lines and products.

Besides rearranging the plants, some companies have begun to reassign service personnel to the product lines rather than maintaining functional groupings of support activities. Assigning purchasing, scheduling, manufacturing engineering, and maintenance personnel, for example, to product lines reduces the problems associated with allocating such costs. The shift to product line profit centers and the specific assignment of overhead costs shifts the orientation of management from cost minimization to profit maximization.

Finally, increasing the use of computer technology for in-process controls, monitoring of manufacturing performance, and providing management information will impact management accounting dramatically. In-process controls aimed at reducing process variability should result in less variances

One cost accounting system need not serve and be absolutely internally consistent with all three purposes of cost accounting.

and the need for tracking same. The ability to obtain real-time performance data and take quick corrective actions argues for collecting data at a very low level of detail, even on individual items.

FROM ONE SYSTEM TO MULTIPLE SYSTEMS

The typical manufacturing cost accounting system uses one system for the purposes of cost management and control, product costing, and inventory valuation.

Cost Management and Control

Costs are originally accumulated in the department where they are incurred, whether in a service department or a production department. Cost control historically has meant comparing the costs incurred in the department of origination with budgeted costs for the same category of expense. Budget versus actual variance reports, by department, are typical control tools. Generally, departments are motivated to minimize their costs to produce favorable variances. For example, a purchasing department may compromise on product quality to achieve favorable purchase price variances. The maintenance department may avoid overtime to prevent an unfavorable expense variance even though that prevents equipment from being put back on line and product produced.

Production departments, too, may behave in dysfunctional ways due to inappropriate costing and performance measures. Poor quality products may be passed on to succeeding departments to avoid material usage variances. Labor may be encouraged to produce more product than required so as to achieve targeted levels of labor efficiency and overhead absorption. While at the same time, unnecessary work-in-process and finished goods inventories may be produced.

Many cost control reports are prepared and distributed to the responsible cost center manager on a monthly basis (usually well after the end of the month) reflecting the company's normal monthly cycle of financial reporting. To the extent that a company has a limited number of production cost centers, the specificity of the data is limited and the ability to retrace variances to their root cause is very difficult.

Classical cost accounting uses one system to control costs at the operating level and to accumulate costs for product cost and financial accounting requirements. However, one cost accounting system need not serve and be absolutely internally consistent with all three purposes of cost accounting systems.

Operating cost control is a very short-term oriented activity. Managers need to know the operations that are not performing as expected and why. They need to look at the job, operator, machine, number of units affected, and what is the cost consequence when the problem occurs. Daily performance measures of the critical success factors of the business are required. These measures should focus on the responsibility center where the costs originally are incurred. One, or a few, production cost center(s) make this focus difficult. In contrast, multiple costs centers make it possible to more clearly hone in on the location and, ultimately, the causes of operating control problems.

The distinction between variable and fixed costs also is important. Some costs are going to vary with production, others will be relative to some cost driver other than production units, and still other costs, in the short run, will be fixed. Cost center managers have to know how costs should behave in order to be able to interpret cost performance. They also should receive cost information frequently in order to monitor how well they are doing.

Product Cost Determination

Classical cost accounting systems do a very poor job product costing. In fact, these systems do a grave disservice to managers who do not understand their inadequacies and use the product cost information as generated. If a firm is in business to produce and sell products, then all costs really are product costs. The distinction between product and period costs used for inventory evaluation and financial reporting purposes is inappropriate for product cost determination.

The manufacturing costs represent only a portion of the total costs of a firm. Engineering, marketing, accounting, and general management costs also relate to the products being produced. An engineering department exists to create new products and modify existing ones. Some product lines have short lives and require high engineering expenses. Others have longer lives and less development. Similarly, market development, promotion and advertising, distribution, and sales expenses are not equal for all products. The system must be able to identify all costs required to design, purchase, manufacture, market and sell the product. Failure to take these cost differences into account puts at risk the understanding of a product's cost.

The second major point regarding product costs is that costs range from being variable and directly identifiable to being fixed and requiring allocation methods to attach the costs to products. That degree of variability and direct identification must clearly be understood.

In the short run, the truly variable costs will probably include only materials and certain operating expenses that vary with manufacturing activity. A second level of expense includes uniquely identifiable fixed expenses of labor and facilities. To the extent that the service activities such as purchasing, scheduling and control, manufacturing engineering, and mainte-

nance have been incorporated into the product line, they are examples of uniquely identifiable fixed costs. The unique facilities are those equipments and other costs directly related to the product line.

A third level of product costs are the allocated costs from outside the product lines—including engineering, marketing, accounting, and general management. As with any allocated cost, the basis upon which

these allocations are made and the assumptions which underride them must clearly be understood. For example, if engineering or marketing allocations are relatively high, then management also might consider actually assigning the engineering and marketing units to the product lines so as to better understand their cost association.

Many companies fail to consider the balance sheet impact of their

ALLEN-BRADLEY: TODAY'S FACTORY OF THE FUTURE

One of the most talked about factories of the future is the Allen-Bradley "factory within a factory" facility in Milwaukee. Based on volume estimates and market prices, this business generates approximately $40 million a year in sales. It is capable of taking an order on one day, producing upwards of 500 different parts the following day (in order sizes from one up to the capacity of the facility), and shipping all of the orders the following day. There is some plastic and steel raw material inventory but virtually no work-in-process or finished goods inventory. At the end of the day, the flow line is empty and orders have been shipped. Material is the primary component of product cost. There are some variable operating expenses but a major portion of the costs, including the few factory technicians and the

Allen-Bradley's $15 million factory.

physical plant, are fixed. Allen-Bradley chooses to expense labor and overhead as period costs. They do not go through the traditional allocations of service department costs to production departments, and then assign the overhead costs to the products based on direct labor. For one thing, there is virtually no labor. For another, there is no inventory to attach costs to.

Allen-Bradley certainly knows its material cost for each of the items it can build in that factory. It knows what variable costs of manufacturing it incurs while the factory is operating as well as its fixed labor and other fixed costs. It also knows the investment that it has in inventory—not much—and in fixed assets—significant.

Allen-Bradley also understands the relationship of the prices of its various products to their costs, both in the short run and long term, and the best mix of products to run across its facility to maximize performance.

They are able to identify quality problems such as scrap when they occur because the production line gets shut down automatically, and the effects of mix changes relative to the optimum mix because they know how much cost they would incur under both.

In essence, Allen-Bradley has a total understanding of the costs and assets associated with its world contactor factory within a factory. They do not need standard costs for variance analysis, full costs for inventory valuation, and average costs for a product line consisting of 500 different items.

product lines and products, yet some products turn over very quickly and require little investment in inventories. Others turn over more slowly and require significantly higher investments. In the new manufacturing environment, product lines have different levels of investment in property, plant and equipment. The failure to take such differences into account and charge the product lines an appropriate capital charge for assets employed, or to relate product line and product profitability to assets employed, will cause managements to continue to rely on incomplete information and potentially make invalid decisions.

Product costs do not need to be determined every month along with the traditional monthly closing schedule. Some world class manufacturers maintain current cost books where they continually incorporate changes in material price, design changes, revised routings, and other factors into their cost calculations. This insures accurate information for any management decision requiring product cost input. On the other hand, in times of relative stability, it may be appropriate to only periodically go through and re-determine product costs. This might be done on a semi-annual or even an annual basis in some circumstances.

The last point regarding product costs is in the long run all costs are variable at the total business unit

The cost accounting system should identify all costs required to design, purchase, manufacture, market and sell a product.

level. If you were to stop producing all products, then obviously all other costs can, in time, be eliminated. Similarly, at the product line level, the uniquely identifiable variable and fixed costs can be eliminated. Some allocated cost categories may,

in fact, be affected by the elimination of a product line and, similarly, identifiable assets disappear. At the individual product level, uniquely identifiable costs and assets can be eliminated. Shared fixed costs and allocated expenses may be more problematic, especially if other products that use them are to be retained.

In sum, product costs are much broader than the financial accounting definition. Product costs have varying levels of cost characteristics and assets associated with them, and there are different degrees of variability depending upon the time horizon of the decision in question.

There is no reason that the product cost calculation used for product cost decision-making need necessarily be consistent with the definition for financial reporting.

Inventory Valuation

An important function of any accounting department is to comply with the corporate and regulatory reporting requirements. Most companies report, at least internally, on a monthly basis. A public company has fiduciary responsibilities to report on a quarterly basis. This necessitates complying with generally accepted accounting practices.

For financial reporting purposes, inventory is supposed to be valued on a full cost basis. That means, to financial accountants, the full manufacturing costs. However, if one is operating in a new manufacturing environment where speed of production is very fast and levels of inventory very low, then inventory valuation becomes a less significant issue and alternative valuation techniques for product cost determination purposes can be applied. There are manufacturing companies today with no work-in-process or finished goods inventory at the end of the day and, therefore, the assignment of cost to products and the utilization of a full cost construction becomes irrelevant. To the extent that a company does have inventories, reasonable bases for assigning overheads to products that are acceptable to the accountants, in the aggregate, are all that is necessary.

Although the same purposes exist for cost accounting systems today as they always have, companies need not continue to use one system to serve all their purposes.

A nine-alley reservoir holds different sizes of molded housings.

If they do, they will not get the best benefits for each purpose. Rather, a single database used by multiple systems will maximize the effectiveness and benefit for each purpose.

CHANGING SYSTEMS CHARACTERISTICS

There are three basic distinctions between cost accounting systems. The first is between job order and process costing. Job order cost accounting systems collect costs by specific job, batch, or shop order. At any point in time, it is possible to determine the amount of charges made to a particular job order. At the end of the job, all job costs should have been charged to it. At the other extreme, process accounting systems assume that the products being costed are homogenous enough that the average cost per unit is meaningful. As a result, it is unnecessary to collect costs for individual jobs or batches. Many companies that manufacture different products, apparently consider their products similar enough to use process costing.

Compared to job costing, process costing normally requires less paperwork and detail, but it has certain deficiencies. Under a process costing system, management is unable to explicitly identify actual costs with individual items. Therefore, if a particular product incurs any unusual costs, such as excessive scrap or rework, its costs would be averaged with the other products' costs. Averaging simplifies but makes cost less specific and less informative.

A second distinction is actual versus standard costs. An actual cost accounting system tracks actual costs through the system. Actual material costs are attributed to a job or a process, actual labor likewise, and overhead is assigned to the product via a job or process cost allocation procedure.

A standard cost accounting system, on the other hand, uses predetermined standards for material, labor, and overhead. These standards are, in turn, used in the accounting process for moving elements of cost between raw material, work-in-process, finished goods, and cost of goods sold. The actual costs incurred are then com-

VP Larry Yost, demonstrates the electromechanical motor contactors.

pared at some level of detail with the standard to produce variances. The most usual variances include material price and usage, labor rate and efficiency, and overhead spending and volume variances. Variance analysis is a fundamental aspect and benefit emanating from a standard cost accounting system. It often is used to direct management's attention to those areas considered most out of control, as indicated by the magnitude of the variances.

The third distinction is between full cost and variable cost. Full cost accounting systems accumulate material, labor, and both variable and fixed overheads, and then assign them to the product for inventory valuation purposes. A variable cost accounting system excludes fixed overhead costs from product costs. Some companies, for example, do exclude depreciation and factory administration from their definition of product cost. A company that excludes all of its fixed overhead costs from its product cost calculation and, as a result, only includes variable material, labor, and variable overhead, would be using a pure variable cost construction. Because companies historically are driven by the financial accounting requirement of valuing inventory at full cost for external reporting purposes, most companies use a full

cost accounting systems for both internal and external reporting.

The research we have recently concluded for the National Association of Accountants reveals that, for the most part, companies use standard, full cost accounting systems. Also, companies will use either a job or process accounting system depending upon whether the manufacturer has a job, batch, or project orientation or more of a repetitive or process orientation. However, many companies do use a process construction even though they produce a number of distinct and unrelated products.

American industry uses standard, full cost accounting systems primarily to provide cost information for inventory valuation and financial reporting, and secondly, for cost management and control purposes. To use existing cost accounting information for decision-making, requires great facility on the part of the decision maker to extract and manipulate the data into appropriate and relevant information. In fact, the most useful and necessary information may not even be found in the firm's cost accounting system.

The new manufacturing environment should result in major changes to a firm's cost accounting system. Standard costs for planning purposes still will be important but their use for control will be less so. Companies still will want to go through the process of estimating the cost that they expect to incur for each product including material from a bill of materials, labor—if any—from a routing, and other directly identifiable and allocated costs. However, using standard costs to produce variances becomes unnecessary. If the manufacturing process is of the high quality level intended, actual costs incurred should approximate the standard costs estimated for planning purposes. Variances should be small and, therefore, unnecessary to track, at least from an accounting sense. Variances from plant production performance such as scrap and rework will be tracked but on an operating rather than a financial basis, and on a real-time rather than on a delayed basis.

Standard cost accounting systems also have been used to track labor variances. To the extent that direct labor component of product cost is less significant, and what exists is fixed, the concept of a labor efficiency variance is no longer relevant.

Instead of focusing on variances, world class manufacturers need to focus on actual costs and cost trends. What is important is how much is actually being spent for material, labor, other manufacturing and nonmanufacturing expenses and, more importantly, how those costs are trending over time.

Thus, we will see a de-emphasis on standard costs and particularly variance analysis in the new factory and much greater emphasis on actual costs and how they are changing.

The focus on full costing, particularly for inventory valuation and financial reporting, will no longer be necessary nor relevant in a JIT production and inventory environment. Just-in-time receipt of materials and purchased parts will result in virtually no raw material inventories. Tight flow lines will eliminate work-in-process inventories between operations. Fast response time will reduce or eliminate the necessity for keeping finished goods inventory to be able to respond to customer demand. In a just-in-time production and inventory environment, there is high inventory turnover and low levels of inventory and, therefore, little or no need to use full cost construction, at least for that purpose.

It is important for managers to understand the various layers that constitute a product's total cost and their cost characteristics, both in the short and long run. In the short run, few costs are variable and contribution margins are high. In the long run, all costs are variable. As a result, when making long-term decisions more costs need to be categorized as either variable or avoidable.

For short-run decisions, variable costs and assets are relevant. For longer-run decisions, full costs, including non-manufacturing as well as manufacturing costs, and all assets are relevant to each individual unit produced. Therefore, we believe there should be a return to job costing practices in the new manufacturing environment. The pattern of standard, full cost, process costing systems, used by many companies, must be turned upside down. Cost accounting systems must be designed to focus on actual costs, different layers of cost variability, and the individual product. This is a dramatic change for many companies' cost accounting system dimensions.

THE NEW COST ACCOUNTING

Cost accounting in the new manufacturing environment will be dramatically different from classical cost accounting practices. It will reflect the higher product quality, greater manufacturing process reliability, lower inventory levels, greater product variety, and greater use of automation and information technology. No longer will one cost accounting system serve all management's needs. Rather, two primary systems will be developed: one for cost control at the source on a real time basis, and the second for product cost determination and managerial decision making, with a longer term orientation. Inventory valuation, rather than being the primary objective, as is the case with today's cost accounting systems, will be a secondary concern, if at all. Instead of standard, full cost, process oriented systems, the new manufacturing environment will use *actual, differential cost and asset, job order systems.*

We believe these changes will enhance the role and responsibility of the management accountant in the new manufacturing environment. ∎

Robert A. Howell, DBA, CMA, is president of Howell Management Corp., and professor of management and accounting at the Graduate School of Business Administration, New York University.

Stephen R. Soucy, MBA, CPA, is a consultant at Howell Management Corporation.

Plant floor operations monitored.

HOW COST ACCOUNTING DISTORTS PRODUCT COSTS

The traditional cost system that defines variable costs as varying in the short term with production will misclassify these costs as fixed.

BY ROBIN COOPER AND
ROBERT S. KAPLAN

In order to make sensible decisions concerning the products they market, managers need to know what their products cost. Product design, new product introduction decisions, and the amount of effort expended on trying to market a given product or product line will be influenced by the anticipated cost and profitability of the product. Conversely, if product profitability appears to drop, the question of discontinuance will be raised. Product costs also can play an important role in setting prices, particularly for customized products with low sales volumes and without readily available market prices.

The cumulative effect of decisions on product design, introduction, support, discontinuance, and pricing helps define a firm's strategy. If the product cost information is distorted, the firm can follow an inappropriate and unprofitable strategy. For example, the low-cost producer often achieves competitive advantage by servicing a broad range of customers. This strategy will be successful if the economies of scale exceed the additional costs, the diseconomies of scope, caused by producing and servicing a more diverse product line. If the cost system does not correctly attribute the additional costs to the products that cause them, then the firm might end up competing in segments where the scope-related costs exceed the benefits from larger scale production.

Similarly, a differentiated producer achieves competitive advantage by meeting specialized customers' needs with products whose costs of differentiation are lower than the price premiums charged for special features and services. If the cost system fails to measure differentiation costs properly, then the firm might choose to compete in segments that are actually unprofitable.

FULL VS. VARIABLE COST

Despite the importance of cost information, disagreement still exists about whether product costs should be measured by full or by variable cost. In a full-cost system, fixed production costs are allocated to products so that reported product costs measure total manufacturing costs. In a variable-cost system, the fixed costs are not allocated and product costs reflect only the marginal cost of manufacturing.

Academic accountants, supported by economists, have argued strongly that variable costs are the relevant ones for product decisions. They have demonstrated, using increasingly complex models, that setting marginal revenues equal to marginal costs will produce the highest profit. In contrast, accountants in practice continue to report full costs in their cost accounting systems.

The definition of variable cost used by academic accountants assumes that product decisions have a short-time horizon, typically a

Robin Cooper and Bob Kaplan are taking research out of the academic setting.

month or a quarter. Costs are variable only if they vary directly with monthly or quarterly changes in production volume. Such a definition is appropriate if the volume of production of all products can be changed at will and there is no way to change simultaneously the level of fixed costs.

In practice, managers reject this short-term perspective because the decision to offer a product creates a long-term commitment to manufacture, market, and support that product. Given this perspective, short-term variable cost is an inadequate measure of product cost.

While full cost is meant to be a surrogate for long-run manufacturing costs, in nearly all of the companies we visited, management was not convinced that their full-cost systems were adequate for its product-related decisions. In particular, management did not believe their systems accurately reflected the costs of resources consumed to manufacture products. But they were also unwilling to adopt a variable-cost approach.

Of the more than 20 firms we visited and documented, Mayers Tap, Rockford, and Schrader Bellows provided particularly useful insights on how product costs were systematically distorted.[1] These companies had several significant common characteristics.

They all produced a large number of distinct products in a single facility. The products formed several distinct product lines and were sold through diverse marketing channels. The range in demand volume for products within a product line was high, with sales of high-volume products between 100 and 1,000 times greater than sales of low-volume products. As a consequence, products were manufactured and shipped in highly varied lot sizes. While our findings are based upon these three companies, the same effects were observed at several other sites.

In all three companies, product costs played an important role in the decisions that surrounded the introduction, pricing, and discontinuance of products. Reported product costs also appeared to play a significant role in determining how much effort should be assigned to marketing and selling products.

Typically, the individual responsible for introducing new products

Management accounting thinking because of its focus on short-term costing has missed the most important aspect of product decision making.

also was responsible for setting prices. Cost-plus pricing to achieve a desired level of gross margin predominantly was used for the special products, though substantial modifications to the resulting estimated prices occurred when direct competition existed. Such competition was common for high-volume products but rarely occurred for the low-volume items. Frequently, no obvious market prices existed for low-volume products because they had been designed to meet a particular customer's needs.

ACCURACY OF PRODUCT COSTS

Managers in all three firms expressed serious concerns about the accuracy of their product-costing systems.

For example, Rockford attempted to obtain much higher margins for its low-volume products to compensate, on an ad hoc basis, for the gross underestimates of costs that it believed the cost system produced for these products. But management was not able to justify its decisions on cutoff points to identify low-volume products or the magnitude of the ad hoc margin increases. Further, Rockford's management believed that its faulty cost system explained the ability of small firms to compete effectively against it for high-volume business. These small firms, with no apparent economic or technological advantage, were winning high-volume business with prices that were at or below Rockford's reported costs. And the small firms

seemed to be prospering at these prices.

At Schrader Bellows, production managers believed that certain products were not earning their keep because they were so difficult to produce. But the cost system reported that these products were among the most profitable in the line. The managers also were convinced that they could make certain products as efficiently as anybody else. Yet competitors were consistently pricing comparable products considerably lower. Management suspected that the cost system contributed to this problem.

At Mayers Tap, the financial accounting profits were always much lower than those predicted by the cost system, but no one could explain the discrepancy. Also, the senior managers were concerned by their failure to predict which bids they would win or lose. Mayers Tap often won bids that had been overpriced because it did not really want the business, and lost bids it had deliberately underpriced in order to get the business.

TWO-STAGE COST ALLOCATION SYSTEM

The cost systems of all companies we visited had many common characteristics. Most important was the use of a two-stage cost allocation system: in the first stage, costs were assigned to cost pools (often called cost centers), and in the second stage, costs were allocated from the cost pools to the products.

The companies used many different allocation bases in the first stage to allocate costs from plant overhead accounts to cost centers. Despite the variation in allocation bases in the first stage, however, all companies used direct labor hours in the second stage to allocate overhead from the cost pools to the products. Direct labor hours was used in the second allocation stage even when the production process was highly automated so that burden rates exceeded 1,000%. Figure 1 illustrates a typical two-stage allocation process.

Of the three companies we examined in detail, only one had a cost accounting system capable of reporting variable product costs. Variable cost was identified at the budgeting stage in one other site, but this information was not subsequently used for product costing. The inability of the cost system to report variable cost was a common feature of many of the systems we observed. Reporting variable product costs was the exception, not the rule.

Firms used only one cost system even though costs were collected and allocated for several purposes, including product costing, operational control, and inventory valuation. The cost systems seemed to be designed primarily to perform the inventory valuation function for financial reporting because they had serious deficiencies for operational control (too delayed and too aggregate) and for product costing (too aggregate).

THE FAILURE OF MARGINAL COSTING

The extensive use of fixed-cost allocations in all the companies we investigated contrasts sharply with a 65-year history of academics advocating marginal costing for product decisions. If the marginal-cost concept had been adopted by companies' management, then we would have expected to see product-costing systems that explicitly reported variable-cost information. Instead, we observed cost systems that reported variable as well as full costs in only a small minority of companies.

The traditional academic recommendation for marginal costing may have made sense when variable costs (labor, material, and some overhead) were a relatively high proportion of total manufactured cost and when product diversity was sufficiently small that there was not wide variation in the demands made by different products on the firm's production and marketing resources. But these conditions are no longer typical of many of today's organizations. Increasingly, overhead (most of it considered "fixed") is becoming a larger share of total manufacturing costs. In addition, the plants we examined are being asked to produce an increasing variety of products that make quite different demands on equipment and support departments. Thus, even if direct or marginal costing were once a useful

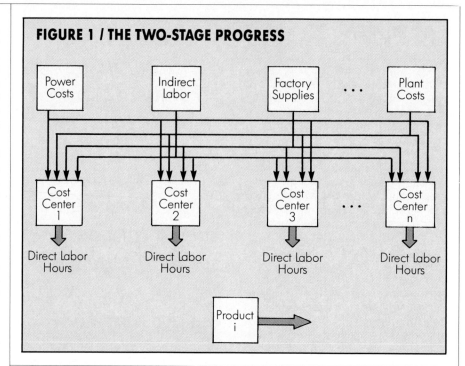

FIGURE 1 / THE TWO-STAGE PROGRESS

recommendation to management, direct costing, even if correctly implemented, is not likely a solution—and may perhaps be a major problem—for product costing in the contemporary manufacturing environment.

THE FAILURE OF FIXED-COST ALLOCATIONS

While we consistently observed managers avoiding the use of variable or marginal costs for their product-related decisions, we observed also their discomfort with the full-cost allocations produced by their existing cost systems. We believe that we have identified the two major sources for the discomfort.

The first problem arises from the use of direct labor hours in the second allocation stage to assign costs from cost centers to products. This procedure may have been adequate many decades ago when direct labor was the principal value-adding activity in the material conversion process. But as firms introduce more automated machinery, direct labor is increasingly engaged in set-up and supervisory functions (rather than actually performing the work on the product) and no longer represents a reasonable surrogate for resource demands by product.

In many of the plants we visited, labor's main tasks are to load the

machines and to act as trouble-shooters. Labor frequently works on several different products at the same time so that it becomes impossible to assign labor hours intelligently to products. Some of the companies we visited had responded to this situation by beginning experiments using machine hours instead of labor hours to allocate costs from cost pools to products (for the second stage of the allocation process). Other companies, particularly those adopting just-in-time or continuous-flow production processes, were moving to material dollars as the basis for distributing costs from pools to products. Material dollars provide a less expensive method for cost allocation than machine hours because, as with labor hours, material dollars are collected by the existing cost system, A move to a machine-hour basis would require the collection of new data for many of these companies.

Shifting from labor hours to machine hours or material dollars provides some relief from the problem of using unrealistic bases for attributing costs to products. In fact, some companies have been experimenting with using all three allocation bases simultaneously: labor hours for those costs that vary with the number of labor hours worked (e.g., supervision—if the amount of labor in a product is high, the amount of supervision related to that product also is likely to be high), machine hours for those costs that vary with the number of hours the machine is running (e.g., power—the longer the machine is running the more power that is consumed by that product), and material dollars for those costs that vary with the value of material in the product (e.g., material handling—the higher the value of the material in the product, the greater the material-handling costs associated with those products are likely to be.)

Using multiple allocation bases allows a finer attribution of costs to the products responsible for the incurrence of those costs. In particular, it allows for product diversity where the direct labor, machine hours, and material dollars consumed in the manufacture of different products are not directly proportional to each other.

For reported product costs to be correct, however, the allocation bases used must be capable of accounting for all aspects of product diversity. Such an accounting is not always possible even using all three volume-related allocation bases we described. As the number of product items manufactured increases, so does the number of direct labor hours, machine hours, and material dollars consumed. The designer of the cost system, in adopting these bases, assumes that all allocated costs have the same behavior; namely that they increase in direct relationship to the volume of product items manufactured. But there are many costs that vary with the diversity and complexity of products, not by the number of units produced.

THE COST OF COMPLEXITY

The complexity costs of a full-line producer can be illustrated as follows. Consider two identical plants. One plant produces 1,000,000 units of product A. The second plant produces 100,000 units of product A and 900,000 units of 199 similar products. (The similar products have sales volumes that vary from 100 to 100,000 units.)

The first plant has a simple production environment and requires limited manufacturing-support facilities. Few setups, expediting, and scheduling activities are required.

The other plant presents a much more complex production-management environment. Its 200 products have to be scheduled through the plant, requiring frequent setups, inventory movements, purchases, receipts, and inspections. To handle this complexity, the support departments must be larger and more sophisticated.

The traditional cost accounting system plays an important role in obfuscating the underlying rela-

The strategic importance of product costing is the focus of Professor Cooper's research efforts.

At the companies visited and studied, we found that a large and growing proportion of total manufacturing costs is considered "fixed." In reality, they are the most variable and rapidly increasing costs for the firm.

tionship between the range of products produced and the size of the support departments. First, the costs of most support departments are classified as fixed, making it difficult to realize that these costs are systematically varying. Second, the use of volume-related allocation bases makes it difficult to recognize how these support-department costs vary.

Support-department costs must vary with something because they have been among the fastest growing in the overall cost structure of manufactured products. As the example demonstrates, support-department costs vary not with the volume of product items manufactured, rather they vary with the range of items produced (i.e., the complexity of the production process). The traditional definition of variable cost, with its monthly or quarterly perspective, views such costs as fixed because complexity-related costs do not vary significantly in such a short time frame. Across an extended period of time, however, the increasing complexity of the production process places additional demands on support departments, and their costs eventually and inevitably rise.

The output of a support department consists of the activities its personnel perform. These include such activities as setups, inspections, material handling, and scheduling. The output of the departments can be represented by the number of distinct activities that are performed or the number of transactions handled. Because most of the output of these departments consists of human activities, however, output can increase quite significantly before an immediate deterioration in the quality of service is detected. Eventually, the maximum output of the department is reached and additional personnel are requested. The request typically comes some time after the initial increase in diversity and output. Thus, support departments, while varying with the diversity of the demanded output, grow intermittently. The practice of annually budgeting the size of the departments further hides the underlying relationship between the mix and volume of demand and the size of the department. The support departments often are constrained to grow only when budgeted to do so.

TABLE 1 / COMPARISON OF REPORTED PRODUCT COSTS AT SCHRADER BELLOWS

Product	Sales Volume	Existing Cost System		Transaction-Based System		Percent of Change	
		Unit Cost[a]	Unit Gross Margin	Unit Cost[a]	Unit Gross Margin	Unit Cost	Unit Gross Margin
1	43,562	7.85	5.51	7.17	6.19	(8.7)	12.3
2	500	8.74	3.76	15.45	(2.95)	76.8	(178.5)
3	53	12.15	10.89	82.49	(59.45)	578.9	(645.9)
4	2,079	13.63	4.91	24.51	(5.97)	79.8	(221.6)
5	5,670	12.40	7.95	19.99	0.36	61.3	(93.4)
6	11,169	8.04	5.49	7.96	5.57	(1.0)	1.5
7	423	8.47	3.74	6.93	5.28	(18.2)	41.2

[a]The sum of total cost (sales volume × unit cost) for all seven products is different under the two systems because the seven products only represent a small fraction of total production.

Support-department costs are perhaps best described as "discretionary" because they are budgeted and authorized each year. The questions we must address are: What determines the level of these discretionary fixed costs? Why, if these costs are not affected by the quantity of production, are there eight people in a support department and not one? What generates the work, if not physical quantities of inputs or outputs, that requires large support-department staffs? We believe the answers to these questions on the origins of discretionary overhead costs (i.e., what drives these costs) can be found by analyzing the activities or transactions demanded when producing a full and diverse line of products.

TRANSACTION COSTING

Low-volume products create more transactions per unit manufactured than their high-volume counterparts. The per unit share of these costs should, therefore, be higher for the low-volume products. But when volume-related bases are used exclusively to allocate support-department costs, high-volume and low-volume products receive similar transaction-related costs. When only volume-related bases are used for second-stage allocations, high-volume products receive an excessively high fraction of support-department costs and, therefore, subsidize the low-volume products.

As the range between low-volume and high-volume products increases, the degree of cross-subsidization rises. Support departments expand to cope with the additional complexity of more products, leading to increased overhead charges. The reported product cost of all products consequently increases. The high-volume products appear more expensive to produce than previously, even though they are not responsible for the additional costs. The costs triggered by the introduction of new, low-volume products are systematically shifted to high-volume products that may be placing relatively few demands on the plant's support departments.

Many of the transactions that generate work for production-support departments can be proxied by the number of setups. For example, the movement of material in the plant often occurs at the commencement or completion of a production run. Similarly, the majority of the time spent on parts inspection occurs just after a setup or changeover. Thus, while the support departments are engaged in a broad array of activities, a considerable portion of their costs may be attributed to the number of setups.

Not all of the support-department costs are related (or relatable) to the number of setups. The cost of setup personnel relates more to the quantity of setup hours than to the actual number of setups. The number of inspections of incoming material can be directly related to the number of material receipts, as would be the time spent moving the received material into inventory. The number of outgoing shipments can be used to predict the activity level of the finished-goods and shipping departments. The assignment of all these support costs with a transactions-based approach reinforces the effect of the setup-related costs because the low-sales-volume items tend to trigger more small incoming and outgoing shipments.

Schrader Bellows had recently performed a "strategic cost analysis" that significantly increased the number of bases used to allocate costs to the products; many second-stage allocations used transactions costs to assign support-department costs to products. In particular, the number of setups allocated a sizeable percentage of support-department costs to products.

The effect of changing these second-stage allocations from a direct labor to a transaction basis was dramatic. While the support-department costs accounted for about 50% of overhead (or about 25% of total costs), the change in the reported product costs ranged from about minus 10% to plus 1,000%. The significant change in the reported product costs for the low-volume items was due to the substantial cost of the support departments and the low batch size over which the transaction cost was spread.

Table 1 shows the magnitude of the shift in reported product costs for seven representative products. The existing cost system reported gross margins that varied from 26% to 47%, while the strategic analysis showed gross margin that ranged from − 258% to + 46%. The trends in the two sets of reported product profitabilities were clear: the existing direct-labor-based system had identified the low-volume products as the most profitable, while the strategic cost analysis indicated exactly the reverse.

There are three important messages in the table and in the company's findings in general.

☐ Traditional systems that assign costs to products using a single volume-related base seriously distort product costs.

☐ The distortion is systematic. Low-volume products are undercosted, and high-volume products are overcosted.

☐ Accurate product costs cannot, in general, be achieved by cost systems that rely only on volume-related bases (even multiple bases such as machine hours and material quantities) for second-stage allocations. A different type of allocation base must be used for overhead costs that vary with the number of transactions performed, as opposed to the volume of product produced.

The shift to transaction-related allocation bases is a more fundamental change to the philosophy of cost-systems design than is at first realized. In a traditional cost system that uses volume-related bases, the costing element is always the product. It is the product that consumes direct labor hours, machine hours, or material dollars. Therefore, it is the product that gets costed.

In a transaction-related system, costs are assigned to the units that caused the transaction to be originated. For example, if the transaction is a setup, then the costing element will be the production lot because each production lot requires a single setup. The same is true for purchasing activities, inspections, scheduling, and material movements. The costing element is no longer the product but those elements the transaction affects.

In the transaction-related costing system, the unit cost of a product is determined by dividing the cost of a transaction by the number of units in the costing element. For example, when the costing element is a production lot, the unit cost of a product is determined by dividing the production lot cost by the number of units in the production lot.

This change in the costing element is not trivial. In the Schrader Bellows strategic cost analysis (see Table 1), product seven appears to violate the strong inverse relationship between profits and produc-

tion-lot size for the other six products. A more detailed analysis of the seven products, however, showed that product seven was assembled with components also used to produce two high-volume products, (numbers one and six) and that it was the production-lot size of the components that was the dominant cost driver, not the assembly-lot size, or the shipping-lot size.

In a traditional cost system, the value of commonality of parts is hidden. Low-volume components appear to cost only slightly more than their high-volume counterparts. There is no incentive to design products with common parts. The shift to transaction-related costing identifies the much lower costs that derive from designing products with common (or fewer) parts and the much higher costs generated when large numbers of unique parts are specified for low-

volume products. In recognition of this phenomenon, more companies are experimenting with assigning material-related overhead on the basis of the total number of different parts used, and not on the physical or dollar volume of materials used.

LONG-TERM VARIABLE COST

The volume-unrelated support-department costs, unlike traditional variable costs, do not vary with short-term changes in activity levels. Traditional variable costs vary in the short run with production fluctuations because they represent cost elements that require no managerial actions to change the level of expenditure.

In contrast, any amount of decrease in overhead costs associated with reducing diversity and complexity in the factory will take many months to realize and will require specific managerial actions. The number of personnel in support departments will have to be reduced, machines may have to be sold off, and some supervisors will become redundant. Actions to accomplish these overhead cost reductions will lag, by months, the complexity-reducing actions in the product line and in the process technology. But this long-term cost response mirrors the way overhead costs were first built up in the factory—as more products with specialized designs were added to the product line, the organization simply muddled through with existing personnel. It was only over time that overworked support departments requested and received additional personnel to handle the increased number of transactions that had been thrust upon them.

The personnel in the support departments are often highly skilled and possess a high degree of firm-specific knowledge. Management is loathe to lay them off when changes in market conditions temporarily reduce the level of production complexity. Consequently, when the workload of these departments drops, surplus capacity exists.

The long-term perspective management had adopted toward its products often made it difficult to use the surplus capacity. When it was used, it was not to make prod-

Direct costing, even if correctly implemented, is not a solution and is perhaps a major problem for product costing.

Fred Smith Assoc.

Professor Kaplan has an MS degree in engineering from MIT and a Ph.D. in operations research from Cornell.

ucts never to be produced again, but rather to produce inventory of products that were known to disrupt production (typically the very low-volume items) or to produce, under short-term contract, products for other companies. We did not observe or hear about a situation in which this capacity was used to introduce a product that had only a short life expectancy. Some companies justified the acceptance of special orders or incremental business because they "knew" that the income from this business more than covered their variable or incremental costs. They failed to realize that the long-term consequence from accepting such incremental business was a steady rise in the costs of their support departments.

WHEN PRODUCT COSTS ARE NOT KNOWN

The magnitude of the errors in reported product costs and the nature of their bias make it difficult for full-line producers to enact sensible strategies. The existing cost systems clearly identify the low-volume products as the most profitable and the high-volume ones as the least profitable. Focused competitors, on the other hand, will not suffer from the same handicap. Their cost systems, while equally poorly designed, will report more accurate product costs because they are not distorted as much by lot-size diversity.

With access to more accurate product cost data, a focused competitor can sell the high-volume products at a lower price. The full-line producer is then apparently faced with very low margins on these products and is naturally tempted to deemphasize this business and concentrate on apparently higher-profit, low-volume specialty business. This shift from high-volume to low-volume products, however, does not produce the anticipated higher profitability. The firm, believing in its cost system, chases illusory profits.

The firm has been victimized by diseconomies of scope. In trying to obtain the benefits of economy of scale by expanding its product offerings to better utilize its fixed or capacity resources, the firm does not see the high diseconomies it has

THE IMPORTANCE OF FIELD RESEARCH

The accompanying article, co-authored with Robin Cooper, is excerpted from *Accounting & Management: Field Study Perspectives* (Boston, Mass., Harvard Business School Press, 1987) William J. Bruns, Jr. and Robert S. Kaplan (eds.). The book contains 13 field studies on management accounting innovations presented at a colloquium at the Harvard Business School in June 1986 by leading academic researchers from the U.S. and Western Europe. The colloquium represents the largest single collection of field research studies on management accounting practices in organizations.

The HBS colloquium had two principal objectives. First, the authors were to understand and document the management accounting practices of actual organizations. Some of the organizations would be captured in a process of transition: attempting, and occasionally succeeding to modify their systems to measure, motivate and evaluate operating performance. Other organizations were studied just to understand the system of measurement and control that had evolved in their particular environment.

A second, and even more important, objective of the colloquium was to begin the process by which field research methods in management accounting could be established as a legitimate method of inquiry. Academic researchers in accounting have extensive experience with deductive, model-building, analytic research with the design and analysis of controlled experiments, usually in a laboratory setting; and with the empirical analysis of large data bases. This experience has yielded research guidance and criteria that, while not always explicit, nevertheless are widely shared and permit research to be conducted and evaluated.

At a time when so many organizations are reexamining the adequacy of their management accounting systems it is especially important that university-based researchers spend more time working directly with innovating organizations. We are pleased that MANAGEMENT ACCOUNTING, through publication of this article, is help-

ing to publicize the existence of the field studies performed to date.

The experiences described in the accompanying article, as well as in the other papers in the colloquium volume, indicate a very different role for management accounting systems in organizations than is currently taught in most of our business schools and accounting departments. We believe that present and future field research and case-writing will lead to major changes in management accounting courses. To facilitate the needed changes in curriculum and research, however, requires extensive cooperation between university faculty and practicing management accountants. As noted by observers at the Harvard colloquium:

There is a tremendous store of knowledge about management accounting practices and ideas out there in real companies. Academicians as a whole are far too ignorant of that knowledge. When academics begin to see the relevance of this data base, perhaps generations of students will become more aware of its richness. Such awareness must precede any real progress on prescribing good management accounting for any given situation.

To observe is also to discover. The authors have observed interesting phenomena. We do not know how prevalent these phenomena are or under what conditions they exist or do not exist. But the studies suggest possible relationships, causes, effects, and even dynamic process in the sense that Yogi Berra must have had in mind when he said, "Sometimes you can observe a lot just by watching."

With the research support and cooperation of the members of the National Association of Accountants, many university professors are looking forward to watching and also describing the changes now under way so that academics can begin to develop theories, teach, and finally prescribe about the new opportunities for management accounting. □

Robert S. Kaplan

introduced by creating a far more complex production environment. The cost accounting system fails to reveal this diseconomy of scope.

A COMPREHENSIVE COST SYSTEM

One message comes through overwhelmingly in our experiences with the three firms, and with the many others we talked and worked with. Almost all product-related decisions—introduction, pricing, and discontinuance—are long-term. Management accounting thinking (and teaching) during the past half-century has concentrated on information for making short-run incremental decisions based on variable, incremental, or relevant costs. It has missed the most important aspect of product decisions. Invariably, the time period for measuring "variable," "incremental," or "relevant" costs has been about a month (the time period corresponding to the cycle of the firm's internal financial reporting system). While academics admonish that notions of fixed and variable are meaningful only with respect to a particular time period, they immediately discard this warning and teach from the perspective of one-month decision horizons.

This short-term focus for product costing has led all the companies we visited to view a large and growing proportion of their total manufacturing costs as "fixed." In fact, however, what they call "fixed" costs have been the most variable and rapidly increasing costs. This paradox has seemingly eluded most accounting practitioners and scholars. Two fundamental changes in our thinking about cost behavior must be introduced.

First, the allocation of costs from the cost pools to the products should be achieved using bases that reflect cost drivers. Because many overhead costs are driven by the complexity of production, not the volume of production, nonvolume-related bases are required. Second, many of these overhead costs are somewhat discretionary. While they vary with changes in the complexity of the production process, these changes are intermittent. A traditional cost system that defines variable costs as varying in the short term with production volume

will misclassify these costs as fixed.

The misclassification also arises from an inadequate understanding of the actual cost drivers for most overhead costs. Many overhead costs vary with transactions: transactions to order, schedule, receive, inspect, and pay for shipments; to move, track, and count inventory; to schedule production work; to set up machines; to perform quality assurance; to implement engineering change orders; and to expedite and ship orders. The cost of these transactions is largely independent of the size of the order being handled; the cost does not vary with the amount of inputs or outputs. It does vary, however, with the need for the transaction itself. If the firm in-

Pneumatic products are manufactured by one of the companies in the study.

troduces more products, if it needs to expedite more orders, or if it needs to inspect more components, then it will need larger overhead departments to perform these additional transactions.

SUMMARY

Product costs are almost all variable costs. Some of the sources of variability relate to physical volume of items produced. These costs will vary with units produced, or in a varied, multiproduct environment, with surrogate measures such as labor hours, machine hours, material dollars and quantities, or elapsed time of production. Other costs, however, particularly those arising from overhead support and marketing departments, vary with the diversity and complexity in the product line. The variability of these costs is best explained by the incidence of transactions to initiate the next stage in the production, logistics, or distribution process.

A comprehensive product cost system, incorporating the long-term variable costs of manufacturing and marketing each product or product line, should provide a much better basis for managerial decisions on pricing, introducing, discontinuing, and reengineering product lines. The cost system may even become strategically important for running the business and creating sustainable competitive advantages for the firm. ∎

Robin Cooper is an associate professor of business administration at the Harvard Business School and a fellow of the Institute of Chartered Accountants in England and Wales. He writes a column, "Cost Management Principles and Concepts," in the Journal of Cost Management *and has produced research on activity-based costing for the CAM-I Cost Management System Project.*

Robert S. Kaplan is the Arthur Lowes Dickinson Professor of Accounting at the Harvard Business School and a professor of industrial administration at Carnegie-Mellon University. Currently, Professor Kaplan serves on the Executive Committee of the CAM-I Cost Management System Project, the Manufacturing Studies Board of the National Research Council, and the Financial Accounting Standards Advisory Committee.

[1]Mayers Tap (disguised name) is described in Harvard Business School, case series 9-185-111. Schrader-Bellows is described in HBS Case Series 9-186-272.

The Four-Stage Model of
Cost Systems Design

Firms must pass through four phases to achieve integrated MIS.

Accurate product costing is essential today. Above, Harley-Davidson engine and transmission plant.

BY ROBERT S. KAPLAN

My article, "One Cost System Isn't Enough," advocated that companies develop new cost systems to produce useful information for operational control and for analyzing the profitability of products, product lines, and customers. The article suggested that these new systems were initially to be separate from the one used to prepare external financial statements.

Many financial executives have not been enthusiastic about this recommendation. They believe that companies cannot run with multiple financial and cost systems. They feel that their company must march to a single drummer so that it would be infeasible to produce external financial statements with one system; attempt to motivate and evaluate managers with a sec-

ond system; and make strategic decisions on pricing, distribution channels, product mix, product design, and process technology with yet a third. While not defending the adequacy of their existing official cost system, either for operational control or for strategic profitability analysis, these executives want any cost system improvements made for managerial purposes to become part of a single official system.

I would like to extend the thoughts expressed in my earlier article to explain that multiple cost systems are not the final objective but only an intermediate and practical stage on the way to a more effective set of integrated management information systems. But I believe it is a stage that companies must pass through. Attempting to skip this experimental stage by leaping directly to the "promised land" of an entirely new, managerially relevant financial system almost surely will lead to a system with serious limitations for operational control or for strategic profitability analysis, perhaps both.

THE FOUR-STAGE MODEL

Stage 1: Poor Data Quality. The best way to make my ideas clear is by means of a four-stage model of cost systems. The first stage, Poor Data Quality (see Figure 1), describes systems in which significant errors are introduced when recording or processing basic transactions. Symptoms of Stage 1 systems are unexpected variances occurring at the end of each accounting period when physical inventories are reconciled against book values, large writedowns of inventory after internal and external audits, many post-closing adjustments and error corrections, and a general lack of integrity and auditability of the financial system. These problems arise because Stage 1 systems either don't capture material, labor, or operating expense transactions accurately or don't count all the outputs produced by the manufacturing process.[1]

Not all companies start with Stage 1 systems. Such systems are more likely to be found in small or newly organized enterprises that have paid insufficient attention to data entry, system design, or internal controls.

Stage 2: External Reporting. Most companies have Stage 2 cost systems, (see Figure 1/Cost Systems Go Through Four Stages of Development). The financial statements prepared from Stage 2 systems require few post-closing adjustments, meet auditability standards with adequate data integrity and internal controls, support fast monthly closings, and engender a general belief within the corporation that the financial statements produced by the system are reliable. While functioning well for external reporting purposes, it is these Stage 2 systems that we have criticized as being inadequate for managerial purposes. Some time in the past, these systems may have been designed for and served managerial purposes. Today, however, these systems have serious limitations for operational control, and for accurate product costing and profitability analysis.[2]

The limitations for operational control arise from several sources. First, Stage 2 systems are not timely. Almost all organizations have a monthly (or four-week) financial reporting cycle. Allowing for the additional time to collect and process end-of-month transactions, and to perform the necessary adjusting and closing entries, financial reports typically appear in the second or third week of the subsequent accounting period. For operations being conducted continually across a diverse product line, finding out about department level material and energy variances five weeks late is not considered a valuable or vital component of the organization's feedback and control system.

Second, Stage 2 systems also are inadequate for operational control because of their high level of aggregation. Particularly with process-like cost systems, variances are reported at departmental levels and can not be assigned to the particular products and batches that caused the favorable or unfavorable results. Thus, limited opportunities for learning and improvement are signaled by the periodic financial summaries.

Third, the systems focus on aggregate financial results,[3] and not the actual activities that produce these results. At a time when organizations are attempting to implement total quality control, just-in-time, and computer-integrated production systems, a narrow focus on traditional summaries of financial data provides inadequate feedback on the progress of departments in implementing these operating improvements.[4]

Fourth, many of the periodic operating reports are contaminated with extensive allocations of costs. Thus, managers are held responsible for the expenses of resources even when the quantity consumed of these resources by their departments has not been accurately measured. The financial system has substituted allocation for accurate measurement, without recognizing

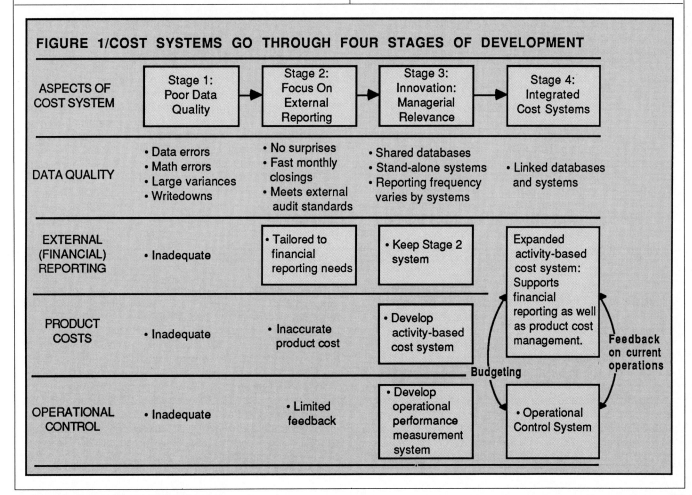

FIGURE 1/COST SYSTEMS GO THROUGH FOUR STAGES OF DEVELOPMENT

ASPECTS OF COST SYSTEM	Stage 1: Poor Data Quality	Stage 2: Focus On External Reporting	Stage 3: Innovation: Managerial Relevance	Stage 4: Integrated Cost Systems
DATA QUALITY	• Data errors • Math errors • Large variances • Writedowns	• No surprises • Fast monthly closings • Meets external audit standards	• Shared databases • Stand-alone systems • Reporting frequency varies by systems	• Linked databases and systems
EXTERNAL (FINANCIAL) REPORTING	• Inadequate	• Tailored to financial reporting needs	• Keep Stage 2 system	Expanded activity-based cost system: Supports financial reporting as well as product cost management.
PRODUCT COSTS	• Inadequate	• Inaccurate product cost	• Develop activity-based cost system	
OPERATIONAL CONTROL	• Inadequate	• Limited feedback	• Develop operational performance measurement system	• Operational Control System

Budgeting

Feedback on current operations

that allocations provide virtually no basis for evaluating the performance of departments and managers.

Finally, most periodic summaries of department performance retain the cost accounting vestiges of earlier production environments (volume and absorption variance, purchase price variances, labor and machine efficiencies) in today's environment where attempts by individual departments to eliminate unfavorable performance along these dimensions can produce disastrous results for the organization as a whole.

Stage 2 systems also are inadequate for product costing and profitability analysis. The systems rely on only a few allocation bases for assigning indirect costs to products, product lines, and customers. Stage 2 product costing systems allocate indirect and support costs to products and customers using measures such as direct labor, machine time, material quantities, and sales revenue. These measures all vary proportionately with the number of units produced (or sold). While adequate for assigning those indirect costs that are in fact consumed in proportion to the number of units of products produced and sold,[5] such allocation bases introduce considerable distortions when also used to assign costs that vary with the number of batches of products made, the number of different products made, the number of different channels and customers served, and, in general, all organizational costs that do not vary with the volume of products produced or sold.

To overcome the managerial limitations of Stage 2 systems, the "One Cost System Isn't Enough," article encouraged companies to develop specialized systems for operational control and for strategic profitability analysis. Because existing Stage 2 systems remain adequate for financial reporting, we recommended that companies retain, temporarily, their current system for preparing external reports and to develop local, customized systems for operational control and for profitability analysis.

Stage 3: Innovation. We refer to this evolutionary phase as Stage 3, Innovation: Managerial Relevance.

The operational control information in Stage 3 systems emphasizes direct measures of operating performance such as quality, timeliness, flexibility, and customer service. The Stage 3 systems supplement these operational and physical measures with financial summaries of short-run performance. The financial summaries build upon the extensive information already being produced from computerized production control and operating systems. For many operations, financial information can be produced daily, hourly, or even batch by batch with virtually no increase in information collection costs.

The financial summaries will be highly accurate, reflecting actual outputs produced and batch-by-batch costs of the actual (measured) resources consumed, computed at either standard or current actual prices. Rather than computing variances between actual and historical standard costs, the current costs can be compared with the trend of the actual costs of the most recent items produced. Graphical presentation of data, highlighting trends and forecasts, replaces the extensive jumble of six-digit numbers that now clutter the monthly variance reports of Stage 2 systems. The goal of these short-run financial summaries is not to control employees but to provide information to guide their learning and improvement activities.[6]

In summary, Stage 3 operational control systems provide continual summaries of operating data and costs of those resources whose consumption varies in the short run with the volume and mix of outputs produced. Such systems can be implemented today. One chemical plant currently records 40,000 observations on its processes every two hours, and its finance staff has built on this database to produce daily income and expense summaries for individual departments.[7]

Independent of the effort to implement more timely, accurate, and relevant operational control systems, companies also can start to build activity-based cost (ABC) systems. These systems will more accurately assign the indirect and support expenses of the organization's resources to the products, product lines, divisions, distribution channels, and customers that either create the demands for or benefit from these resources. The assignment of expenses will be more accurate than those made in Stage 2 cost systems because activity-based systems are not limited to allocation bases that vary proportionally to the number of units produced.[8]

Thus, expenses may be assigned based on their actual consumption by batches produced, by different components or products, by different product lines or by different channels and customers.[9] As with operational control systems, ABC systems for strategic analysis can be developed and implemented today using data already being collected by existing systems, supplemented by information collected through on-site observation and interviews.

Activity-based costing systems differ from operational control systems in several important ways. First, because ABC systems are designed to facilitate decisions on product design, and strategic decisions on manufacturing processes, pricing and product mix, virtually all organizational expenses will be considered variable with respect to the decisions made. Operational control systems, focusing on short-run process efficiencies, will classify many organizational expenses as fixed with respect to fluctuations in daily and weekly activity levels, and focus primarily on short-run variable resource consumption. Second, as already noted, operational control systems will report continually, certainly at least daily, whereas the product costs computed by ABC systems, while used for analytic studies throughout the year, may only be reestimated annually. Strategic decisions on customers and product lines are not made daily or even monthly so that it is usually not necessary to reestimate the parameters used to compute product and customer-related costs more often than annually.[10]

Third, operational control systems must report accurately on actual resource consumption by processes and departments, with no allocations included. The expense analysis, for an ABC profitability study, however, requires that all expenses be associated with the activities performed and products produced. Even if accurate metering of resource consumption does not exist, the ABC analysis will require that subjective, best-estimate judgments be made to assign expenses to activities and products. Also, expenses will be associated with products, channels, and customers, even when managerial responsibility and control overlaps or is shared across various aspects of production, distribution, and sales. Operational control systems should be organized by managerial responsibility but ABC systems assign expenses across the value chain to compute the profitability of individual products, product lines, channels, and customers.

Thus, operational control and ABC systems differ significantly in assumptions about expense variability, frequency of reporting and updating, requirements for accuracy, the role for subjective judgments of resource consumption, and on the scope of the system. Attempting to meet these diverse—even contradictory—demands with a single systems design seems well beyond the capabilities of any existing system. Therefore, companies in Stage 3 should retain their existing system for financial reporting but start to develop local, managerially relevant operational control and activity-based cost systems in individual sites.

To minimize costs and obtain maximum data integrity, the information to these localized systems may be downloaded from existing financial accounting, production, marketing, logistics, and sales systems. But the intelligence and processing for operational control and profitability analysis will likely reside in localized processing units. A single systems design that will be adequate for an individual plant's and division's operational control and ABC systems cannot be specified at this time. Such a generalized system specification can only emerge after a period of experimentation. But such experimentation will be inhibited if local systems must be integrated into the official company-wide reporting system.

Stage Four: Integration. The next stage of development, Stage 4: Integrated Cost Systems, will derive information to prepare external financial statements from the activity-based and operational control systems developed during Stage 3. As companies experiment with, gain confidence in, and eventually standardize their strategic profitability systems and their operational control systems, they can replace their Stage 2 financial reporting system with reconciliation modules that prepare GAAP external reporting statements from data already being collected for the managerial systems.

Inventory valuation, including concerns such as lower of cost or market and obsolescence, can be performed using the unit, batch, and product specific assignment bases in the activity-based cost system.

Expenses that have been assigned down to individual

In ABC systems, best judgment is used to assign expenses to products like motorcycles in Harley-Davidson final assembly plant, York, Pa.

products, but which cannot (according to GAAP) be allocated to inventory, will be stripped away, and expenses that could not be causally assigned to individual products under an ABC analysis, but which according to GAAP must be allocated to inventoried products, can be allocated using an arbitrary allocation base (much as is done today for all indirect expenses).

The actual expenses needed to prepare periodic financial statements can be captured from the operational control systems that are monitoring daily, weekly, and monthly spending activities. Thus, in Stage 4, financial statements are prepared from systems explicitly designed to provide managerially relevant information. The Stage 4 approach is exactly counter to the present Stage 2 philosophy where companies attempt, unsuccessfully, to develop managerially relevant information from systems that primarily satisfy external requirements.

In addition to preparing financial statements from the managerial systems, Stage 4 systems will integrate information between the operational control and activity-based systems. The activity-based expense analysis system will prepare budgets for operating departments based on forecasts of product volume and mix, and the use of particular production processes and procedures. If substantial changes occur in product mix and volume, or in the nature of the production processes, new budgets can be prepared from the activity-based system. During the year, the operational control system can compare actual spending to the expense forecasts prepared by the activity-based system.

Feedback will operate from operational control to activity-based as well, with the operational control system providing information on actual resource consumption of operating activities during the year. Thus, many of the estimates in the activity-based system can be updated based on current actual operating data.

ANALYSIS, FEEDBACK, MEASUREMENT

In summary, the Stage 4 system will have two integrated managerial systems—one for product and customer profitability analysis, and one for on-line feedback and performance measurement. Periodic financial statements will be prepared by excerpting information from the two systems and reconciling to meet externally determined reporting standards. Only one set of product costs will exist, in contrast with Stage 3 systems where the product costs used to prepare financial statements may differ from those derived from a more accurate analysis of the demands made by individual products on indirect and support resources.

Some people, however, wish to move directly to Stage 4 systems without having to transit through the confusion of multiple reporting systems of Stage 3. At this time, and with our present state of knowledge of what is possible and beneficial from newly designed operational control and activity-based systems, I am skeptical that we can develop the detailed systems specifications for a Stage 4 system. Some current attempts at Stage 4 systems provide daily feedback on cost center and departmental spending, including flexible budgets to control for volume and mix of products produced and even use different or multiple cost drivers in different cost centers. But these systems provide poor estimates of product costs, and little to no information on the profitability of product lines, customers, and distribution channels.

The flexible budget, so useful for short-term expense analysis, assumes that many organizational expenses are fixed independent of the volume and mix of production. The cost drivers used to budget operating expenses in a cost center are almost always unit related: labor or machine hours, material quantities, or units produced. The systems find it difficult, if not impossible, to assign expenses to products that are not proportional to the number of units produced. Thus, batch-level, product-specific, or even product-line related expenses end up in the fixed cost overhead pool where they are not assigned accurately to individual products or lines.

The questions to ask when contemplating such systems include: Are the cost drivers for individual cost centers all unit related? How are product costs that do not vary with the volume of production of individual products assigned or allocated to products? Are some product costs considered "fixed"? Do the periodic financial data dominate nonfinancial operating data in assessing the performance of cost center and departmental managers?

Alternatively, some companies are experimenting with using their newly developed activity-based systems to provide operational control information. The problem here is just the reverse of that encountered when attempting to use an operational control system for product costing. Now, the expenses that were considered variable for strategic profitability analysis will also be treated as variable for efficiency measurements during short time periods.

This assumption will not be accurate and large spending or efficiency variances will appear when actual product volumes and mix, or production processes, differ considerably from that assumed when performing the activity-based budget analysis. Also, in attempting to have all costs appear variable, cost system designers may be influenced to use unit-based cost drivers (number of insertions in a PC board) even for expenses that might be characterized better by batch level (starting a production lot) or product specific (engineering change orders) cost drivers. In any case, compromises get made in an attempt to perform both managerial functions — operational control and strategic profitability analysis — with a single system.

OBSOLETE COST SYSTEMS

Beliefs engendered from 60 years of using one system to produce both financial accounting and management accounting information are difficult to overcome. Contemporary changes in the demands made on our management accounting systems and in the technology available to produce customized information have made obsolete the cost system design decisions that were sensibly and correctly made decades ago.

I believe that the best cost system designs will come from organizations that allow local, customized systems to be developed as prototypes. The benefits of developing prototype Stage 3 operational control and ABC systems include a much lower cost for development and implementation, the flexibility and ease of modifying single purpose systems, and the considerable opportunities for organizational learning and acceptance with the new approaches. Attempts to bypass this experimentation period prematurely, by buying or building standardized systems to be used by all organizational units, may be successful. But more likely, they may succeed only in providing the organization with a Stage 2 system operating on a 1990 computer system: fast, accurate data, but not very useful for operational control or for knowing in which products, services, and customers the company is making and losing money. ∎

Robert S. Kaplan is the Arthur Lowes Dickinson Professor of Accounting at the Harvard Business School and a professor of industrial administration at Carnegie Mellon University.

[1]Examples of such systems can be found in Harvard Business School Cases "Multislide," (HBS Case # 9-175-020), Barnes and Jones, (HBS Case # 9-181-053), Ransom Furniture (HBS Case # 9-175-067), and Mueller Lemkuhl (HBS Case # 9-187-048).

[2]Many companies are currently updating their Stage 2 systems to reduce incompatibilities among their diverse financial systems. Especially when companies are highly decentralized, have overseas operations, or have grown through acquisition, the localized financial systems do not share common data formats or common definitions for the charts of accounts, and cannot be easily consolidated into an integrated corporate-wide system. Thus, these companies are improving the compatibility of their financial systems but not making fundamental improvements in their managerial relevance.

[3]H. Thomas Johnson, "Activity Based Information: A Blueprint for World Class Management Accounting," MANAGEMENT ACCOUNTING®, June 1988.

[4]In some instances, the financial summaries can run completely counter to the actual operating improvements being achieved.

[5]These costs, varying with the number of units produced or sold, are the costs typically classified as "variable" by traditional cost accounting systems.

[6]This role for short-run cost information has been articulated by R. Jaikumar, "An Architecture for a Process Control Costing System," Chapter 7 in *Measures for Manufacturing Excellence.*

[7]"Texas Eastman Company," HBS Case # 9-130-039.

[8]The distinction between unit-based and other bases (such as batch or product sustaining) for assigning expenses to products is described in Robin Cooper, "Cost Classification in Unit-Based and Activity-Based Manufacturing Cost Systems," HBS Working Paper 1989.

[9]The assignment of marketing and selling expenses to product lines and distribution channels is described in "Winchell Lighting (A)," (HBS Case # 9-187-074). Order processing and special production order expenses are assigned to individual customers in "Kanthal (A) and (B)," (HBS Cases # 9-190-002 and 190-003).

[10]The ABC cost estimates may need to be modified more frequently if the company is making substantial product design, technological, or marketing changes.

Is this article of interest to you? If so, circle appropriate number on Reader Service Card.

	Yes	No
	76	77

Section 7

Implications: Performance Measurement

Section 7 continues an examination of implications for future cost accounting systems resulting from changes occurring in the new manufacturing environment. These three articles review changes needed in the area of performance measurement.

In the lead article, Robert A. Howell and Stephen R. Soucy discuss changes needed in management reporting systems. They cite two flaws in current reporting systems: reports irrelevant to the needs of management and unused reports that are repetitive in content. The authors feel that the new environment makes the risk associated with decisions greater than ever before and stress the importance of relevant and timely information that is effective in evaluating performance and identifying opportunities for action. They see the optimal system as one that provides both operating and financial information tailored to the various levels of the organization.

Howell and Soucy review the nature of information needs in the new manufacturing environment as they relate to operations reporting, business unit reporting, and corporate reporting. In operations reporting, the key is operating and financial information focusing on critical factors that identify specific problem areas and track performance over time. Operating and financial information reflecting critical success factors, although reported less frequently and in less detail, is needed for business unit reporting. Corporate reports should be concise and include an analysis and review of operations, selected critical success factors, a financial summary, and a forecast. Two exhibits provide illustrative examples of the authors' recommendations.

C.J. McNair and William Mosconi see the performance measurement system as providing the first step on the path to manufacturing excellence—supplying the best product at the lowest price. They state that performance measurements should capture the key elements of the manufacturing strategy, expose nonvalue-added costs for elimination, provide accurate and timely data on cost drivers, and serve as accurate records for product costing decisions. The authors cite four critical success factors that need to be measured at every level of activity—people, quality, delivery, and cost. They emphasize that many traditional reporting systems focus solely on cost and ignore the three nonfinancial measures.

McNair and Mosconi provide useful criteria for evaluating management accounting and control systems in an advanced manufacturing environment, including rapid feedback, sensitivity to profit, reclassification of costs, and enhanced traceability of costs. They feel these characteristics are an inherent part of a well-functioning performance measurement system. The authors' findings came from a field study of firms that had instituted just-in-time techniques, of which five examples are reported in the article. McNair and Mosconi observe that changes in performance measurement systems were necessary complements to the introduction of advanced technologies and process modifications. They conclude that although change was slow and reactive, it was occurring.

The final article, also by Howell and Soucy, describes the new kinds of operating control mechanisms required in the world-class manufacturing environment. The authors cite three reasons why the development of operating measures has not kept pace with the changing environment: obsolete cost accounting systems are still the primary tool for manufacturing performance measurement; traditional measures, focusing on labor, standards, and overhead absorption, are still the basis for evaluating manufacturing performance; and managerial accountants are not closely involved with operations. The authors call for integration of more nonfinancial and subjectively determined measures and for more timely and flexible systems.

Howell and Soucy discuss in turn five major nonfinancial areas of operating control for world-class manufacturers—quality, delivery, inventory, material utilization/scrap, and machine availability/performance. Their discussion provides many examples of operating measures needed in the new manufacturing environment, which are summarized in a table. The authors see the challenge for management accountants to be developing these new measures of operating control and integrating them into a centrally maintained and readily available source of information for the control and decision-making processes.

Additional Readings from *Management Accounting*

Brayton, Gary N., "Productivity Measure Aids in Profit Analysis," January 1985, pp. 54-58.

Doost, Roger K. and Evans Pappas, "Frozen-to-Current Cost Variance," March 1988, pp. 41-43.

Keegan, Daniel P., Robert G. Eiler, and Charles R. Jones, "Are Your Performance Measures Obsolete?" June 1989, pp. 45-50.

Lippa, Victor, "Measuring Performance with Synchronous Management," February 1990, pp. 54-59.

Taussig, Russell A. and William L. Shaw, "Accounting for Productivity: A Practical Approach," May 1985, pp. 48-52.

Tietze, Armin R. and Delphine R. Shaw, "OPUS: A New Concept for Mastering Cost," August 1986, pp. 27-31.

MANAGEMENT REPORTING

In the New Manufacturing Environment

BY ROBERT A. HOWELL AND
STEPHEN R. SOUCY

Many U.S. manufacturers are changing dramatically the way they operate their factories in an effort to improve their competitive position in an increasingly demanding marketplace. These changes include placing more emphasis on customer responsiveness (quality, delivery, and service), product line profitability, product contribution, operating effectiveness (lower inventories, shorter cycle times, lower cost of nonquality, higher throughput, lower operating expenses), and asset management (equipment, fixed asset, and space utilization).

What's hindering many companies' efforts, however, is the lack of an effective management reporting system that evaluates performance and identifies opportunities for action. We have observed many companies with management reporting systems that produce little or no information, fail to identify the user of the information properly and to tailor the content and presentation to suit his needs, and do not reflect the new competitive environment.

Managers can manage effectively only if they get the information they need to evaluate, decide, and implement the appropriate course of action for their businesses. Today, many managers make decisions based strictly on instinct, despite what the data indicates. Other managers do not make decisions against their instincts because the "evidence" does not support the decision or the necessary information is unavailable.

In such an environment, it is obvious that the risk of making the wrong decision or the risk of not

> *Management accounting reports today often are irrelevant and repetitious.*

making any decision at all is greater than ever before. Management accountants must address the issue of management information. If they don't, their company's ability to be competitive may be compromised.

IRRELEVANT AND REPETITIVE REPORTING

Two principal flaws in current management reporting are: reports produced often are irrelevant to the needs of management, and half of all reports are either not used or are repetitive in content.

A manufacturing executive recalled a conversation he had with a plant manager. The executive started to ask for some information regarding... but even before he finished his sentence, the plant manager said, "Wait, whatever you need, I've got it right here." He pulled out a six-inch-thick binder and gave it to the executive. The executive said he didn't have two days to spend looking through the binder. He wanted to know the plant's profitability by major product line. "Sorry, not available. We

might be able to get a report in a couple of weeks but only based on standards, and that won't be too accurate."

A conversation we had with the cost accounting manager of a large auto parts supplier, virtually surrounded by reams of computer paper, revealed that he had "more data than anyone could possibly ever need!" Yet a production manager in that same company said the accounting department produced relatively useless data and certainly not the information he used to run the factory.

We also are concerned with the volume of information that accounting departments produce today. We estimate that half of all reports are either not used or are repetitive in content and should be eliminated.

Many of the reports and schedules produced by management accountants are no longer necessary. For example, when a company was battling bankruptcy it created Schedule 345, a weekly cash receipts and disbursements report for the purpose of keeping the CEO informed of the daily cash position. Today, the prosperous company with millions in cash still spends hours putting it together and no one uses it.

Most manufacturing companies still have one-third to one-half of their production reporting schedules focusing on labor efficiency and utilization. Fifteen years ago, when labor was 30% to 40% of total cost, the reports were relevant. Today, labor is 5% to 10% of total cost and the production manager is not concerned with labor utilization, but quality, delivery, scrap, inventory, and cycle time. Is the source of the production manager's management information the ac-

To be competitive, manufacturers need an effective management reporting system.

counting department? No, accounting reports often are relegated to the circular file. The production manager's information comes from his own PC.

REPORTS TAILORED TO USERS' NEEDS

There are three principal reporting levels within an organization: operations, business unit, and corporate (Figure 1). Understanding the information needs of each level will improve the accounting department's ability to provide relevant and timely reports.

Operations Reporting. The operations level is responsible for specific products and manufacturing performance. An operations manager needs two categories of information: operating and financial. It must focus on the critical factors affecting the business and be available on a timely basis. Three major kinds of operating information are useful: product lines, profitability, expenses and assets. The product line's performance includes responsiveness to customers and mea-

sures of product quality, and delivery. Quality measurements must address vendor performance, incoming inspection, in-process performance, and customer reaction. In the short-run, operations managers need to know if any problems exist so that corrective action may be taken and any disruption in the supply chain avoided.

Managers need to know whether customers' delivery and service expectations are being met. Information relating to on-time delivery, order-fill rate, and customer satisfaction should be closely monitored.

Delivery and service performance measures also apply to the company's internal "customers" that represent each step in the manufacturing process. For example, the lathe operation "sells" its product to the drill operation which in turn sells its finished product to the assembly line and so on. Each area's satisfaction, represented by schedule attainment, needs to be closely monitored. The schedule chain begins with incoming materials thus requiring the measurement of vendor delivery performance.

The operations manager also is responsible for major categories of cost, particularly those influenced and controlled in the short run. In many modern factories, these costs include material usage, scrap rates, and manufacturing yield, and such operating expenses as supplies and utilities. Thus, the manager must track how well these categories of costs are being controlled.

For many firms, material constitutes a significant proportion of manufacturing product costs, making scrap a significant control issue. Scrap rates of 5% to 10% and higher in some businesses are not unusual. The firm's objective should be to reduce scrap to its absolute minimum. Knowing where scrap is created is the first step toward achieving this objective.

Similarly, operating expenses and energy can add up to large amounts. Often they are ignored because there is the belief that either they are relatively small in terms of unit cost, as in the case of operating supplies, or are relatively uncontrollable as in the case of energy.

Aggregating the operating expenses to highlight their cumula-

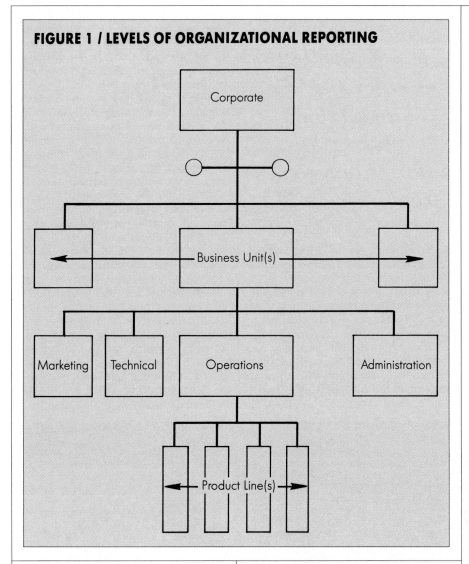

FIGURE 1 / LEVELS OF ORGANIZATIONAL REPORTING

tive effect, and disaggregating the energy costs, in an attempt to establish cause and effect relationships can help the operations manager control these key expenses categories.

One broad financial measure that has been effectively applied at the plant level of many businesses is the "cost of quality" or nonquality. Companies that identify the major components of the costs resulting from poor quality, take corrective action to reduce them, and track their progress in doing so, can significantly reduce costs and improve their product quality.

The calculation of "nonvalue added" costs is similar to the concept of the cost of quality and is an attempt to identify all of the costs of manufacturing and nonmanufacturing that do not add any intrinsic value to the products being produced. The objective is, obviously, to eliminate these costs.

The product line manager also must increase his responsibility for the assets he controls. Thus, it is essential he receives exacting records of inventory levels, activity, and location to ensure that either the absence of inventory does not interfere with the production process or the existence of higher than required inventories is corrected. Increased investments in property, plant, and equipment emphasize the need to track equipment utilization and performance, and to maintain meticulous and detailed preventative maintenance schedules and repair records. The overriding objective of tracking and reporting operating measures of performance is to identify problems before they occur and to use the information to signal uncontrolled situations that need prompt corrective action.

Operating information should be provided to the operations manager as frequently as daily or according to shifts. The information should be detailed and even include the individual part number and operation. Such detail, obviously, runs the risk of reports with information overload. Therefore, limits should be established to avoid unnecessary and repetitive information.

Some companies are placing output parameters in their daily operations reporting package. If a measure is out of a preestablished range, the information is reported to the operations manager immediately. By the time the plant manager starts his shift he will have received reports of the development of problems according to product and operation.

Operations reports should focus primarily on actual results and actual trends and not budget-versus-actual variance analysis. For example, in the case of material usage and scrap, the use of budget-versus-actual variance analysis may result in the conclusion that a positive variance relative to budget is favorable performance, even if significant scrap still is being produced. Using zero scrap as a target results in any variance being identified as unfavorable. World class manufacturers use the concept of "continual improvement." That means identifying and highlighting all scrap until none remains.

The operations manager needs exact operating information on a short-term basis. Actual trends should be tracked rather than compared to a predetermined budget.

Operating measures of performance are more important for the operations manager than financial measures. Because the operating transactions drive the financial measures they can be collected faster and distributed earlier to the operations manager. Nevertheless, the operations manager should understand that the goal of business is to make money and actions at the operations level greatly influence the ability to do that.

The operations manager must know whether the controllable financial objectives are being met. Materials, operating supplies, energy, and inventory levels are major determinants of line managers' cost performance and should be tracked on a regular basis.

Periodically, perhaps quarterly, the operations manager should get reports summarizing expenses incurred that fall into the categories of either managed or discretionary costs and fixed costs.

In addition to a company's manufacturing operations, there are usually several centralized service departments such as purchasing, scheduling, manufacturing engineering, and maintenance. There are also nonmanufacturing departments such as engineering, marketing and sales, and administration that require periodic management reports. Some of these departments' costs are "driven" by levels of activity, and managers need to understand how the costs that are actually incurred are related to those levels of activity. The departments' costs that are still manageable, or discretionary, also need to be reported and evaluated periodically. But there is no requirement that these departments' costs need to be reported on a monthly basis, especially if they do not change much from month to month.

In sum, the purpose of operating and financial measurement at the department level is to identify specific problem areas as they emerge and to track performance over time. The goal: to quickly identify and resolve problems and continually improve operating and financial performance.

Business Unit Reporting. A business unit is a free standing business entity that has overall responsibility for a number of product lines serving one or a number of markets. An operating division is a typical example. In some companies, even a plant would qualify as a business unit.

While the operations manager is concerned with the performance of the particular plant, the business unit manager looks at the broader financial, investment, and operating issues for his unit's product lines and markets.

The business unit manager requires less detail than the operations manager about specific product lines and plant performance. The business unit manager, however, does need information about various product lines' economic characteristics and operating performance to enable him to make the correct capital investment, pricing, and strategic choices. Such decisions are more long-term in nature and, therefore, information is

Accounting reports are relegated to the circular file; the production manager's information comes from his own PC.

gathered and presented to business unit managers less frequently than for the product line manager.

As with the operations manager, the business unit manager needs both operating and financial information. In the case of operating information, we like to think in terms of critical success factors rather than operating measures of performance—although essentially they are the same. Critical success factors are considered those areas of the operation that will—if handled well—result in a high-level of performance overall.

The first critical success factor for a business manager to have information about is the status of backlog, incoming orders, and shipments. This information is presented in the aggregate as well as broken down by product lines. Tracking orders, shipments, and other key measures can signal changes in the marketplace, competitive position, and internal performance of a unit and allow management the opportunity to react.

A second set of critical success factors revolves around the customer's receptivity to the units' products and services. Measures of customer satisfaction, and quality and delivery performance in the aggregate and by product lines are important. Quality and delivery are most important to customers. Qual-

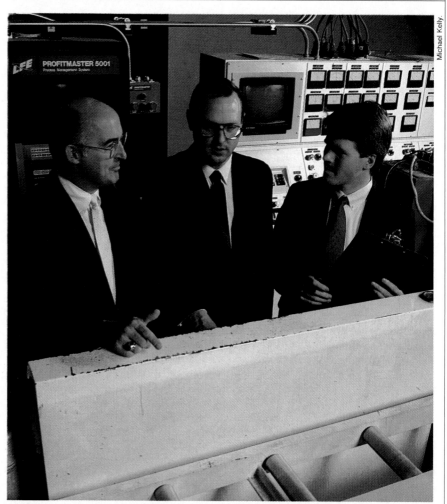

Authors Bob Howell (l.) and Steve Soucy (r.) with Chuck Poirier, group v.p. of Packaging Corporation of America.

ity measures such as customer returns, complaints, credits (related to poor quality), and customer satisfaction surveys quantify quality as perceived by customers. Quality measures such as scrap, cost of quality, rework, material yield, and reject rate reflect an internal quality rating.

Aggregated delivery measures such as number of vendors qualified, percentage of incoming materials rejected, percentage of orders delivered on time, and average level of order fulfillment are examples of schedule performance. Average cycle time for products manufactured and average setup times also are the kinds of customer quality and delivery statistics that may be useful signals and targets for the business unit manager.

Similarly, in the areas of material utilization, scrap, and yield, aggregate results and results by product line and trend data will help the business unit manager track progress.

While business unit managers should not be required to review detailed quality and delivery data, changes in aggregated level of data must be clearly defined by the root causes (detail). But managers also should be open to monitor detail information about such significant issues as quality and delivery performance for the top 10 customers and plant performance (best and worst).

The business manager also needs to track other expense areas and assets including total inventory, inventory turns in the aggregate and by product line, and types of inventory within product lines. Cycle count accuracy and levels of inventory write-downs are monitored.

In addition to tracking overall business financial results, the business unit manager must focus on key areas of financial performance. Among the most important information he or she reviews is product, product line, and customer profitability.

Product line and product profitability information is necessary to address key issues such as outsourcing parts or total products, selecting market, product line and product emphasis, pricing decisions, capital investments, and performance evaluation. Many companies do not do a very good job of determining product profitability and, as a result, face a higher risk

Labor represents only 5% to 10% of a manufacturer's total cost.

of making the wrong decision because of inadequate or incorrect data.

Most companies' differentiation between variable and fixed costs and period costs are based on traditional practices that no longer reflect the realities of the manufacturing environment. A product line or product, in the short run, may incur variable costs of material and some operating supplies. Costs such as labor and overhead are quite fixed. In the longer run, material, labor, and overhead at the factory level can be altered and, therefore, can be thought to be variable.

In addition, engineering, marketing, and administrative costs, associated with a particular line or product need to be considered in the definition of product costs.

Finally, product line related investments such as inventory and equipment also must be considered. The traditional definition of variable manufacturing costs as being the only relevant cost for decision-making purposes or full manufacturing costs as a definition of product cost are both inaccurate, especially in the context of the changing manufacturing environment where fewer costs are variable and the allocation basis of full costing often failed to even approximate the actual cost to produce.

Similarly, business unit managers have to understand the profitability of different customers. This

only can be accomplished if the broader definition of product costs is adequately determined and is related to the prices paid by individual customers. We are aware of companies that knew how much they sold to each customer but did not determine how profitable the sales to each customer were to the company. Consequently, large volume customers were treated as though they were the most profitable when they were not. Requests from lower volume customers were responded to less quickly even though they bought higher profit products and represented more profitability to the firm.

Business unit managers should focus on key areas of expense such as material costs, and overhead expense whether related to production or nonmanufacturing areas of overhead. Many companies fail to consider these major cost categories because they are resigned to the fact that such costs are uncontrollable or difficult to lower. This is usually not the case. These costs should be monitored and evaluated periodically.

The business unit manager must put more emphasis on asset management and cash flows. For example, compare two products of equal revenue and profit characteristics. Product one, due to high seasonality, requires an average inventory equal to 40% of product sales. Product two, on a JIT schedule, averages three days' inventory (all raw material). Incredibly, many systems fail to reflect the significant difference between the two products. Management continues to tie up inventory and cash in product one because of its return on sales. While many companies will argue that they measure profits on some asset base (total assets, assets employed, net assets), few know the return on assets performance according to product line or product.

The problem is compounded when fixed assets such as equipment and plant requirements are taken into consideration. Because of the difficulty in attributing certain pieces of equipment to particular product lines, little attention has been given to fixed assets when evaluating product line performance.

Many companies are now dedicating factories or areas within factories to the production of specific

TABLE 1 / SUMMARY REVIEW AND ANALYSIS OF OPERATIONS

ABC Grain Company, Corn Processing Division,
(Period Ended September 30, 1987)

Critical Success Factors ($000)

Actual	Plan	Variance	Division	Actual	Plan	Variance
	Current Month				**9 Mos. Year to Date**	
Actual	**Plan**	**Variance**	**Division**	**Actual**	**Plan**	**Variance**
64,450	79,500	(15,050)	Net sales	566,170	650,000	(83,830)
15,810	21,365	(5,555)	Contribution margin: $	141,080	190,230	(49,150)
25%	27%	−2%	% of net sales	25%	29%	−4%
(1,055)	800	(1,855)	Operating income: $	(24,525)	24,500	(49,025)
−2%	1%	−3%	% of net sales	−4%	4%	−8%
(1,065)	745	(1,810)	Net income: $	(24,835)	23,995	(48,830)
−2%	1%	−3%	% of net sales	−4%	4%	−8%
−3%	2%	−6%	Return on assets employed % (Annualized)	−9%	8%	−17%

Volume

Actual	Plan	Variance	Division	Actual	Plan	Variance
11,360	13,595	(2,235)	Sales bushels	99,700	106,225	(6,525)
11,795	11,980	(185)	Production bushels	97,590	108,670	(11,080)

Contribution $ by product group

Actual	Plan	Variance	Division	Actual	Plan	Variance
5,534	6,410	(876)	CSU	49,378	57,069	(7,691)
1,897	1,709	188	Unmodified common starch	16,930	15,218	1,711
3,794	4,273	(479)	Modified common starch	33,859	38,046	(4,187)
(949)	(2,051)	1,102	Oil well	(8,465)	(18,262)	9,797
16	0	16	PG	141	(2)	143
2,514	3,397	(883)	Dextrin	22,432	30,247	(7,815)
(1,818)	299	(2,117)	Amioca (Waxy)	(16,224)	2,663	(18,887)
1,657	2,243	(586)	Amylomaize	14,785	19,974	(5,189)
370	500	(130)	Starch by-products	3,301	4,451	(1,150)
3,004	4,089	(1,086)	Distress	26,805	36,412	(9,607)
(209)	496	(704)	Feed	(1,862)	4,414	(6,275)

Balance sheet

Actual	Plan	Variance	Division	Actual	Plan	Variance
			Net receivables: $	68,490	76,512	8,022
			days outstanding	33	32	(1)
			Net inventory: $	86,618	87,642	1,024
			inventory days	55	49	(7)
			Working capital: $	118,047	124,568	6,521
			% of net sales	16%	14%	−1%
			Assets (Funds) employed	387,140	402,454	15,314
(4,652)	8,432	(13,084)	Cash provided (Required)	(15,462)	67,246	(82,708)

products or product lines. These "focused factories" make it possible to evaluate the fixed asset requirements of particular product lines. As a result, products that require more equipment, plant space (including warehouse), and other assets are identified and management can better assess the relative return of each product line.

Corporate Reporting. Corporate management must have enough information about the business units' performance, product line, and product performance to be able to deal with significant problems and opportunities. Yet, at the same time, corporate executives should not be burdened with detail. They must be able to see the major issues facing the firm.

Corporate executives should receive four principal kinds of information. The first report should be a summary from the business unit manager that reviews the operation, analyses results, and addresses significant strategic and management issues. Second, the package should include a limited number of critical success factors the corporate executive can quickly relate to and use to assess performance. Third, financial results should be summarized in a managerial rather than financial accounting format. Finally, there should be a forecast of future expectations. Table 1 is an example of a one page summary report.

Each business unit should provide a brief but thorough review, analysis, and summary of operations for the most immediate reporting period, the year-to-date, the following period, and the remainder of the year. It should be prepared by the business unit's senior manager, and, in highlight form, identify the significant issues, problems, and opportunities facing the business unit. Issues could include: changes in the overall business climate, significant competitive moves, and/or internal developments that could have a major impact on the business unit. All businesses are confronted with problems and it is important that business unit managers identify those most critical. This report consolidates top business management's thoughts on the business for the benefit of senior management.

Previously, we discussed the importance of business unit managers identifying their critical success factors for their areas of operation. Actual results and continual improvement reports for these areas should be reported regularly to corporate management. The reports

Half of all reports produced today are either not used or are repetitive in content and should be eliminated.

could use graphs and trend lines to clearly communicate this information.

Many companies' internal reporting practices reflect external financial reporting requirements. As a result, the reports that are distributed among the corporate levels are similar to those produced for external financial reporting purposes. We recommend that on a regular basis corporate manage-

ment receive an income statement, balance sheet, and operating cash flows for each business unit.

Income statements are typically prepared for both internal and external use in compliance with generally accepted accounting principles. This is not necessary for internal reporting purposes, and in fact, can be dysfunctional. Income statements for internal reporting purposes should emphasize the degree of variability of the costs involved. That is, use more of a variable costing/contribution methodology than the traditional product/period distinction of financial reporting. It is easier to understand the economics of a business and make economic comparisons between businesses using the contribution format than if the traditional accounting format is used.

The *balance sheet* should focus on working capital and property, plant, and equipment. Together they represent assets used by the

FIGURE 2 / MANAGEMENT REPORTING FRAMEWORK

	Operations	Business Unit	Corporate
Operating Measures	Customer Responsiveness Quality Delivery & service	Critical Success Factors Backlog & Orders Shipments	Review/Analysis/Summary of Operations
	Operations Scrap/yield Supplies Energy	Quality Delivery Scrap	Critical Success Factors
	Assets Inventory turnover Equipment use/performance	Inventory Space Equipment	
Financial Measures	Specific Expenses Scrap Supplies Energy	Profitability Analysis Products Customers	Financial Results Profit Asset management Cash flow management
	Comprehensive Expenses Cost of quality Nonvalue added costs	Financial Results Profit Expense management Asset management Cash flow management	Financial Forecasts
	Departmental Expenses Purchasing Scheduling Manufacturing engineering Maintenance		

business unit.

Working capital is closely related to business activity. For example, as a business grows in sales volume, its accounts receivable should increase proportionately. The same situation occurs with costs of goods sold and inventory—provided inventory turnovers remain relatively constant. As inventories grow, so will accounts payable and expenses.

There usually is a normal relationship between the level of working capital and sales volume for every business. The idea of the ratio of working capital to sales, though not often emphasized, is a powerful one. Many companies have far too many resources invested in working capital and fail to manage it as aggressively as they should. By concentrating on this relationship, and emphasizing the importance of driving the relationship of working capital to sales down, working capital management can be improved.

In the changing manufacturing environment, fixed assets (property, plant, and equipment) also are increasing. In many companies, fixed assets have become significantly larger than working capital especially in companies that have done a good job of driving down working capital through such practices as just-in-time inventory management.

Working capital and property, plant, and equipment are the assets used by a business unit. Comparing the profitability of the unit to the assets employed gives a good immediate measure of performance. Return on assets employed, however, does have many limitations. Two of the most often cited are the tendency toward short-term results and the historical base that is used for accounting measures, which during inflationary periods will not reflect real economic performance. In such cases, inflation-adjusted statements can and should be prepared.

A *cash flow statement* should be prepared for each business unit. Many companies do not concern themselves as they should with unit cash flows. Consider the net income of a business unit adjusted for any noncash expenses, as cash from operations, then add or subtract from it any net changes from working capital or property, plant, and equipment. For growth businesses, additional working capital

Measuring product quality is a priority for many U.S. firms.

is usually required. Most businesses, except in their waning years, do exhibit a net increase in property, plant, and equipment. Operating cash flow is, however, a measure that is difficult to manipulate by accounting methods.

Each business unit should prepare a set of management-oriented financial statements with information about cost variability, asset management, and cash flows. Senior corporate management should get a quick and accurate understanding of the economic performance of each business unit.

Finally, the business unit management should submit to senior executives a financial forecast for the ensuing period and remainder of the year. This forecast should describe future income stream, asset requirements, and cash flows. A statement of why economic conditions are expected to change should be included so that the reader understands the relationship between the forecast and performance-to-date.

GOOD MANAGERS MADE BETTER

The new manufacturing environment demands an effective management reporting system. Too often, we have seen managers handed reports in a financial accounting format that contain too much data and detail. The reports fail to communicate and make it difficult for managers to evaluate, decide, and take action.

The creation of a management reporting system (Figure 2) that provides both operating and financial information, is tailored to the various levels of an organization, has more detail at the operations level, and is more summarized but still understandable and useful to senior executives is a challenge. But we urge management accountants to seize the opportunity and wean themselves from the classical budget versus actual and variance methodology. They should move toward an actual trend and continual improvement in the reporting orientation. ∎

Robert A. Howell, DBA, CMA, is clinical professor of management and accounting, New York University, and president of Howell Management Corp.

Stephen R. Soucy, MBA, CPA, is a consultant at Howell Management Corp.

"Management Reporting in the New Manufacturing Environment" *is the final article in a series of five articles on management accounting in the new manufacturing environment, published in* MANAGEMENT ACCOUNTING *and coauthored by Dr. Howell and Mr. Soucy.*

MEASURING PERFORMANCE IN AN ADVANCED MANUFACTURING ENVIRONMENT

Shrinking margins are triggering reactive decision making.

BY C.J. MCNAIR AND WILLIAM MOSCONI

Improvements in technology and procedures always have been associated with higher standards of living in the United States. The ability to innovate has been touted as one of our major strengths, and we have relied upon "Yankee ingenuity" to solve our problems and provide us with a competitive edge in the world marketplace.

It seems ironic, therefore, that our current lack of competitiveness is due in large part to technological improvements in manufacturing processes and procedures. Perhaps, as suggested by Richard J. Schonberger in *World Class Manufacturing: The Lessons of Simplicity Applied*, this turnabout can be traced to postwar complacency which turned the task of running a manufacturing enterprise into gentlemen's work. Manufacturing firms were no longer run by the experienced manager who had dedicated his career to a single entity, but rather by people two and three times removed from the manufacturing process, many of whom had never even stepped foot onto the manufacturing floor.

Today, the scene is changing. Once again, managers are beginning to manage their companies rather than just the numbers. Many are doing it to survive, others because they recognize they must adapt to the new manufacturing environment if they are to maintain their competitive edge. In order to achieve manufacturing excellence, though, companies must begin to proactively and intelligently incorporate advanced manufacturing techniques and performance measurement system changes into their strategic plans.

THE PATH TO MANUFACTURING EXCELLENCE

Advanced manufacturing technologies and process modifications are changing how companies do business, and are forcing companies to make complementary changes in their performance measurement systems. Organizations striving for manufacturing excellence and the attainment/maintenance of a competitive edge in the marketplace must proactively manage the change from traditional manufacturing and accounting techniques to those that support excellence, efficiency, and effectiveness in the new environment.

Manufacturing excellence arises from one basic goal—to provide the best product at the lowest price. The manufacturing objectives arising from this goal include high quality, low cost, and high customer responsiveness. A pursuit of excellence entails, therefore, high performance on more than one product attribute and is achieved by providing the customer with a product that surpasses all others in value and reliability.

The performance measurement system provides the first step on the path to manufacturing excellence. These measurements should capture the key elements in the manufacturing strategy, expose nonvalue-added costs to aid in their elimination, provide accurate and timely data on cost drivers, and serve as accurate records for product costing decisions. In sum, they should ensure attainment of company goals.

People, quality, delivery, and cost are the four critical success factors that need to be measured at every level of activity. Unfortunately, accountants traditionally have been myopic, focusing solely on cost and ignoring the "nonfinancial" critical success factors. Yet the companies accountants work in are multifaceted, needing more than cost information to survive.

In order to achieve manufacturing excellence, companies not only need high levels of performance on all four critical success factors. Their management accounting and control systems should include performance measurements on multiple aspects of the organization. Some criteria for evaluating management accounting and control systems in an advanced manufacturing environment are:

- Rapid feedback;
- Sensitivity to profit contribution of various activities and products;
- Flexible and migratory measurement systems;
- Holistic product costing and control measures;
- Identification, measurement, and elimination of nonvalue-added costs;
- Focus on variance reduction in such areas as quality, cycle time,

It is unclear whether the technology has actually changed the environment, or if it has served to amplify existing shortcomings.

and product complexity, (e.g., total parts);
- Reclassification of costs based on assignability and value-adding characteristics;
- Enhanced traceability of costs to specific products and processes to decrease allocations and their distortions.

These characteristics are an inherent part of a well functioning performance measurement system, and are intricately linked to the critical success factors. They provide the framework for designing a performance measurement hierarchy for integrating and coordinating activities in an organization. This hierarchy would be a set of interdependent subsystems of performance measurements designed to meet the operating objectives and information needs at the market, business, plant, and shop levels.

A performance measurement system should monitor changes in market demands, establish and evaluate progress toward business objectives, assure attainment of performance targets at the plant level, and serve as performance indicators on the manufacturing process itself.

A REVOLUTION

The original objective of our study was to examine only changes in cost accounting systems in a just-in-time (JIT) setting. However, it was soon recognized that the revolution and change taking place in the field went far beyond this level of analysis. JIT is just one step in a migration path of technologies leading toward manufacturing excellence. Therefore, we

expanded our study to capture the range of technologies and their impact on the management accounting and control system.

Five companies were studied—designated as Company A through Company E.

Company A is a $337 million enterprise involved in the design, manufacturing, and marketing of complex precision metal products and components for foreign and domestic industrial and consumer markets. The plant studied is part of the diesel systems division of the automotive products group.

Due to downturns in the domestic diesel market, Company A is facing a period of declining profits and sales. This situation has triggered the conversion to JIT work cells, as the company seeks to reduce costs and increase quality in order to survive.

In addition, it is using MRP II for scheduling, installing statistical process control throughout the plant, adopting a vendor certification program, and employing robotics and flexible manufacturing systems in isolated areas (e.g., are automating only where necessary). Within the management accounting and control systems specifically, local solutions are being used that have not been formally accepted or approved by corporate management.

Company B is a member of the electronics and telecommunication industry. The plant used in this study produces printers, keyboards, display terminals, and controllers. It provides nearly $200 million per year in revenues. A slowdown in the growth of the computer industry, as it moves into maturity, has created the need to control costs and standardize products. A JIT line was designed and partially installed in the Company B plant, in a true "factory-within-a-factory" setting, complete with performance measurement systems and incentives. Currently, MRP II is used plant-wide, the corporate vendor certification program is moving forward, and robotics are being employed at various locations throughout the plant.

Company C is a leader in the electronics industry. Two plants were visited during the course of this study; both produce PC components, such as tape drives, memory, and printers. The majority of the data collection was focused in the tape drive assembly plant, which has sales exceeding $170 million per year and employs over 800 workers. This site has the most highly developed JIT lines, as well as advanced MRP II systems, and has made significant changes in its management accounting and control systems.

As a result of the ability to measure the critical success factors and focus improvement in this manner, cycle time has been reduced from an average of 22 days to 1 day, overhead per unit has been decreased 30%, and a two-tiered overhead system has been devised to compensate for distortions inherent in using a direct labor base in a JIT setting. The objectives stated for Company C's control systems are simplicity and relevance.

Company D manufactures integrated circuits at the site we studied. It is currently changing its manufacturing processes over to a "focused factory" approach using work cells to replace traditional functional departments. To date, 29 cost blocks have been converted to 11 work cells. The primary objectives in this changeover are to decrease the cycle time by improving the linearity of production, reduce inventories, eliminate excess scrap, and improve product quality. The most significant change to the management accounting and control systems is the use of cycle time variances, the substitution of actual costs for standards, and the de-

---

The firms in our study have not determined how to quantify the qualitative benefits provided by advanced technologies.

---

velopment of an hourly rate for applying, evaluating, and controlling cell costs.

Company E is a large multinational producer of office equipment, computers, and related items. The site used in this study builds laptop computers for the domestic market using computer-integrated manufacturing (CIM). At this site, accounting measurement has become routinized and automated, which is best described as a "no-brainer" situation. The primary emphasis is on zero defect production, decreased cycle times, and the development of a "direct charging" accounting system designed to assign overhead costs directly to the products/processes creating them. The management accounting and control system is a complex, transaction intensive system focused on highlighting the value added to the fi-

nal product by each process and person.

WHAT WE FOUND

The majority of the companies that adopt advanced manufacturing technologies in their production processes are doing so on a limited basis as a means of responding to increasing competition and decreasing margins. Companies C and E appear to have a more integrated approach to technology adoption and are known for their proactive management styles and dedication to innovation. Even in these firms, the speed of adoption of such technologies suggests that shrinking margins are triggering reactive decision making.

Secondly, it appears that the changes in the management accounting and control systems are best described as "islands of accounting" that match the degree and type of automation used. It would appear that the progression in the management accounting and control system is mirroring the technology migration path.

Companies are recognizing that the existing system does not form a basis for adequate coordination and control in a modern environment. It is unclear from the data whether the technology has actually changed the environment or if it has instead served to amplify existing shortcomings.

Most of the firms we studied are

MEASUREMENTS USED BY TECHNOLOGY

COMPANY	BASIC CONTROL	MRP	JIT	CIM
A	Modified	Mature	None	Not Relevant
B	Traditional	Advanced	Pre-Pilot	Not Relevant
C	None	Essential (Evolved)	Advanced	Not Applicable
D	Traditional/Pre-Pilot	Immature	Pre-Pilot	Not Relevant
E	None	Evolved	Not Relevant	Complex/Transactions Intensive

adopting an actual cost system, although the abandonment of the traditional standard cost accounting system is not obvious. Given the costs of maintaining the information system, and the confusion created by the existence of multiple data sources, it seems likely that this multiplicity of measurements is only a temporary phenomenon.

The continuing demand by corporate controllers and management for the traditional standards-based reports hinders the adoption of innovative, and critically needed, changes in the accounting systems, such as the use of actual costs. Until top management becomes comfortable with the concept of an adaptive performance measurement system, it will be difficult for individual plants and divisions to adopt sweeping accounting reforms.

The use of JIT techniques does appear to be moving control closer to the point of production, and to be more clearly matching responsibility with controllability of costs. Company A has instituted a "checkbook" for cost control within the work center, which focuses solely on direct (e.g., traceable) costs for supervisor evaluation. Company A's internal reports are being revamped to isolate the overhead that is controllable only at the plant management level. These items are being reported as a lump sum figure in a contribution, margin-based reporting system. The responsibility for controlling these costs belongs to top management.

There is tremendous diversity in the level of acceptance of JIT and other advanced manufacturing techniques at the various sites. While all of the management personnel interviewed touted their JIT/CIM lines as revolutionary and leading edge, actual adoptions and change are quite rudimentary for the most part, and encompass only a small percentage of the companies' total productive capacity. Company C was the only firm to have a mature JIT environment.

Project justification remains an unsolved problem. Managers are adopting technology based primarily on intuition and faith. They are abandoning the traditional capital budgeting techniques where necessary, or if this cannot be done within the existing corporate structure, they are completing the necessary

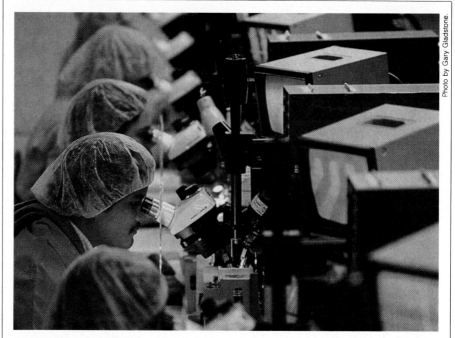

Manufacturing microchips.

forms using cash flows fabricated to meet investment criteria. It appears that, to date, the firms in our study have not determined how to quantify the qualitative benefits provided by these technologies.

SLOW AND CAUTIOUS

In summary, the progress made in advanced manufacturing technologies appears to be inconsistent and isolated within the organizations studied. Islands of technology characterize the majority of the production facilities examined. Notable exceptions also have been detailed, indicating that the statement, "JIT is a journey, not a technique," may be the most appropriate way to characterize the adoption process.

Although the MACS at each site is being modified, once again an "islands" portrayal is most accurate. We find this encouraging, rather than discouraging, in its implications for the future. Change is happening slowly and cautiously, but it is happening.

The most distressing finding is the reactive nature of the change process in most organizations. Theoretically, companies should proactively manage the adoption of technology and accounting system modifications based on the organization's strategic objectives.

In reality, however, accounting changes and technology adoptions

appear to be reactive. Firms facing declining profits are adopting technology in an attempt to regain viability in the marketplace, and the accounting system modifications, in all cases, are happening after the technology is already in place.

Proactive management suggests that changing measurements and incentives are critical for successful technology adoption. As the diffusion of technology accelerates, it will be necessary to more actively manage the process of change in the performance measurement/ management accounting system. The management accountant will need to expand his horizons, become an agent for organizational change, and assume a key position in the management of the firm. ∎

William Mosconi, CPA, CPIM, is in charge of the Manufacturing Applications practice of Coopers & Lybrand in the New York metropolitan region. His major consulting experience with C&L has been in high technology, electronics, computing, and telecommunications manufacturing.

C.J. McNair, Ph.D. is an assistant professor of accounting and MIS at the Pennsylvania State University. Her major research efforts have focused on the impact of technology on the management accounting system as well as the effects these accounting systems have on behavior in organizations.

OPERATING CONTROLS

in the New Manufacturing Environment

Antiquated operating measures promote inaccurate analysis, poor operating decisions, and inappropriate resource allocations.

BY ROBERT A. HOWELL AND STEPHEN R. SOUCY

Traditional operating control measures used to motivate, evaluate, and control yesterday's manufacturing operations are not applicable today. Given the contradictory operating objectives and conditions of the two manufacturing environments, one fundamentally unchanged set of operating measurements cannot yield the quality information needed to successfully manage today's operations.

The manufacturing transformation in many companies has been slowed, if not set back, as antiquated sets of operating performance yardsticks promote inaccurate analysis, poor operating decisions, and inappropriate resource allocations.

Management accountants need to understand that U.S. manufacturing is facing a revolution not unlike that of the standardization of manufacturing in the early 1900s. In that era, standard costs, variance analysis, labor efficiency, and overhead absorption measures were developed and maintained to

provide managers with operating data to manage the process.

Today, the focus of manufacturing has changed. Yet, many accounting departments have not updated their control mechanisms

Technician tests circuit board.

Editor's Note: "Operating Controls in the New Manufacturing Environment" is the third in a series of five articles on current cost management practice in automated manufacturing environments. The first two articles were published in July and August.

Inspecting turbine blades.

and processes. Operating controls need to reflect the concerns of new manufacturers. They need to be timely, accurate, and relevant. Many companies that are considered superior manufacturers and world class competitors have discarded or subordinated traditional performance measures, and replaced them with measures that reflect the new manufacturing environment. Issues such as quality, delivery, inventory, and machine performance are replacing measures of labor productivity, machine and capacity utilization, and standard cost variances. Many companies now employ a detailed cost-of-quality figure in their monthly reporting package as well as reporting statistical process control results, customer complaints, and other nonfinancial measures on a daily and weekly basis.

In response to the changing environment, many operating managers have begun to maintain their own PC-based controls. The challenge for management accountants is to get involved. They need to get into the factory in order to understand how it operates and how they can contribute to making their company a world class competitor. Accountants need to re-establish their role as a primary source of information within the organization. It is important that information be centrally maintained and readily available. The controller only can achieve this objective by taking a leadership role in the development and continual evolution of information disseminated for control and decision-making processes.

Five major nonfinancial areas of operating control for world class manufacturers are quality, delivery (including throughput and cycle time), inventory, material utilization/scrap, and machine availability/performance. Management accountants need to capture these factors in the control process. This calls for the integration of more nonfinancial and more subjectively determined measures into the traditional reporting and evaluation process. This also will require systems that are significantly more timely and flexible, in both reporting and analysis.

OPERATING MEASURES

There are several reasons why the development of operating measures has not kept pace with the changing manufacturing environment.

1. *Obsolete cost accounting systems are still the primary tool for measuring manufacturing performance.* Most manufacturers have cost accounting systems that have been used and relied upon for years. These systems have not been modified to reflect the changing manufacturing environment (see "Cost Accounting for the New Manufacturing Environment," *Management Accounting*, August 1987). Despite changes in manufacturing objectives, the greater variety of products and customers, and the increased level of automation and sophistication of the manufacturing process, these systems are still the basis for operating measures used to monitor manufacturing performance.

2. *Traditional measures are still the basis for evaluating manufacturing performance.* Companies continue to evaluate manufacturing performance on the basis of labor utilization, standard versus actual performance, and overhead absorption. In the new manufacturing environment, labor is less significant, more fixed and professional. A company that focuses on labor utilization drives managers to produce product, and create unnecessary inventory. Standard costing, therefore variance analysis, is no longer relevant because automation and statistical

process control results in a very reliable and consistent process. Variances cease to exist. Overhead is a more complex managerial issue as a result of increased product diversity, and higher levels of automation. Focusing on overhead absorption prompts managers to produce in advance of customer requirements. Today, the objective is not to absorb overhead, it is to minimize overhead.

3. *Managerial accountants have not been closely involved with operations.* The typical management accountant has little direct communication with operations. Accountants often are physically separated from the manufacturing operations, and the time spent sorting through miles of computer runs, tracking and reporting every dollar spent by every cost center, and the routine of monthly closing has encouraged this unintended alienation from operations.

It is tragic that as the manufacturing operations are changing, the management accountant is not there to observe, understand, and relate the changes to his role in the company. As a result, the effectiveness of today's cost-based measures has been significantly undermined.

QUALITY

High quality is clearly a major objective of world class manufacturers. Companies such as Ford, Hewlett-Packard, and Harley Davidson are recognizing that in order to continue to be competitive, a company must start by producing a quality product at a competitive cost.

Companies are addressing the issue of quality in three specific ways. First, they are dedicating the resources to design, plan, and build quality into the product instead of ensuring quality of the product via after-the-fact inspection. This objective requires coordination among the engineering, production, and service departments to design a product that can be produced at a high-quality level, a reasonable cost, and fulfill the needs of the customer. A company that fails to incorporate all three in the initial stages of the product development process is likely to realize produc-

COST OF QUALITY

The costs associated with quality of conformance generally can be classified into four types: prevention costs, appraisal costs, internal failure costs, and external failure costs. The prevention and appraisal costs occur because a lack of quality or conformance can exist. The internal and external failure costs occur because a lack or quality of conformance does exist.

- *Prevention costs* are associated with designing, implementing, and maintaining a quality system. These costs include engineering quality control systems, quality planning by various departments, and quality training programs.
- *Appraisal costs* are incurred to ensure that materials and products that fail to meet quality standards are identified prior to shipment. These costs include inspection of raw materials, laboratory tests, in-process and finished goods, quality audits, and field testing.
- *Internal failure costs* are associated with materials and result in manufacturing losses. They include the cost of scrap, repair, and rework of defective products.

Bob Howell (l.) with a Premix, Inc., manager readdressing the factory's operating control measures.

- *External failure costs* are incurred because inferior quality products are shipped to consumers. They include the costs of handling complaints, warranty replacement, and repairs of returned products and conceptually, lost sales.[1]

The management accountant needs to collect, analyze and report these costs and cost categories to management. Their significance must not be underestimated. The majority of companies we have been involved with have realized a cost of quality in the range of 20-30% of total cost. Numbers that get a lot of attention quickly. ∎

[1]Harold P. Roth and Wayne J. Morse, "Let's Help Measure and Report Quality Costs," *Management Accounting*, August 1983, p.50.

tion problems, excess inventory, and customer dissatisfaction.

Second, companies are emphasizing quality much earlier in the manufacturing process. Many companies are working with their vendors to ensure that manufacturing begins with high quality inputs. Some companies have established vendor certification programs and others inspect all incoming materials. The cost of inspecting all or most of the incoming materials may appear to be an inordinate expense, but if you consider that material is frequently the single largest cost category, any value added to the material along with the material itself is lost if the incoming part is bad.

While vendor quality is one important place to advance the control of quality, companies also are using statistical process controls

(SPC) and other in-process control checks to build in quality rather than waiting until the product is fully manufactured before subjecting it to final tests. In-process control mechanisms allow operating personnel to quickly isolate a quality problem, stop production, and resolve the issue before the problem results in significant scrap, rework, or other effects of poor quality.

The third approach to quality management is the shift in the responsibility for quality to the production function. In many businesses, production is evaluated solely on its ability to produce. Quality, while not disregarded, is not their directive. It is the job of quality control to prevent rejects from being shipped, without regard for meeting production targets. If production is held responsible for quality management and accountable

for producing quality products, the focus shifts from gross output to quality output. The issue of whose job it is to produce quality products becomes irrelevant–everyone is responsible.

While a handful of companies have made significant progress in the quality effort, to date the measurement of quality, which is essential to making and maintaining improvements, has not evolved as rapidly as some of the more conceptual and strategic initiatives.

Successful monitoring of quality assumes that the necessary data are available, which is not always true. Without specific and timely information on defects and field failures, improvements in quality are seldom possible. Not surprisingly, information on defects and field failures at the poorest managed companies is virtually nonexistent, and assembly-line defects and service call rates are seldom reported. "Epidemic" failures (problems that a large proportion of all units had in common) are frequent. Design flaws remain undetected. At one domestic producer, nearly a quarter of all 1979-81 warranty expenses came from problems with a single type of compressor.[1]

The management accountant can have a meaningful role in developing quality measures and implementing their use. Principal focus areas:

■ Customer Acceptance,
■ In-Processing Audit,
■ Vendor Quality/ Incoming Inspection, and
■ Cost of Nonconformance.

Customer acceptance may be measured in terms of numbers of customer complaints. The measurement system should include procedures to follow up sales and gain assurance that the customer is satisfied. Some companies are keeping track of the number of customer complaints they receive in evaluating the success of their quality program. Other companies survey their customers on a regular basis to get feedback in addition to customer complaints. This provides a customer satisfaction index that can indicate the existence of quality problems before they reach the bottom line. Other objective measures of quality include field service expenses, warranty claims, and returns and allowances.

The second major source of quality measurement encompasses the wide range of in-process quality controls. Quality audit programs enable a company to randomly measure quality at specific points in the manufacturing process to ascertain conformance to the specified quality levels. Obviously, the degree to which companies have in-process controls is influenced by the extent of the quality audit program. Many companies, however, have literally hundreds of control points at which they are now measuring. At any of these points production can be stopped until the problem is resolved.

The third major area of quality measurement involves vendors and incoming materials. Many companies have developed systems that rate their suppliers on the basis of quality as well as delivery and price. These systems get quite elaborate but are intended to have the vendor assume the responsibility for delivering products within specification. Those companies that have not reached the point of formalizing their vendor inspection process, but are still very conscious of the importance of incoming materials, have increased their incoming material inspection–sometimes up to 100%.

The cost of nonconformance, the last area of measurement, represents the aggregation of all the explicit costs that are attributable to producing a nonquality product. Cost of nonconformance is a comprehensive, company-wide, financial score card for quality. It attempts to capture all quality related costs, not just those that pertain to a specific product or process. It also puts a dollar value on what is most often thought of as an operating performance measure. Many researchers and practitioners have developed a conceptual framework and an itemized list defining the cost of nonconformance. (See "Cost of Quality" p. 27.)

> *Too few managers realize or appreciate the dollars lost to scrap on an annual basis.*

The need for measuring and controlling quality, both on an operational and financial basis, is great and affords the management accountant the opportunity to be centrally involved with probably the most important objective of American businesses today.

DELIVERY

A second major operating measurement is delivery performance. The objective is to establish and maintain process consistency and reliability, allowing marketing to quote accurate delivery schedules. Once consistency and reliability are established, then speed or throughput should be emphasized.

World class manufacturers are establishing targets of 100% on-time delivery and 100% orders filled. They are rearranging the factory in order to increase throughput and reduce cycle times. Manufacturers also are focusing on set-up times and making quick changeovers, characteristics normally associated with Japanese manufacturers.

Among the measures of delivery performance is the on-time delivery performance record. This, of course, necessitates establishing delivery due dates against which actual delivery can be measured. Targets must be realistic "as soon as possible" and "yesterday" are inappropriate, and operations must document and monitor the reasons behind the delay.

Percentage of orders filled may be measured according to dollars of orders filled, line items, or specific number of items–whichever is considered most effective.

The third major delivery measure is the *length of time, or cycle time*, required from the placing of an order by a customer to shipment. Some companies have gone from cycle times of six and seven months to five or six weeks as a result of focusing on this measure and making the necessary changes to accomplish improvements. The cycle time also can be segregated into greater detail, such as purchase order lead time and production cycle time. Purchase order lead time is the time it takes to provide manufacturing with the resources needed to begin production. Production cycle time is the time it takes to make the product available for shipment from the dispensation of material to the production floor. The myriad of available "clocks" enable management to focus on where value is being detained and what potential opportunities exist for greater efficiency.

INVENTORY

Historically, inventory control has primarily focused on the accuracy of the aggregate inventory balance to avoid unfavorable year-end adjustments. Inventory turnover measures and, to some extent, the detailed record keeping of specific part/product inventories have been secondary concerns.

World class manufacturers are discovering that the cost of holding inventory greatly exceeds the traditional cost definition—average inventory times cost of capital. Benefits such as reduced off-site and on-site storage requirements, material inspection and handling costs, and obsolescence—a much greater risk today due to shorter product life cycles—provide a significant opportunity for cost reduction. Improved product flows (efficiency), cleaner facilities, and quicker identification of quality problems also are benefits of reducing the levels of raw material, work-in-process, and finished good inventory.

The objectives of inventory management in many world class manufacturers is no longer to optimize the inventory level as defined by the economic order quantity model—but to minimize the inventory. For example, one manufacturer has reduced the space allotted to inventories from two-thirds of one facility to 15% of a facility half the former size. Another manufacturer achieved 100 times inventory turnover.

From an operating standpoint, the best way to attack the inventory problem is the traditional "divide and conquer" approach. Detailed recording and control of inventory by part/product and location is a necessity in order to focus management attention on where the inventory problems lie. A number of companies admit they can not control their inventory because they do not know what or where it is. Breaking down the aggregate inventory balance into part/product detail also allows management to directly associate the level of inventory and inventory-related costs with a particular product line. With operating measures such as absolute balances and turnover rates by the breakdowns available to management, serious attention can be dedicated to eliminating inventory.

Inventory reduction is a key operating as well as a financial objective in the new manufacturing environment. The solution requires input from all areas of an organization. To decrease finished goods turnover, greater communication

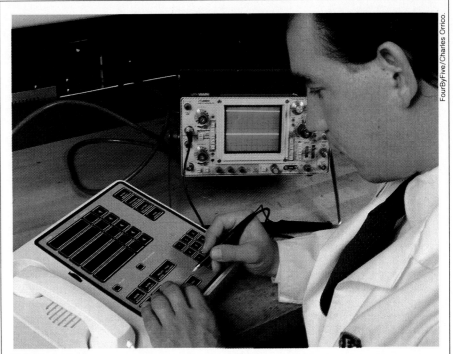

Telephone tester.

between sales and manufacturing is required. To reduce raw material and work-in-process inventory, management must address the problems that underlie the existing inventory balances such as unreliable vendors, engineering change notices, schedule changes, equipment breakdowns, and quality problems—all of which require a company to maintain excessive inventory balances.

In the U.S., inventory always has been thought of as a necessary evil. Smart domestic and overseas manufacturers that successfully analyze and control what causes inventory find that it no longer is necessary—it's just an evil.

MATERIAL COST/ SCRAP CONTROL

One area of common ground between the new and old manufacturing environments is the significance of material in manufacturing costs. In many companies, material cost control is the function of the purchasing department. By motivating purchasing through purchase price variances, management seeks to keep material costs at a minimum. In other organizations, the issue of material cost control has taken on a whole new dimension. Purchasing decisions are not made on the

basis of lowest cost, but on specific guidelines that include quality and delivery as well as cost. Besides being the single most significant cost, material, along with certain operating expenses such as power and supplies, is the primary variable cost in the new factory. By not controlling total material cost, managements fail to take full advantage of the operating leverage associated with the highly automated factory.

An important, but frequently ignored, aspect of total material cost is scrap. In many manufacturers, scrap is included in the standard cost of the product. A company with sales of $1 billion, cost of materials of $300 million, and a standard scrap rate of 5% would lose $15 million per year in scrap. Given that a billion-dollar business might have a 5% after-tax profit, or $50 million, the $15 million worth of scrap is very significant. Yet many accounting systems bury scrap in the standard cost, providing only variances from standard for management review and analysis. World class manufacturers are recognizing that scrap is a significant cost, and are segregating the full expense on department, plant, division, and corporate management reports. Too few managers realize or appreciate the dollars lost to scrap on an annual basis.

Scrap, other than a pure financial loss, also has a great impact on the operating efficiency of a plant. Machine and labor time spent on producing items scrapped obviously is lost, but the disruption to the process also causes operating inefficiencies such as downtime, rework and schedule adjustments (to replace the scrapped product).

As with inventory, the way to monitor scrap is through detailed reporting that quantifies total scrap losses by product and by operation. Isolating the cause of scrap is the first step. The way to manage scrap is to identify when it occurs, where, and why–then do something about it.

An appropriate measure of scrap is the percentage of scrap to good pieces. In some process businesses, the measure can be the relationship of output yield to input re-sources. Some companies actually set up scrap reclamation areas where all scrap, whatever its cause, are sent for review and disposition. Other companies establish very short review periods with the requirement that all material dispositions be made within 72 hours of their incurrence. While scrap is certainly a problem, it is also an opportunity. Many Japanese companies profess to cherish scrap because it provides an opportunity to improve the process.

Ironically, if the new manufacturing environment really means high incoming quality and tight in–process control, then you would expect that scrap would be at a minimum. That is the ultimate goal and, in fact, some world class manufacturers have set zero scrap as their objective. That means no scrap allowances. Until a manufacturer gets there, however, the measurement of scrap is critical.

MACHINE MANAGEMENT AND MAINTENANCE

A major trend in the new manufacturing environment is increased automation. Considering that single pieces of equipment can cost $1 million and flexible manufacturing systems $20 to $25 million, companies are realizing a higher proportion of investment and product cost represented by capital equipment. This obviously places increased importance on the management and maintenance of this resource.

The first step in evaluating and controlling the investment and performance of equipment is by understanding the relative capacities of the various pieces of equipment. Many companies distinguish between bottleneck and nonbottleneck operations in an attempt to single out those pieces of equipment that are most critical to plant capacity. If capacity can be increased at a bottleneck operation, total output can be increased. The relevant measure with regard to a bottleneck is its use. If the equipment limits the total output of the plant, it is expected that the equipment will be 100% used, excluding maintenance downtime. This is not a relevant measure for nonbottleneck operations. All you really want to do with nonbottlenecks is to use them to the extent that it is necessary to support production through the bottleneck operations. To produce goods at any higher rate would only build inventories.

A critical measure of equipment performance is equipment availability or its inverse, downtime. The issue really is availability. Equipment must be ready at all times when it is needed. It should not be down for repairs. However, downtime when it is not needed, is irrelevant. Therefore, it should not be considered an example of poor machine management. The whole area of the measurement of equipment availability, or readiness to serve, and downtime when it is needed and not ready, is an important area of inquiry and measurement for the management accountant.

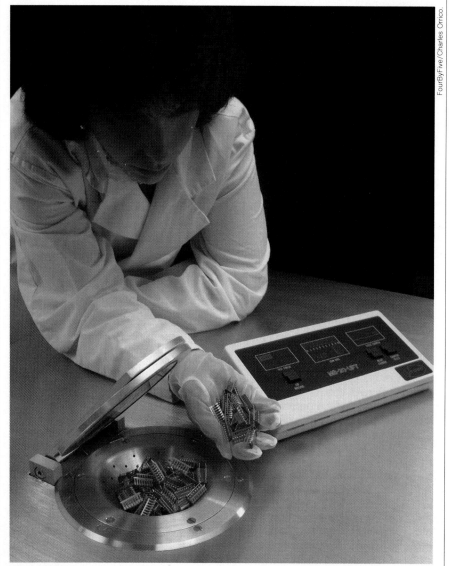

I.C. chip test.

The last area of measurement pertaining to machines is the development of historical records of machine maintenance. It's similar to keeping records on an automobile–how frequent the automobile is oiled, the spark plugs and filters changed, tires rotated and the engine thoroughly checked to ensure that it is capable of running properly and efficiently. With these records, managers are in a much better position to ascertain the availability of the equipment and the appropriateness of replacing it. Also, with highly disciplined machine maintenance programs, companies are realizing higher quality and greater consistency from their manufacturing process.

MEASURES OF THE NEW MANUFACTURING ENVIRONMENT

Quality, delivery, inventory, material cost and scrap, and machine performance are very important areas of operating performance in the new manufacturing environment (See Table 1).

Quality and delivery, at a reasonable price, are what the customer ultimately is seeking. To measure performance, thereby motivating management decisions, along those dimensions will ensure a continuing stream of customers. These measures relate the business to the customer, a liaison that must be stressed continually.

Low inventories, material cost, and minimal scrap are primary measures of the manufacturing performance of a business. These measures reflect directly on the efficiency of the manufacturing process. The company that has low inventories, material cost, and scrap rates is on its way toward becoming a lowest cost, and therefore most productive, manufacturer.

The focus on equipment performance recognizes the increasing investment in fixed assets that would support a more equipment intensive manufacturing environment. Assuring that it is utilized, is available when required, and is carefully maintained to minimize its lifetime costs will go a long way toward minimizing total manufacturing costs.

As new measures are developed, traditional measures of performance—direct labor productivity,

---

TABLE 1/
OPERATING MEASURES IN THE NEW MANUFACTURING ENVIRONMENT

Quality

Customer complaints
Customer surveys
Warranty claims
Quality audits
Vendor quality
Cost of quality
   Scrap
   Rework
   Returns and allowances
   Field service
   Warranty claims
   Lost business

Inventory

Turnover rates by location
   Raw materials
   Work-in-process
   Finished goods
   Composite
Turnover rates by product
Cycle count accuracy
Space reduction
Number of inventoried items

Material/Scrap

Quality—incoming material inspection
Material cost as a percentage of total cost
Actual scrap loss
Scrap by part/product/operation
Scrap percentage of total cost

Equipment/Maintenance

Equipment capacity/utilization
Availability/downtime
Machine maintenance
Equipment experience

Delivery/Throughput

On-time delivery
Order fill rate
Lead time—order to shipment
Waste time—lead time less process time
Cycle time—material receipt to product shipment
Set-up time
Production backlog (in total and by product)

---

standard versus actual performance, and overhead absorption—are de-emphasized.

As labor diminishes, it becomes less critical to manage from a cost perspective and more critical to view it as a resource. As automation increases the consistency and reliability of manufacturing performance, operating variability disappears. Overhead absorption is no longer the issue. The issue is to use the fixed costs efficiently. That is not accomplished by building inventory and attaching overhead costs to the product rather by using the operating measures we have described to monitor and control overhead costs in the absolute. ∎

Robert A. Howell, DBA, CMA, is president of Howell Management Corp. and professor at New York University.

Stephen R. Soucy, MBA, CPA, is a consultant at Howell Management Corp. Dr. Howell and Mr. Soucy are two of the authors of the NAA Bold Step research study Management Accounting in the New Manufacturing Environment.

---

[1]David A. Garvin, "Quality On The Line" *Harvard Business Review,* September-October 1983.

Section 8

Implications: Investment Management

The concluding section reviews the changes needed in cost accounting information to support investment management in the new manufacturing environment. The final article also summarizes the existing product costing, performance measurement, and capital investment practices of world-class American manufacturers.

Robert A. Howell and Stephen R. Soucy again provide their perspective on the new environment; this article focuses on the capital investment decision. They believe management accountants will need to reassess the entire capital budgeting process. The authors say the discounted cash flow model will remain relevant but that the nature of the inputs used in the model will change. They see three reasons for these necessary changes: investments becoming more significant; equipment becoming more technically and operationally complex; and cash returns occurring over a longer time period. They depict investments in the new manufacturing environment as more expensive, longer term, riskier, and of greater intangible benefit.

Howell and Soucy provide examples of investments at three different levels of scale—robots, flexible manufacturing systems, and greenfield factories. A table indicates the kinds of direct, indirect, and intangible returns associated with each, and a figure demonstrates how the level of scale interacts with payback periods and uncertainty of cash flows. The authors discuss three concepts that will take on increased importance in the new environment—terminal values, moving baselines, and post-investment audits. They close by describing the future role of the management accountant as more analytical and communicative, more understanding of operating characteristics and benefits, and more willing to gather information from outside the existing cost accounting system.

James Brimson examines current depreciation methods and technology cost, defined as plant and equipment and information systems. He uses an example to illustrate how technology cost currently is buried in overhead and to explain

six reasons for reconsidering depreciation methods: depreciation should reflect relationships between assets and the manufacturing process; the economic magnitude of technology cost is significant; production-based methods are more appropriate than time-based methods; estimates derived from realistic cost behavior patterns are preferable for controlling operations; cost basis does not reflect the economic value of technology; and conservatism encourages expensing rather than amortizing start-up costs.

Brimson feels that technology cost should be treated as a direct cost just as materials and labor are and cites five reasons for doing so: technology is a significant component of manufacturing cost; technology change is more rapid than physical obsolescence; cost behavior patterns are different in a computer-controlled environment; technology is involved directly in the conversion process; and automation reduces the cost of collecting the required data. Brimson says the goal of a technology accounting system is to assign capital investment costs more accurately to the products that benefit from them.

The final article, by James A. Hendricks, examines the existing cost accounting practices of a sample of world-class American manufacturing companies. In early 1988 he surveyed Fortune 500 industrial firms likely to have substantial amounts of factory automation. The questionnaire, which attained a 51% response rate, obtained data on types of factory automation, capital investment justification, product costing procedures, and operating performance measures. The article provides several figures that summarize the major findings.

Hendricks indicates these needed changes in cost accounting practice: in investment justification, expanded use of DCF techniques utilizing realistic hurdle rates and risk analysis, with better quantification of intangible benefits; in product costing, use of departmental or work cell overhead rates and multiple overhead bases using machine-based rates; in performance measurement, focus on quality, material control, delivery, inventory, and machine performance.

Hendricks found most changes reported in his survey had occurred in the previous three to five years. He concluded that although progress is slow, respondents are aware of the changes occurring in the new manufacturing environment and are studying the issues and planning to make appropriate changes.

Additional Readings from *Management Accounting*

Bennett, Robert E. and James A. Hendricks, "Justifying the Acquisition of Automated Equipment," July 1987, pp. 39-46.

Michaels, Lawrence T., "A Control Framework for Factory Automation," May 1988, pp. 37-42.

Pipkin, Al, "The 21st Century Controller," February 1989, pp. 21-25.

Seed, Allen H., III, "Improving Cost Management," February 1990, pp. 27-30.

Sullivan, William G. and James M. Reeve, "XVENTURE: Expert Systems to the Rescue," October 1988, pp. 51-58.

CAPITAL INVESTMENT IN THE NEW MANUFACTURING ENVIRONMENT

BY ROBERT A. HOWELL AND
STEPHEN R. SOUCY

Management accountants: Don't rely exclusively on traditional cost systems to justify investments.

Automation is probably the most evident change in the new manufacturing environment. The objective of automation, besides adding capacity, is to produce high quality goods consistently, quickly, and economically. Effective use of automation can leverage the success achieved through more fundamental efforts aimed at achieving higher quality, lower inventory, streamlined production flow lines, simplified processes, and other major trends in the factory. Thus, automation can enhance the overall competitiveness of a company.

In spite of the obvious advantages of investing in automation, issues central to the investment decision have changed dramatically over the past 20 years. The new manufacturing environment presents new issues of scope, timing, and uncertainty that require management accountants to reassess

Automated final assembly and test module at IBM Lexington.

the whole capital budgeting process.

Although automation often is viewed as a "cure-all" for competitive deficiencies, this view is incorrect. The key to effective and successful automation is to first analyze, understand, and if necessary, redesign and simplify the manufacturing process. Many companies are achieving significant benefits, without significantly automating, by simply rearranging the plant floor, eliminating nonvalue activities such as inventory storage and material handling, and establishing more streamlined and flexible process flows. Once the effort to simplify and improve the process is complete, automation can leverage the benefits by performing the operations faster, more reliably, and within tighter tolerances. While automation is not the cure-all, wise investment in automated equipment, systems, production lines and factories is an integral part of any effort to achieve and maintain a competitive advantage.

THE INVESTMENT DECISION

The investment decision evaluates whether an investment's returns exceed its costs. While the issue of returns versus costs is still the fundamental question, the nature and risks associated with those investments has changed dramatically in the new manufacturing environment.

First, investments are becoming more significant. Stand-alone pieces of equipment, such as robots and computerized numerical control machines, can sell for up to $1 million. Flexible manufacturing systems—a machine or group of machines linked together to perform a series of operations automatically for one or more product lines such as Allen-Bradley's "factory within a factory" world contactor facility–can cost anywhere from $10 to $50 million. Investments in fully automated factories, such as the IBM Proprinter facility, can cost more than $100 million.

Second, the equipment involved is more complex, technically and operationally, than traditional pieces of equipment. The benefits associated with advanced automation are more indirect and intangible. Where emphasis in the 1950s

The key to successful automation is to first analyze, understand, and, if necessary, redesign and simplify the manufacturing process.

was direct cost savings, today investments are designed to improve quality, delivery, and customer satisfaction. This new focus requires that management accountants devise new models and methodologies to capture these benefits to establish the value contributed by the investment.

Finally, the cash returns required to justify the investment are received over a longer period of time because of the high investment cost. It is critical to establish the nature, amount, and timing of future after-tax cash flows in order to arrive at an accurate estimate of the discounted cash value. As we have described, investments in advanced automation are more expensive, longer term, and more risky. This new environment requires management to place more attention, understanding, and control over the investment justification process.

THE CAPITAL INVESTMENT MODEL

We assert that the basic capital budgeting model—discounted cash flow value analysis—is still the appropriate tool to analyze capital investments in the new manufacturing environment. However, what needs to be reconsidered by management accountants are the inputs used in the analysis: investments, operating cash flows, terminal value, and the discount rate. The nature of these inputs has changed dramatically in the new manufacturing environment.

Investments today are larger, more complex, and require a longer implementation period than traditional capital investments. General Motors' Saturn project, initially proclaimed as "the key to GM's long-term competitiveness," was expected to require five years before it was ready for production. On a smaller scale, Allen-Bradley took two years to implement fully its "factory within a factory" world contactor facility.

Also, investments no longer can be considered "givens" in the capital budgeting model. Much of the cost of the investment is in engineering, software development, and implementation. Allen-Bradley's capital investment in its world contactor facility was $8 million, yet its overall cost was $15 million. The Saturn project at GM was originally slated to cost $5 billion to produce 400,000 cars per year. Today, the projected cost is $1.7 billion for the "first phase" for a production volume of 250,000 cars.

Longer-term horizons, intangible benefits, and greater uncertainty also are characteristics of the cash flows from advanced automation. These factors create an even more difficult assignment for the management accountant.

Traditional investment analysis focused primarily on immediate direct benefits from labor, scrap, inventory, and capacity. Such was the case because these benefits were, in fact, the primary and significant values derived from capital investments. Intangible benefits were not material and therefore did not warrant analysis or consideration.

Today, the situation is significantly different. The principal objectives and benefits of many capital investments are quality, delivery, throughput, and flexibility, as well as cost. Thus, while direct savings such as labor, scrap, and inventory may be reduced, much of the value resulting from automation remains uncovered if only the direct savings are considered.

TYPES OF INVESTMENTS AND RETURNS

Table 1 distinguishes several types of investments and returns that characterize the

CAPITAL INVESTMENT ANALYSIS

Investments	Robot	FMS	Factory
	Plant & Equipment	Plant & Equipment	Plant & Equipment Working Capital Operating Losses
Returns			
Direct	Labor Scrap	Labor Scrap Inventory	Labor Scrap Inventory
Indirect		Support Functions: Purchasing/Scheduling/ Handling/Maintenance/ Quality Control	
Intangibles		Quality Delivery	Quality Delivery Throughput Flexibility A Competitive Advantage

new manufacturing environment. At the base level are the smaller, individual pieces of equipment, such as computer-aided design, computer-aided engineering, numerically controlled machines, and robots, which are generally justified on the basis of direct cost savings. For example, if a robot replaces a worker on a paint line, the worker's wages and benefits, and the reduction in scrap pieces resulting from worker error can be calculated and compared with the cost of the robot to determine the net present value of the investment. It may be unnecessary to consider intangible benefits such as the quality, reliability, consistency, and the flexibility of the equipment.

A second level of investment in advanced automated equipment is the flexible manufacturing system (FMS). The direct benefits of labor savings and scrap reduction may be insufficient to justify the magnitude of investment in flexible manufacturing systems. However, there are considerable indirect savings and intangible benefits that need to be recognized and incorporated into the analysis.

When the larger investment reduces the number of direct labor employees and their associated expenses, there will be implications of that reduced labor force on such support areas as personnel and payroll. When the automated

equipment reduces the level of scrap, purchasing, production scheduling, and inventory control requirements will be favorably impacted. When computer-controlled equipment allows for quick changeovers, support functions that formerly spent a considerable amount of time executing setups will no longer be necessary. If, in fact, the equipment is more reliable so that it provides greater throughput and faster setups, there are significant implications for the level of inventory that must be maintained.

As companies consider invest-

ments in larger, more integrated systems, the analysis must reach beyond the traditional cost savings to the multitude of more qualitative, expense and revenue categories affected. All investments may contribute, in varying degrees, to such intangible benefits as flexibility, reliability, delivery, and quality of manufacturing, but the contribution currently is missed in many capital budgeting analyses.

The broadest category of investment in the new manufacturing environment is the "greenfield" factory. This is the situation where a company decides that to be competitive it must completely change the way it manufactures, resulting in a new factory designed and built from scratch. An investment of such scope is clearly strategic.

The impact on direct material and labor, indirect support activities, and inventories must be estimated, but, again, will not be sufficient to justify the investment. The reason a company makes such an investment is because it provides a clear competitive advantage. It was that logic that prompted IBM to build a new facility to produce the Proprinter. The new plant produces a computer printer as efficiently, inexpensively, and with as high reliability as any other product of its kind in the industry.

GE decided to rebuild its Appliance Park in Kentucky to stay ahead of its competition in terms of cost and quality. In the case of these large investments, intangible benefits, primarily impacting reve-

FIGURE 1/CAPITAL INVESTMENT ANALYSIS DISCOUNTED CASH FLOW MODEL

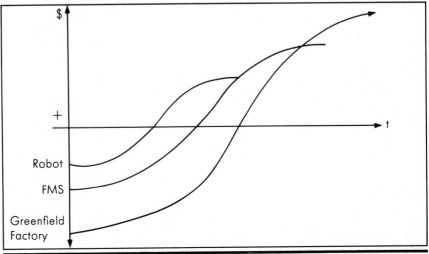

nues, must be brought into account.

This experience suggests that as a company moves from smaller, less sophisticated, and less costly investments the criteria that is used to justify investments will change. Although, it is appropriate to assess the indirect and intangible benefits associated with smaller and less expensive investments. Many companies have recognized that there are one or two critical operations in the manufacturing process such that if one NCC machine or robot could perform the operation within tighter tolerances and with greater reliability, the value added would be principally in the quality and reliability the machine allows rather than the one or two people it displaces. Thus, for any significant investment, all of the elements of direct and indirect savings, and tangible and intangible benefits, must be identified and considered.

Figure 1 demonstrates the three types of investment in the context of the basic capital budgeting model. As one moves along the scale of investments, the cash outlays are larger, the payback periods are longer, the investments typically rely on more indirect and intangible benefits and there is a higher level of uncertainty with the cash flows. It is important for management accountants to take these issues into consideration when applying capital budgeting techniques to investments in automated equipment.

In a study commissioned by the National Association of Accountants (NAA) and Computer Aided Manufacturing-International (CAM-I), the researchers found that the majority of manufacturers use an unadjusted payback period of between two and four years when evaluating advanced manufacturing equipment.[1] This constraint, given the long-term characteristics of advanced automation and the inability of many manufacturers to accurately establish and quantify the benefits of advanced automation, often undermines such investments.

TERMINAL VALUE

An important element of the investment justification process is the determination of the in-

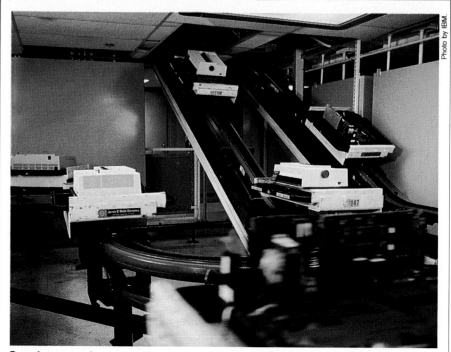

Proprinters moving on overhead conveyor lines at IBM's automated plant.

vestment's terminal value, which is defined as the cash value at the end of its useful life or the analysis period used in the capital budgeting model. The terminal value often can be the swing number in the investment decision. The terminal value requires management accountants to forecast technological, economic, operational, strategic, and market developments over the investment's life in order to make a reasonable estimate of its potential value. Thus, the uncertainty accorded operating cash flows is magnified when applied to terminal values.

Managers have been known to exclude or excessively discount the terminal value of an investment in the capital budgeting analysis due to the level of uncertainty accorded its return. While terminal value is a function of many independent issues, to ignore the benefit is incorrect.

To address the issue of uncertainty for investments, cash flows, terminal values, and discount rates (below), management accountants need to expand the use of probability and sensitivity analysis in the investment justification process. Input from customer service, sales, distribution, marketing, manufacturing, purchasing, and engineering, as well as finance, must be incorporated when establishing the projected cash flows.

Traditionally, if a potential benefit could not be reasonably estimated then no value was given. Of course, no value is the value zero and by taking a "proper and conservative" approach to such analyses, many companies forego significant investment opportunities. Preparers and evaluators of capital investment proposals must recognize the necessity for making reasonable, subjective determinations when assessing the costs and contributions of an investment. Management must then evaluate the sensitivity of the results to changes in significant inputs. This provides management with some degree of confidence that even if a critical assumption is incorrect by a certain percentage, the decision to make the investment would not change.

The final aspect of the capital investment analysis is the discount or hurdle rate. Its determination is not directly impacted by changes in the new manufacturing environment. However, due to the longer-term orientation of the cash flows from advanced automated equipment, the impact of the discount rate on the decision to invest is greater.

In the survey conducted by the NAA, 36% of the manufacturers reported using discount rates between 13% and 17% and more than 30% used discount rates over 19%.

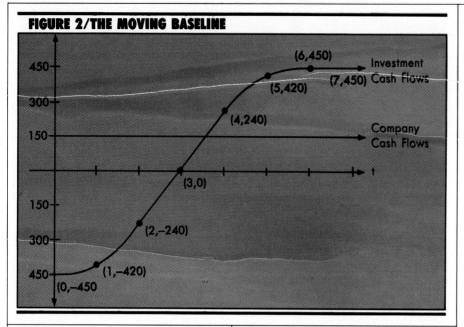

FIGURE 2/THE MOVING BASELINE

This practice occurred at a time when the prime rate was 8% and a reasonable estimate of the cost of capital for most companies would be between 10% and 12%. The significance is that if companies use incorrect or artificially high discount rates, investments with longer paybacks and higher terminal values stand a lesser chance of being accepted than short-term oriented projects.

Thus, the nature, timing, and level of certainty associated with the cash flows from advanced automation result in a dramatically different set of input issues and decisions for the capital investment analyst.

THE MOVING BASELINE CONCEPT

A very critical issue manufacturers need to address is: if the capital investment analysis indicates that the investment in advanced automation is not justified, what is the impact of not making the investment? The idea of a "moving baseline" addresses that question.

The premise is that companies require an investment to show value against the company's current operating position. If a company generates a cash flow of $150,000 annually, an investment must create value by improving the current operating position in order to justify the capital outlay. Such a premise assumes that the current operating position of the company

will remain relatively constant, or status quo, if the investment is not undertaken.

But experience indicates that is not the case and, depending upon an industry's characteristics, not investing in the most technologically advanced equipment may result in losing the company's competitive position—the inability to meet quality, delivery, or cost characteristics of its competitors.

In Figure 2 we assume that the initial investment will cost $450 thousand in year 1 and requires approximately $1 million before it reaches the cash flow breakeven level in year 3. It is important to note that the cash flows projected in Figure 2 represent the incremental cash flows generated by the investment, given current operating conditions. Thus, if the investment

Investment audits serve as an important control mechanism over the cash flows associated with investments in advanced automation.

reduces labor costs by 5%, improves quality by 15%, and throughput by 10% over existing operating conditions, those are the benefits that go into the determination of the overall return. Under such an example, the present value of the cash flows are equal in year 7, and any additional return provides a positive net present value or an internal rate of return greater than the cost of capital.

Now, as stated above, one of the assumptions is that the cash flows are contingent upon the current operating condition of the company being maintained over the life of the investment. Suppose the company does not invest in advanced equipment and its competitors do. There are two possibilities: not investing does not change the competitive balance within the industry and the company can expect to maintain its current operating condition; or not investing alters the competitive position within the industry.

Under the second scenario, the company's cost and/or quality are now out of line with the competition and, as a result, the company loses ground and, assuming no reaction to the change in conditions, becomes increasingly noncompetitive.

This situation is depicted in Figure 3. It assumes that the competition will invest regardless of the company's decision. Under these conditions, if the company invests, it will maintain its operating cash flow of $150 thousand. If the company does not invest, operating cash flows will decrease. In this example, company cash flows turn negative after year 2 and raise serious questions of viability. This is the "moving baseline."

If the company does not invest in available technology its competitiveness and, therefore, profitability will be adversely affected. It is unreasonable and inconsistent to evaluate the capital investment against the status quo. The baseline against which the cash flows need to be evaluated is the "no investment" line.

Figure 3 reflects the impact of the moving baseline on the company as a whole and not the investment in particular. To calculate the impact on the investment remember that: a) the investment cash flows are projected based on the incremental benefits over the status quo, assumed constant over the life of the asset, and b) if the company invests in the equipment it will maintain the cash inflow of $150 thousand (this does not have to equal the cash flows under the status quo assumption). The difference between the cash flows assuming investment: $150 thousand in year 1 through 7, and the cash flows assuming no investment: $75 thousand in year 1, $0 in year 2, ($75) in year 3, etc., reflect the additional benefit of investing in the automated equipment. Thus, the incremental benefit not projected under the original model would be $75 thousand in year 1, $150 thousand in year 2, $225 thousand in year 3, etc. The impact on the investment cash flows is shown in Figure 4.

While the original assumptions resulted in a positive cash flow in year 3 and a positive net present value after year 7, the new assumptions, taking into consideration the moving baseline, reflect a positive cash flow just after year 2 and a positive net present value between years 4 and 5. This outcome results in both a faster payback and a greater net present value than projected under the traditional capital investment model.

Of course, companies should continually question the long-term viability of a business and whether they should continue to invest capital and management effort in the business. While this model focuses on the value of the equipment assuming the decision to stay in the business, if a company wishes to analyze a significant investment without this assumption, the model can be quickly adapted. Companies that fail to consider the implications of the "no investment" alternative characteristically underestimate the potential value added of investments that serve to maintain the company's competitiveness and thereby overall profitability.

POST-INVESTMENT AUDITS

Larger, longer-term, and more uncertain returns heighten the importance of conducting post-investment audits. These audits serve as an important control mechanism over the cash flows associated with investments in ad-

vanced automation. In the study: *Management Accounting in the New Manufacturing Environment*, the National Association of Accountants reported that more than 65% of the survey respondents did not perform post-investment audits or performed audits only on selected investments in advanced manu-

facturing technology. We see this is clearly as an area where companies can improve. While an audit will have no direct impact on any investment decision, there are a number of substantive indirect benefits that warrant the effort.

A post-investment audit, conducted both during the investment

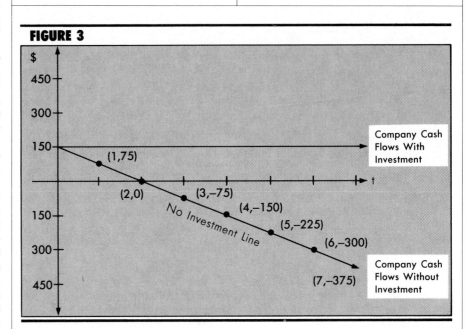

FIGURE 3

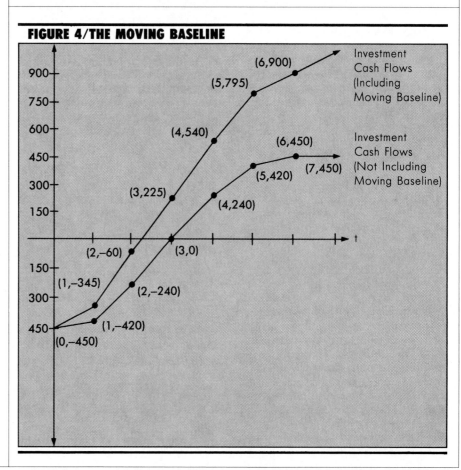

FIGURE 4/THE MOVING BASELINE

process (recall that the investment itself can be extended over a period of years) and after its completion, provides valuable information that can be used to correct problems before the success of the investment is undermined and to provide management with feedback on how well the cash outlays and inflows associated with the investment were estimated.

It is important that the post-investment audit include both an audit of the financial cash flows generated by the investment and the operating benefits forecasted. Companies should consider that if an investment was projected to cost $15 million over two years and return direct cost savings and quantifiable indirect and intangible benefits of

The new manufacturing environment presents new issues to address.

$20 million in the subsequent four years accompanied by additional operating benefits associated with the investment, the post-investment audit should evaluate all areas of performance against the forecast. The audit should detail reasons for any differences. The financial expectations should be assessed against the actual cash flows. The operational expectations, such as the flexibility provided by the investment, are evaluated against the results achieved. The operating expectations often provide the most direct comparison of expected versus realized performance.

Such a control mechanism drives managers to prepare cash flow estimates on sound, supportable assumptions. Situations have been cited where manufacturing often "bumps up" the numbers on capital investment proposals that they feel are necessary to be competitive in order to get them over the "excessive hurdle rate" they are required to meet. On the other hand, the accounting department justifies the significant difference between the hurdle rate and the actual cost of

capital based on offsetting the "bumped up" numbers submitted by manufacturing.

While the combination of the two may or may not work, depending on the relative relationship, it is clearly not the optimal method of making capital investment decisions. What is needed is to have all parties working together to develop the most accurate projection of the future costs and returns possible. The expectation of post audit accountability would go far in minimizing the root of this problem.

ROLE OF THE MANAGEMENT ACCOUNTANT

The role of the management accountant in the capital budgeting process has become more analytical and more communicative than in the past. The management accountant and manager should not rely exclusively on existing cost systems for the information required to justify the investment. Cost systems are frequently developed for financial reporting purposes and have certain constructions embodied in them to provide a full-cost valuation. Those constructions may not be consistent with the implications of a capital investment or, in fact, be detailed enough to help the analyst. The management accountant must be able to go beyond the existing cost system to incorporate into the estimates of cash flows all of the cost and benefits to be effected by a prospective investment.

The management accountant also must play the central role in the capital investment process. Financial expertise is a necessity. But to be effective, he must understand the operating characteristics and benefits of the investment and be willing to get input from all areas within the organization to arrive at the most realistic—not the most conservative—estimate of the investment's value. ∎

Robert A. Howell, DBA, CMA, is president of Howell Management Corp.

Stephen R. Soucy, MBA, CPA, is consultant at Howell Management.

[1]Robert A. Howell, James D. Brown, Stephen R. Soucy, and Allen H. Seed, III, *Management Accounting in the New Manufacturing Environment*, National Association of Accountants, 1987.

Technology Accounting

Technology should be treated as a direct cost, equivalent to direct labor and material.

BY JAMES A. BRIMSON

I n most factories, touch labor and materials are identified as the prime direct costs. All remaining costs are considered overhead and are allocated to the products using direct labor or other production volume bases.

Technology costs, which are defined as plant and equipment and information systems, are buried in overhead. Currently this important cost component, technology, is addressed through depreciation methodologies less comprehensive than what is needed to remain competitive in today's technology dominant environment.

In today's highly automated factories, traditional depreciation methods distort product cost. There are two reasons for this problem. First, companies are basing the selection of depreciation methods and allocation bases on criteria that do not mirror the manufacturing process. Second, the total of technology-related costs is large. The larger the technology cost as a percentage of total costs, the greater the impact of a misallocation on product cost.

A HIGH-TECH PURCHASE

A company's purchase of a five-axis spar machine and its use of inappropriate accounting practices will illustrate the importance of technology accounting.

Table 1 shows the planning assumptions the investment analysis yielded at the time the asset was acquired. The accounting department decided that the spar mill would be depreciated for tax purposes using an accelerated method and straight line for financial reporting over a ten-year period.

The company's plant produced two products with equal production volume. The five-axis spar machine was purchased primarily to support the manufacture of product A. Product B is labor intensive and used minor technology in the manufacturing process. An industrial engineering study revealed the traceable costs (Table 2).

General Electric.

Product costs are distorted in automated factories.

TABLE 1/INVESTMENT ANALYSIS

Equipment description	NC 5 Axis Spar
Date of purchase	23-Feb-88
Original cost	$300,000
Estimated salvage value	$30,000
Depreciable cost	$270,000
Length of term—years	7
Estimated useful life—hours	18,000
Hourly depreciation rate	$15.00
Annual interest rate	15%

NONRECURRING COSTS

Year of asset's life	Re-arrange Facilities	Industrial Engineering	NC Programming	Product Engineering	Total Nonrecurring
1	$40,000	$25,000	$15,000	$40,000	$120,000
2			$20,000	$50,000	$70,000
3			$25,000	$40,000	$65,000
4			$10,000	$20,000	$30,000
5			$5,000		$5,000
6					$0
7					$0
TOTALS	$40,000	$25,000	$75,000	$150,000	$290,000

RECURRING COSTS

Year of asset's life	Machine Operator	Utilities	Facilities	Maintenance	Supplies	Total Recurring
1	$ 30,000	$ 15,000	$ 5,000	$ 30,000	$ 10,000	$ 90,000
2	$ 50,000	$ 20,000	$ 5,000	$ 25,000	$ 20,000	$120,000
3	$ 50,000	$ 20,000	$ 5,000	$ 30,000	$ 30,000	$135,000
4	$ 50,000	$ 20,000	$ 5,000	$ 35,000	$ 30,000	$140,000
5	$ 40,000	$ 18,000	$ 5,000	$ 40,000	$ 20,000	$123,000
6	$ 30,000	$ 15,000	$ 5,000	$ 45,000	$ 15,000	$110,000
7	$ 25,000	$ 12,000	$ 5,000	$ 50,000	$ 10,000	$102,000
TOTALS	$275,000	$120,000	$35,000	$255,000	$135,000	$820,000

and technology is diametric rather than complementary. The economic cause and effect criteria have been violated.

Now let's assume that the product manager for product A is innovative and he decides to invest in a new numerical control machine. The direct labor content is reduced by $10 per unit. However, the depreciation on the machine and higher software and maintenance support will increase the overhead costs by $7 per unit. The company will realize a net savings on product A of $3 per unit from this investment. Product B's cost will remain unchanged. The overhead rate would be recomputed (Table 2).

The accounting system reported a $40 increase in the cost of product B even though its manufacturing process was unaffected. Why? Because the direct labor content of product B is, after the investment, proportionally greater than product A, and it must absorb a greater share of total technology costs. In other words, the cost of product B has increased because of the choice of accounting methods—not economic reality. If product B was a marginally profitable product, the decision might be made to drop this product.

Direct labor and material were charged directly to the individual products. The start-up (nonrecurring) costs were charged to expense during the period in which the costs were incurred. Depreciation (technology) was charged to a plant-wide overhead pool. Technology costs, as a part of overhead, were applied to the products using a predetermined basis such as direct labor. An overhead rate based on direct labor dollars was also computed.

After applying overhead to the products, the reported cost of product A would be $550, and the cost of Product B, $1,300. These reported costs represent a 50% discrepancy from the traceable costs. A primary cause of the distortion is that the overhead rate is inflated by technology cost. Technology costs represent 14% of total cost and 25% of overhead costs. The problem is compounded by allocating the inflated overhead cost to the products using an erroneous direct labor base. In fact, the relationship between labor

TABLE 2/PRODUCT COSTS

Cost Distribution

	PRODUCT	
	A	B
Direct Labor	$ 50	$200
Direct Material	300	300
Technology	200	50
Traceable Overhead	325	225
Non-Traceable Overhead	100	100
Total Product Cost	$975	$875

Overhead Cost Calculation:

$$\frac{\text{All costs less direct labor and material}}{\text{Labor}} = \frac{\$1,000}{\$250} = 400\%$$

NC MACHINE PURCHASED

New Overhead Cost Allocation:

$$\frac{\text{Total cost less direct labor and material}}{\text{Total direct labor cost}} = \frac{\$1,007}{\$240} = 420\%$$

The accounting system would then calculate a new product cost using the revised overhead rate:

	Product A	Product B
Direct Labor	$ 40	$ 200
Direct Material	300	300
Overhead	168	840
Total Product Cost	$508	$1,340

TECHNOLOGY ACCOUNTING TODAY

Technology accounting, as practiced today, is simply capital asset depreciation. Depreciation accounting can be defined as a system that aims to distribute the cost or other basic value of tangible assets, less salvage (if any), over the estimated useful life of the asset in a systematic, rational, and consistent manner. Depreciation expense does not have to correspond with the rate at which the asset's value actually declines.

When a company purchases a capital asset, the determination of a depreciation rate involves several factors:

1. *What number of periods will the asset be used and what will be the amount of depreciation expense during each period.* The company must consider the cost basis, residual value, useful life of the technology, and the depreciation method (for example, machine hours, units of production, straight line, sum of the years, accelerated, etc.).

Typically, the cost basis is computed using the historical acquisition cost of the asset. If significant installation costs are involved, then the start-up costs associated with the installation are included in the cost basis. Next, the useful life of the asset is estimated. Common methods on which to base estimates of useful life include the tax allowed life or the physical life of the asset. The residual value of the asset at the end of its useful life would be based on anticipated wear and tear and market demand.

In the case of the five-axis spar mill, the company selected straight-line depreciation for financial reporting and double declining for tax reporting. A ten-year life is selected because it is the suggested tax allowable service life.

2. *What is the basis for matching technology costs to the product during each period?* Here the company looks at the level of cost center control and the basis of allocation (direct labor, machine hours, and so on). The decision on the level of cost center control dictates the point of cost accumulation. It is typically based on factors such as organizational structure and computational ease. The more aggregate the cost

center definition, the wider the range of products to which the technology costs are applied.

THE PROBLEM: DEPRECIATION ACCOUNTING

Management accountants must reconsider the traditional depreciation methods they now use for the following reasons.

Economic Consequence. Depreciation is simply a device for distributing the cost of a fixed asset over its useful life. We have considerable latitude over how the allocation will be accomplished. Often depreciation methods are selected

because of computational ease, regulatory requirements, and conservatism.

GAAP is another important factor that contributes to the selection of depreciation practices. A primary goal of current cost accounting is to value inventory based on GAAP for financial reporting purposes. It calls for the specified depreciation method to be applied in a systematic, rational, and consistent manner.

Depreciation methods that mask the impact of technology on product cost result in poor decisions. Companies should select the depreciation method that reflects the relationship between an asset and

TABLE 3/DEPRECIATION ACCOUNTING
5-Axis Spar Machine: Straight Line vs. Machine Hours

Year of asset's life	Straight line	Machine hours	Difference	Percentage Difference
1	$ 27,000	$ 22,500	$ 4,500	17%
2	$ 27,000	$ 54,000	$(27,000)	(100%)
3	$ 27,000	$ 65,250	$(38,250)	(142%)
4	$ 27,000	$ 45,000	$(18,000)	(67%)
5	$ 27,000	$ 29,250	$(2,250)	(8%)
6	$ 27,000	$ 18,000	$ 9,000	34%
7	$ 27,000	$ 13,500	$ 13,500	50%
8	$ 27,000	$ 11,250	$ 15,750	58%
9	$ 27,000	$ 6,750	$ 20,250	75%
10	$ 27,000	$ 4,500	$ 22,500	84%
TOTAL	$270,000	$270,000	$ 0	0%

Straight Line: Cost Per Machine Hours Varies

Year of asset's life	Straight line	Estimated hours	Cost per hour
1	$27,000	1,000	$ 27.00
2	$27,000	2,400	$ 11.25
3	$27,000	2,900	$ 9.31
4	$27,000	2,000	$ 13.50
5	$27,000	1,300	$ 20.77
6	$27,000	800	$ 33.75
7	$27,000	600	$ 45.00
8	$27,000	500	$ 54.00
9	$27,000	300	$ 90.00
10	$27,000	200	$135.00

Product Cost Distortion

Month	Straight line	Actual hours	Cost per hour
1	$ 2,250	90	$ 25.00
2	$ 2,250	90	$ 25.00
3	$ 2,250	90	$ 25.00
4	$ 2,250	150	$ 15.00
5	$ 2,250	300	$ 7.50
6	$ 2,250	300	$ 7.50
7	$ 2,250	300	$ 7.50
8	$ 2,250	300	$ 7.50
9	$ 2,250	150	$ 15.00
10	$ 2,250	90	$ 25.00
11	$ 2,250	90	$ 25.00
12	$ 2,250	50	$ 45.00
Total	$27,000	2,000	$ 13.50

the manufacturing process.

Economic magnitude. In a 1987 study on management accounting in the new manufacturing environment, jointly funded by Computer Aided Manufacturing-International and the National Association of Accountants, survey respondents were asked about the importance of changing depreciation techniques. The enthusiasm was underwhelming—less than 10% of respondents believed such changes were necessary.

While there are several reasons for this apathy, an important reason is that the magnitude of technology costs are being significantly understated. Most companies, however, are unaware of the magnitude of technology costs because technology-related costs are scattered in numerous cost categories including maintenance, data processing, NC programming, industrial engineering, and others.

Previously, direct labor was the predominant factor of production and technology costs were minor. As a result, the distortion to product cost caused by improper selection of a depreciation method was minimal. The concept of materiality dominated.

In contrast, technology is now both a significant component of product cost and a major determinant of competitive advantage. Because of its importance, the choice of depreciation methods will have a major impact on product cost. The manufacturer's selection of either straight line or machine hours method for the five-axis spar machine would result in a substantial difference in the amount of cost applied to the product (Table 3).

The impact is magnified when all technology associated costs for the company are considered. For example, assume the average difference between depreciation methods in this example is 60%. If the technology component of total cost is 5%, then the 60% discrepancy in depreciation methods results in only a 3% difference in total cost (60% * 5%). On the other hand, if technology consists of 30% of total product cost, then there is a difference of 18% in total cost (60% * 30%). As technology costs increase in magnitude, the importance of selecting depreciation methods based on economic consequence also increases.

Reject the practice of depreciating many capital assets using time-based methods.

Time-Based Technology Cost. Fixed-time methods of depreciation are popular for two reasons. First, they are conservative because they *guarantee* that the cost will be recovered at the end of the depreciable life. Production-based depreciation methods have higher uncertainty because they are dependent on fore-

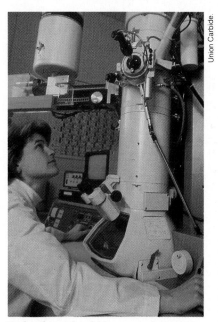

Technology should be treated as a direct cost.

casts of future product demand and are more sensitive to changes in production capabilities and technology.

Second, people equate time with cost. If a machine is not in use, then managers fear that company profitability must be slipping away. Accounting practices contribute to this view. Time-based depreciation equates time with cost. With every tick of the clock, the cost of depreciation must be absorbed. Idle equipment means no revenue is being generated to offset the depreciation expense.

The practice of absorbing overhead on direct labor instead of machine hours exacerbates the time/ cost relationship. If a machine is idle, how will the overhead be absorbed?

Just-in-Time (JIT) protagonists have already demonstrated the fallacy of this view. The end result of keeping machines fully used is inventory that must be financed. Also, inventory results in significant support costs to control, and becomes obsolete over time.

If we return to the premise that a major objective of cost accounting is to reflect the economic consequence, then today's practice of depreciating many capital assets using time-based methods must be rejected. Production volume is variable over time except for continuous production environments. Time-based depreciation methods absorb too much cost during periods of low production and too little cost during peak production periods.

If a company selects straight-line depreciation for the five-axis spar machine, the resulting cost per machine hour will vary significantly between years resulting in a significant difference in product cost as illustrated in Table 3.

In year 3, the cost per machine hour will be $9.31 and in year 10 it will be $135.00. Keep in mind the investment analysis. The machine was purchased predicated on the estimated hours. Products in years with low production volume should not be penalized because it was *planned* that the production volume would be less. In reality, the planned cost over the technology life was $15 ($270,000 / 18,000 machine hours) per machine hour. As long as the machine cost $270,000 and delivers 18,000 machine hours, the cost assigned to products should be $15 per machine hour. The problem extends beyond distortions between years. It also applies within a single year. Consider the distortion that occurs in year four of the example (Table 3).

Technology Cost Precision. To accurately match depreciation costs to products involves precise knowledge of future business conditions, including production volume or number of years a technology will be used. Such predictions are impossible to make. As a result, the matching of technology cost to products must be based on estimates and is necessarily imprecise. However, don't assume that because technology costs are based on imprecise estimates, this information is not useful to managers. Estimates derived from realistic cost behavior patterns provide an excellent basis for making routine decisions and controlling manufacturing operations. These cost behavior patterns and estimated cost are the foundation for calculating product cost.

Cost precision depends on the value of the information in the decision-making process, and cost-versus-benefits of accurate information.

Management accountants need information and decision criteria that are consistent. The five-axis spar machine investment decision required forecasts from the product manager, manufacturing engineers, production schedulers, and others about the type and volume of parts to be processed on the new numerical control machine during the next several years. The return on investment for the new machine was predicated on these assumptions and expectations. If the cost accounting department decides to use time-basis depreciation, the reported cost will bear no relationship to the assumptions used to justify the investment.

Skeptics might say, "so what." The investment and cost systems are separate and distinct. That's true if the goal of cost accounting is to report a product cost in accordance with GAAP requirements. But, if the goal of the cost accounting system is to provide information that can be used to manage cost, then the analysis of deviations between actual operations and the investment plan can provide a basis for implementing corrective action.

If the actual level of production, for example, were significantly below the forecasted production used in the investment analysis, then the technology component of cost will exceed target. Management accountants aware of this early in the life cycle of the five-axis mill will be able to take corrective action such as redesigning products to use the mill.

Whether the benefits of obtaining accurate information is worth the cost is the second important criteria. If not, the use of surrogate bases often provides an acceptable level of precision with a significant reduction in cost accounting costs.

Would the choice of depreciation

TABLE 4/TECHNOLOGY COST PRECISION
Straight-line Depreciation Method

Year of asset life	Straight line	Actual machine hours	Difference
1	$ 27,000	$ 13,729	$ 4,500
2	$ 27,000	$ 36,610	($27,000)
3	$ 27,000	$ 54,915	($38,250)
4	$ 27,000	$ 54,915	($18,000)
5	$ 27,000	$ 41,186	($ 2,250)
6	$ 27,000	$ 22,881	$ 9,000
7	$ 27,000	$ 18,305	$13,500
8	$ 27,000	$ 13,729	$15,750
9	$ 27,000	$ 8,008	$20,250
10	$ 27,000	$ 5,720	$22,500
TOTALS	$270,000	$270,000	$ 0

Machine-Hours Depreciation Method

Year of asset life	Forecasted machine hours	Actual machine hours	Difference
1	$ 22,500	$ 13,729	($ 8,771)
2	$ 54,000	$ 36,610	($17,390)
3	$ 65,250	$ 54,915	($10,335)
4	$ 45,000	$ 54,915	$ 9,915
5	$ 29,250	$ 41,186	$11,936
6	$ 18,000	$ 22,881	$ 4,881
7	$ 13,500	$ 18,305	$ 4,805
8	$ 11,250	$ 18,305	$ 2,479
9	$ 6,750	$ 8,008	$ 1,258
10	$ 4,500	$ 5,720	$ 1,220
	$270,000	$270,000	$ 0

methods be impacted by the error between actual and forecast? Table 4 shows a comparison between actual machine hours and the straight-line depreciation at the end of the spar mill's useful life.

Now, consider if machine hours had been selected as the primary depreciation method. The difference between forecasted and actual hours is shown in Table 4.

The distortion caused by the error between actual and forecast is less if the depreciation method was based on machine hour rather than straight-line depreciation. The reason is that machine hours more closely mirrors the manufacturing process. In practice, the difference would be even less because the estimates would be adjusted throughout the life of the mill as production demands become known.

Cost Basis. The cost basis used

> *Don't use depreciation methods to control risk.*

to compute depreciation expense does not reflect the economic value of technology. Depreciation practices understate the cost basis. The cost of capital equipment capitalized on the balance sheet is normally limited to all the expenditures relating to its acquisition and preparation. These costs form the base for computing the depreciation charge.

With technology investment becoming a principal driver in the economics of manufacturing, it is important to identify all costs that result from the decision to invest in an asset. Such factors as the cost of capital used to finance the acquisition, nonrecurring costs such as software development, industrial engineering, product design, fees paid to consultants, legal, accounting, and process R&D should be associated with the manufacturing process. The recurring costs should include salaries and related fringe benefits, travel, and support services. Such costs are internal to the company and directly related to the development of a new technology.

Understating technology costs masks the importance of these costs. When all these factors are considered, the total cost of the five-axis spar machine exceeds $1.5 million rather than the traditionally reported $270,000.

Emphasis on Conservative Practices. Conservative practices encourage expensing rather than amortizing many start-up costs. Start-up costs are defined as nonrecurring costs incurred in the preparation of new or expanded facilities. These costs accrue from the project's inception until operations begin. The conflict of whether to amortize or expense start-up costs revolves around two primary issues:

■ Start-up costs benefit future periods and should be amortized against revenues in these periods.
■ Capitalizing start-up costs as-

> *The choice of depreciation method will have a major impact on product cost.*

chine. Nonrecurring costs that are amortized and traced to products using machine hours cause significant differences as illustrated in Table 5. Any potentially traceable costs that are treated as an expense in the current period rather than matched to products, result in product cost distortion. The greater the distortion, the less the relevancy of

investment is dependent upon production volume. Risk should be managed through a rigorous review of all activities from start-up to technology retirement as events unfold in relationship to the original plan. If the start-up costs exceed estimates or the production volume is less than anticipated, a new estimate of cost is needed. Don't use depreciation methods to control risk.

TECHNOLOGY COSTS ARE RELEVANT

Technology should be treated as a direct cost, equivalent to direct labor and material for the following reasons.

1. Technology is a significant component of manufacturing cost—it often exceeds the traditional prime cost of direct labor. Advanced manufacturing technologies often replace or increase the productivity of direct laborers. As a result, it is not uncommon for direct touch labor to account for less than 10% of the total product cost at many companies. These costs have been offset by a sharp increase in the equipment and information (technology) component of manufacturing cost. Much of this changed cost behavior is the result of substituting automation for direct labor.

2. Technology is changing at a rapid rate and these breakthroughs are providing processes that promise superior performance at less cost. As a result, major assets are often obsolete before their physical lives are exhausted. The new manufacturing equipment often employs a significant amount of computer technology—a technology in which major productivity advancements are occurring every three years or so. However, it remains a common practice at many manufacturers to depreciate equipment over eight, ten, or even twelve years.

3. The cost behavior patterns of manufacturing in a computer-controlled process are different from those in a labor-intensive environment. Technology controls the pace of manufacturing; the laborer assists and monitors.

4. Technology is directly involved

TABLE 5/NONRECURRING AMORTIZED COSTS			
Five-Axis Spar Machine			
Year of asset's life	Nonrecurring expensed	Nonrecurring amortized	Difference
1	$120,000	$ 24,167	$95,833
2	$ 70,000	$ 48,333	$21,667
3	$ 65,000	$ 59,611	$ 5,389
4	$ 30,000	$ 59,611	($29,611)
5	$ 5,000	$ 45,111	($40,111)
6	$ 0	$ 32,223	($32,223)
7	$ 0	$ 20,944	($20,944)
TOTALS	$290,000	$290,000	$ 0

sumes the venture will be successful and the future earnings will be sufficient to match the known expenses.

One of the main reasons that companies expense start-up costs is that it minimizes taxable income and maximizes cash flow. Also, expensing costs is conservative. If start-up costs are amortized and the automation project is abandoned or turns out not to be profitable, then a company must "write-off" the asset. It is believed that a company is financially healthier by expensing costs that are potentially risky.

There are two major problems with expensing rather than amortizing technology costs. First, major cost distortions can occur. Start-up activities are a result of the decision to invest in the new technology. They would not occur if the investment was not made.

Consider the five-axis mill ma-

the reported cost in the decision-making process.

A second problem is that it confuses the issue of matching and risk. The goal of matching is to understand how costs attach to products. Risk—the probability of achieving desired results—is directly related to anticipated variability of estimates.

In the previous example of the investment in the NC machine, achieving the ROI was primarily dependent upon the estimates of production volume. If these estimates are based on firm orders, then potential variability is minimal. On the other hand, if the production volume is predicated on a new product line the uncertainty and thus the risk is higher.

The issues of risk and matching are separate and distinct. The degree of risk has no bearing on how technology costs attach to products. The profitability of the

in the conversion process. Technology touches the product. The manufacture of products requires a specified amount of technology as a factor of production as well as direct labor. Consider the manufacture of a bearing. The part routing might specify the following operations: turning, heat treat, grinding, honing, and assembly. In addition to identifying the sequence of manufacturing steps, the routing would specify the types of machines, machine time, type of direct labor, and direct labor hours needed to build the bearing. Labor is specified by the routing; material is specified by the Bill of Material; technology is specified in the routing. Thus, the technology component of manufacturing is directly specified and a cost should be directly computed.

5. Information is a by-product of automation. Charging technology costs to products on the basis of production volume rather than time, increases the dependence of accounting information on the availability of accurate data. Manually generated data have questionable reliability. They must be continuously reviewed and corrected,

The depreciation method used should reflect the relationship between the asset and the manufacturing process.

and are usually not timely. Manual data are often inaccurate and costly to collect. The choice of accounting methodologies is influenced by the accuracy and cost of collecting the required data. Time-based depreciation requires minimal ongoing data collection; production-based depreciation requires significant ongoing data collection. However, in an automated environment, the economics of data collection will be improved. The automated processes need to know what part is being processed and what processing is required including the time. This same information could be automatically passed to the cost

management system. With this increased availability and accuracy of shop-floor data, the changing of technology accounting procedures to production-based methods will be economically viable.

THE GOAL

Today's depreciation methods are based on concepts such as: systematic, rational, consistent, computational ease, regulatory requirements, conservatism, and GAAP. As a result, the importance of understanding the economic cause-and-effect relationship between technology and product cost has become a secondary objective.

This violates an important objective of cost accounting, which is to accurately match production costs to those products that benefit from them. Technologies are acquired to support specific activities, such as production requirements, engineering, or support tasks. Therefore, the cost of the asset should be charged to only those products that use it. By lumping technology costs into overhead, the asset costs are distributed over all activities masking the "real" cost of the activity. Better traceability and matching of costs will result in improved decision making.

The exclusion of technology costs as a prime product cost is no longer acceptable because inaccurate information, caused by improper matching of technology costs to products, prompts management to make incorrect decisions. A major distortion to product cost is caused by high overhead rates that are inflated by the potential traceable technology costs. The inflated overhead cost is then allocated to the products using an erroneous allocation base, such as direct labor. The goal of a technology accounting system is to more accurately assign capital investment costs to those products that benefit from them. ∎

James A. Brimson is president of Integrated Cost Management Systems, Inc., in Arlington, Texas. Previously, Mr. Brimson was vice president for Business Development at Computer Aided Manufacturing-International, Inc. Mr. Brimson is a member of NAA's Fort Worth Chapter, through which this article was submitted.

Technology changes so fast it cannot be depreciated over 8-10 years.

Applying Cost Accounting to
FACTORY AUTOMATION

Survey asks: How do you quantify automation benefits?

BY JAMES A. HENDRICKS

How are American manufacturing companies relating their cost accounting practices to the automation of their factories? More companies are automating every day so they can deliver customized products on a timely basis, improve quality, increase manufacturing flexibility, and reduce costs.

The increase in factory automation has exposed and magnified cost accounting problems related to investment justification, product costing, and performance measurement. The solution to these problems lies in the use of cost accounting practices appropriate for automated machine environments.

I determined to find out what large industrial firms were actually doing. Such practice data should be useful in helping to improve cost accounting practices in automated environments and, as a consequence, the ability of American manufacturing firms to compete in world markets.

A pretested questionnaire and three follow-up mailings were sent in March and April 1988 to corporate controllers of 168 Fortune 500 industrial firms in seven industry categories. The industries surveyed were those likely to have substantial amounts of factory automation. They included the aerospace, computers, electronic, industrial and farm equipment, metal products, motor vehicles and parts, and scientific and photographic equipment industries.

Eighty-five usable responses were received, a 51% response rate, indicating substantial interest in cost accounting practices related to automation. The questionnaire topics were: factory automation in the respondent's firm, investment justification, product costing, and performance measures.

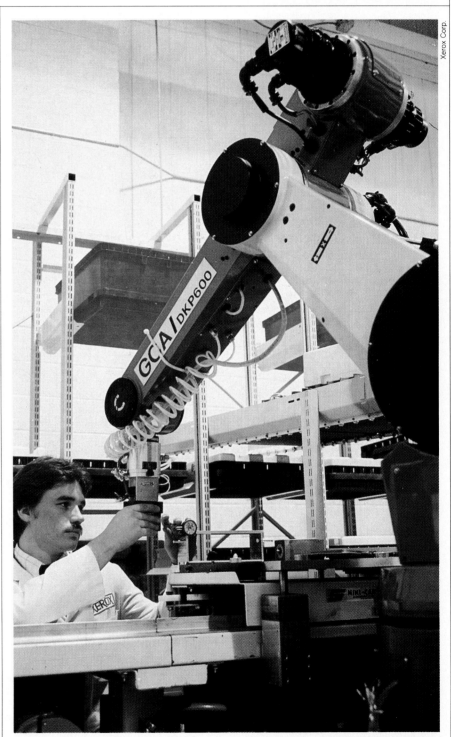

Robotic arm at Xerox factory. Automation is revolutionizing manufacturing and accounting must adapt.

AUTOMATION IN THE RESPONDENTS' FIRMS

The percentages of respondents making use of each type of factory automation are detailed in Figure 1. The percentage with standalone automation is very high, ranging from 60% for Computer-Aided Inspection to 98% for Computer-Aided Design. The percentage of respondents with more integrated types of automation such as flexible manufacturing cells or systems or CIM is considerably lower than for standalone automation. Apparently, companies are evaluating carefully the results of standalone automation before investing heavily in more integrated types of automation. With only one-sixth of the most automated large industrial companies in the United States employing CIM, the progress toward fully automated factories is slow.

INVESTMENT JUSTIFICATION

A major difference between justifying investments for factory automation and those for conventional equipment is that it is more difficult to quantify the more intangible benefits of automated equipment accurately. Because of this difficulty, some managers believe that discounted cash flow (DCF) capital budgeting techniques (internal rate of return and net present value) are not appropriate for evaluating investments in factory automation. They contend that such investments must be made in the belief that if the right strategic investments are made, the future will be as good as the past.

DCF techniques are appropriate, however, because these techniques consider all estimated cash flows and the time value of money—the catch is that managers must make a better effort to quantify the intangible benefits and costs. Assigning a reasonable value to these items is clearly better than assigning a value of zero. In conjunction with a DCF primary capital budgeting technique, payback may be a useful secondary technique because it indicates how long it will take to recover the initial outlay. The primary and secondary capital budgeting techniques used by the survey

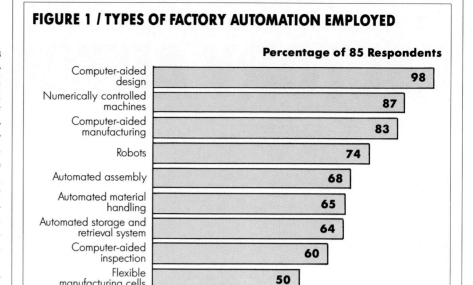

FIGURE 1 / TYPES OF FACTORY AUTOMATION EMPLOYED

Percentage of 85 Respondents

- Computer-aided design: 98
- Numerically controlled machines: 87
- Computer-aided manufacturing: 83
- Robots: 74
- Automated assembly: 68
- Automated material handling: 65
- Automated storage and retrieval system: 64
- Computer-aided inspection: 60
- Flexible manufacturing cells: 50
- Flexible manufacturing system: 31
- Integrated, highly automated factory (CIM): 17

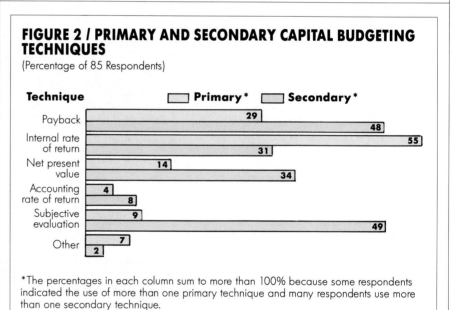

FIGURE 2 / PRIMARY AND SECONDARY CAPITAL BUDGETING TECHNIQUES

(Percentage of 85 Respondents)

Technique — Primary* — Secondary*

- Payback: Primary 29, Secondary 48
- Internal rate of return: Primary 55, Secondary 31
- Net present value: Primary 14, Secondary 34
- Accounting rate of return: Primary 4, Secondary 8
- Subjective evaluation: Primary 9, Secondary 49
- Other: Primary 7, Secondary 2

*The percentages in each column sum to more than 100% because some respondents indicated the use of more than one primary technique and many respondents use more than one secondary technique.

respondents to justify expenditures for factory automation are shown in Figure 2.

Only about two-thirds of the respondents now use a DCF technique as a primary technique in justifying expenditures for factory automation. Further analysis revealed that 14% of the respondents do not use a DCF technique as either a primary or secondary technique, a situation that could cause them to make bad investment decisions. Additionally, almost one-third of the respondents use pay-

back as a primary technique, which should be discouraged because it does not consider the time value of money or cash flows beyond the payback period.

About one-half of the respondents use payback as a secondary evaluative technique, which is appropriate. Also, about one-half use subjective evaluation as a secondary technique in conjunction with a quantitative primary technique, probably because they are not comfortable with their quantification of the more intangible benefits. It is encouraging to note that only a few respondents use subjective evaluation as a primary technique.

Ideally, all expected benefits and costs should be quantified and included in a DCF model when evaluating capital expenditures for factory automation. The benefits that the survey respondents quantify and those they consider qualitatively only are shown in Figure 3.

Many benefits are considered qualitatively only. It is encouraging that about two-thirds of the respondents do consider qualitatively how well automated projects mesh with corporate strategy. If a major automated project is not in line with corporate goals and manufacturing strategy, it should be dropped from further consideration.

Most companies quantify the first five benefits listed in Figure 3 because they are more tangible in nature. If an automated project is not justified after quantification of the more tangible benefits, companies should quantify the intangible benefits. Representatives from engineering, manufacturing, marketing, and management accounting may have to team up to do this because multiple functional areas may be affected.

The use of probability factors for cash flows, sensitivity analysis, or other risk analysis techniques should be helpful for projects with benefits or costs that are uncertain and difficult to quantify. The survey results indicate that improvement needs to be made in this area. More than one-fourth of the respondents do not use a risk analysis technique, and about one-third make a subjective, nonquantitative adjustment for risk. The use of the more sophisticated quantitative techniques, such as determining probability factors for cash flows and simulation, is very limited and is concentrated largely in the electronics industry. But sensitivity analysis is used by about 40% of the respondents to assess risk. The advantage of sensitivity analysis is that the effect on IRR, NPV, or payback can be assessed by changing the estimates for one input factor at a time.

A realistic hurdle rate approximating the weighted-average cost of capital should be used in DCF models when evaluating automated (as well as other) projects. The un-

fortunate result of using artificially high hurdle or discount rates could be the rejection of profitable projects. About three-fourths of the survey respondents using a DCF technique and a hurdle or discount rate use a rate of more than 14%, and one-third use a rate of more than 18%. These high rates apparently include a substantial adjustment for risk because most companies' weighted-average cost of capital was probably less than 10% at the time of the survey.

PRODUCT COSTING

Accurate product costs are needed by managers for new product introduction, pricing, product support, make-or-buy, and product discontinuance decisions as well as for external reporting. If the cost accounting system provides inaccurate product cost information, the potential benefits of factory automation may not be realized. What's more, managers may be saddled with a less than optimal

TABLE 1 / PRODUCT COST BY INDUSTRY
(Percentage of Total Manufacturing Cost)

Industry	Direct Materials	Direct Labor	Manufacturing Overhead
Aerospace	51.7	19.3	29.0
Computers	69.9	7.5	22.5
Electronics	48.6	15.1	36.3
Industrial and farm equipment	46.0	12.8	41.2
Metal products	52.0	15.7	32.3
Motor vehicles and parts	63.8	7.8	28.4
Scientific and photographic equipment	52.3	11.3	36.5
Average for seven industries	54.4	12.9	32.6

FIGURE 3 / BENEFITS CONSIDERED WHEN JUSTIFYING CAPITAL EXPENDITURES
(Percentage of 85 Respondents)

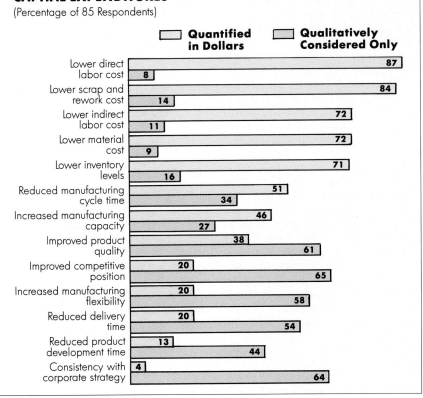

Quantified in Dollars   Qualitatively Considered Only

Benefit	Quantified in Dollars	Qualitatively Considered Only
Lower direct labor cost	8	87
Lower scrap and rework cost	14	84
Lower indirect labor cost	11	72
Lower material cost	9	72
Lower inventory levels	16	71
Reduced manufacturing cycle time	34	51
Increased manufacturing capacity	27	46
Improved product quality	38	61
Improved competitive position	20	65
Increased manufacturing flexibility	20	58
Reduced delivery time	20	54
Reduced product development time	13	44
Consistency with corporate strategy	4	64

pricing structure and product mix.

In the NAA study, *Management Accounting in the New Manufacturing Environment,* the authors suggest that direct labor might compose only 5% of total product cost in heavily automated manufacturing facilities.[1]

As seen in Table 1, direct labor averages almost 13% of product cost in the seven industries surveyed. The conclusion is that except for the computers and motor vehicles and parts industries the production facilities of the industries surveyed are not "heavily automated." The average product cost percentages of about 54% for direct materials, 13% for direct labor, and 33% for manufacturing overhead, however, do represent a substantial shift of production costs over the past decade from direct labor to fixed overhead costs such as depreciation and indirect labor.

Teachers of accounting have long advocated variable (direct) costing for internal use. The justification is that the only relevant costs for product decisions are variable costs because fixed costs have already been incurred and cannot be changed. This short-term perspective is often not appropriate "because the decision to offer a product creates a long-term commitment to manufacture, market, and support that product," resulting in an increase in fixed costs. Thus, short-term variable cost is often an inappropriate measure of product cost.[2] Because of the higher level of fixed costs and lower level of variable costs in automated environments, the use of full (absorption) costing that also allocates fixed overhead costs to products may lead to better product-related decisions.

The survey indicates that most respondents use full costing in automated machine environments, with only 15% using variable costing. Full costing is probably used so heavily because it is mandated for external financial reporting and thus is available for internal use. In addition, full costs are required for cost-plus pricing for government contracts. All of the respondents in the aerospace, computers, and scientific and photographic equipment industries use only full costing.

Because manufacturing overhead is about one-third of total

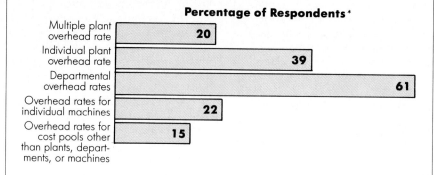

FIGURE 4 / TYPE OF OVERHEAD RATES

Percentage of Respondents*

Multiple plant overhead rate	20
Individual plant overhead rate	39
Departmental overhead rates	61
Overhead rates for individual machines	22
Overhead rates for cost pools other than plants, departments, or machines	15

*Percentages sum to more than 100% because many respondents use more than one type of overhead rate.

product cost and companies rely extensively on full costing, the manner in which overhead costs are assigned from cost pools to products in automated machine environments is very important. The two factors to consider are: the type of overhead rate (cost centers for which overhead rates are established) and the overhead application base.

In automated machine environments, overhead rates can be established for multiple plants, individual plants, departments, individual machines, or for cost pools other than plants, departments, or machines. Multiple or individual plant overhead rates will often result in inaccurate product cost and bad product-related decisions because

dissimilar kinds of activities are aggregated. A better way is to establish overhead rates for separate production processes such as individual departments or work cells within departments. Establishing overhead rates for individual key machines also has been suggested to improve the accuracy of product costs.[3] The types of overhead rates used in the respondents' companies are shown in Figure 4.

The use of multiple and individual plant overhead rates is excessive. In fact, further analysis revealed that about one-fourth of the respondents use only multiple or individual plant overhead rates, with the result that individual product costs could be very inaccurate. The exclusive use of these

FIGURE 5 / OVERHEAD APPLICATION BASES

Percentage of Respondents

Actual direct labor hours	26
Standard direct labor hours	35
Actual direct labor dollars	20
Standard direct labor dollars	34
Actual machine hours	14
Standard machine hours	34
Time in machine center	7
Direct material (units or cost)	26
Units of production	18

rates was particularly high in the computers and electronics industries; none of the respondents in the industrial and farm equipment and scientific and photographic equipment industries use these rates exclusively.

Departmental overhead rates, used by about three-fifths of the respondents, should result in accurate product costs if the department is a relatively small, homogeneous cost center such as a department of N/C machines or an FMS. A positive note is that more than one-fifth of the respondents have established overhead rates for individual machines, and 15% have established overhead rates for cost pools other than plants, departments, or machines, such as groups of machines or work cells within departments. The use of both of the latter types of overhead rates should enhance product-costing accuracy but will cost more to implement.

The second important factor regarding overhead assignment from cost pools to products is the overhead application base. In the past, manufacturing processes were la-

It is difficult to quantify the benefits of automated equipment accurately.

bor intensive so direct labor overhead bases were appropriate. These bases are not appropriate in automated environments because the amount of direct labor is very small and most overhead costs are unrelated to the incurrence of direct labor. In automated environments many overhead costs, including tooling, power, machine depreciation, engineering, supervision, and property taxes, are more closely related to the usage of machine hours than direct labor hours. Using machine-based overhead rates instead of labor-based rates should produce more accurate product costing in automated environments. The per-

centages of respondents using different overhead application bases in automated machine environments are shown in Figure 5.

The use of direct labor overhead bases is excessive. More than half of the respondents in the aerospace, computers, electronics, and motor vehicles and parts industries use labor-based rates to the exclusion of machine-based rates. Inaccurate product costs are likely to result from such a situation because of the low level of direct labor and the substantial overhead costs unrelated to the incurrence of direct labor.

Machine hour overhead bases can be expressed in terms of actual machine hours or standard (engineered) machine hours. Standard machine time is usually determined when the program is written for the manufacturing operations for a part. The availability of standard machine hours over actual machine hours probably explains the heavy use of them as a base. Usually neither actual machine hours nor time in the machine center is measured or recorded. The heaviest use of machine-based overhead rates is in the aerospace, electronics, industrial and farm equipment, and scientific and photographic equipment industries.

A direct material overhead base, used by about one-fourth of the respondents, is appropriate for the assignment of overhead costs, such as material handling, that are related to direct material units or cost. This base is also comparatively easy to employ because the cost system records the usage of direct materials. The units of production base, used by about one-fifth of the respondents, is suitable for reasonably homogeneous parts requiring similar machine operations.

For more accurate product costing, companies should consider using multiple allocation bases simultaneously. For example, a direct labor overhead base could be used for applying overhead costs related to direct labor worked, a machine hour overhead base could be used for applying overhead costs related to machine hours, and a direct material overhead base could be used for applying overhead costs related to the usage of materials. Using multiple overhead bases allows for product diversity and a finer alloca-

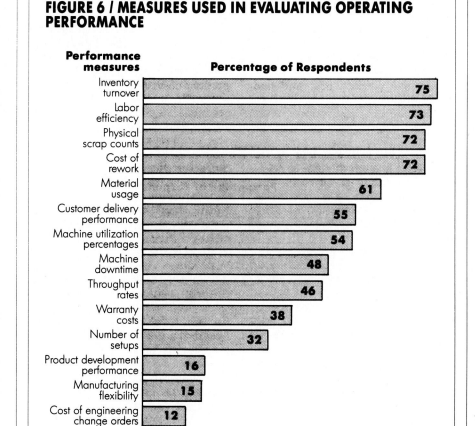

FIGURE 6 / MEASURES USED IN EVALUATING OPERATING PERFORMANCE

Performance measures — **Percentage of Respondents**

Performance measure	Percentage
Inventory turnover	75
Labor efficiency	73
Physical scrap counts	72
Cost of rework	72
Material usage	61
Customer delivery performance	55
Machine utilization percentages	54
Machine downtime	48
Throughput rates	46
Warranty costs	38
Number of setups	32
Product development performance	16
Manufacturing flexibility	15
Cost of engineering change orders	12

tion of costs to products if direct labor hours, machine hours, and material dollars used in the manufacturing process are not directly proportional to one another.[4] At the present time only nine respondents use all three of these overhead bases, but several more are considering the use of multiple overhead bases.

PERFORMANCE MEASURES

Many performance measures appropriate for nonautomated environments are inappropriate for automated environments, for example, labor use, overhead absorption, and variances from standard costs. Concentrating on labor use and overhead absorption may cause managers to produce unnecessarily for inventory. The goal in regard to overhead should be to minimize actual cost, not maximize absorption. Standard cost systems have the major advantage of cost control through variance reporting, but variance analysis is not as important in automated environments because the manufacturing process is usually more reliable and consistent, so variances should be minimal or nonexistent.[5] Nevertheless, 80% of the survey respondents employ standard cost systems in automated machine environments.

Performance measures in automated machine environments should reflect the manufacturing processes, promote decisions in line with the goal of long-term profitability, and help to control operations. Timely, accurate measures that focus on quality, material control, delivery, inventory, and machine performance should replace the outdated performance measures discussed above.[6] Many of these new measures will be more subjective and nonfinancial in nature than the old ones. Representatives from engineering, manufacturing, marketing, and management accounting may need to work together to formulate and implement them. Figure 6 shows the items that the survey respondents measure formally in evaluating operating performance in business units with automated machine environments.

As mentioned previously, quality is extremely important in automat-

Honeywell's Modutrol motor assembly line in Golden Valley, Minn.

ed environments. Quality costs can be classified in four categories: prevention costs, appraisal costs, internal failure costs, and external failure costs.[7] The concern about product quality is reflected in Figure 6 by the fact that approximately three-fourths of the respondents formally measure physical scrap counts and the cost of rework (internal failure cost) and more than one-third measure warranty costs (external failure costs). Many standard cost systems include an allowance for scrap in the standards. As a result, it is often difficult to separate and analyze scrap costs. But because scrap can be a substantial cost, scrap losses should be analyzed in total and by operation and product.[8]

Direct materials are the most significant component of product cost (54%) and direct labor is the least significant component (13%), so performance measurement systems should focus more on material usage and less on labor efficiency. This change has not yet occurred. Figure 6 shows that almost three-fourths of the respondents formally measure labor efficiency, but only about three-fifths formally measure material usage in automated environments. However, the trend

is toward decreased emphasis on measuring labor efficiency; 11 respondents indicated that they have already discontinued this measurement.

With the increased emphasis on meeting customers' needs in a timely manner, manufacturers in automated environments should be concerned about delivery performance in addition to being concerned about the quality of the products delivered. Quality has several characteristics that can be quantified, but delivery-related characteristics are more difficult to quantify. Although delivery information has been considered in a qualitative, informal manner in the past, key characteristics related to delivery should be quantified because of the potentially large effect on revenues.[9] The survey respondents show a high concern for on-time customer deliveries, with more than half formally measuring customer delivery performance. Throughput rates also should be monitored because throughput rates can affect on-time delivery performance. Almost half of the respondents formally measure throughput rates.

Inventory reduction should be a prime objective in automated machine environments. The JIT concept of minimizing inventory levels should replace the use of economic order quantities (EOQ). To reduce finished goods inventory, better sales forecasting and coordination between manufacturing and sales are necessary. To reduce raw material and work-in-process inventories, factors such as inconsistent vendor deliveries, changes in production schedules, equipment breakdowns, and excessive scrap and rework should be analyzed.[10] With the emphasis on controlling inventory costs in automated environments, it is not surprising that inventory turnover is at the top of the list in Figure 6. To be most useful, inventory turnover rates should be calculated by product, location, and other relevant inventory categories.

Because of the large investment required for automated equipment, managers should monitor machine performance indicators such as machine use percentages and machine downtime so that timely corrective action can be initiated if necessary. About half of the respondents formally measure both of these, as well as throughput rates. Manufacturing flexibility is usually monitored on an informal basis; it is most often measured formally by respondents with an FMS or CIM.

Many performance measures appropriate for nonautomated environments are inappropriate for automated environments.

Other performance measures, including number of setups, product development performance, and cost of engineering change orders, are the predominant items that are informally monitored.

A CHALLENGE FOR COST ACCOUNTANTS

Cost accounting practices related to factory automation need to be improved. In the area of investment justification, this implies the expanded use of DCF techniques, better efforts to quantify the more intangible benefits and costs, the expanded use of probabilities or other risk analysis techniques, and the use of realistic hurdle rates. In regard to product costing, companies need to establish overhead application rates for individual departments, work cells within departments, or individual machines rather than for individual or multiple plants. They should use machine-based overhead rates instead of labor-based rates and should consider the use of multiple overhead bases. Performance measures in automated environments need to focus on quality, material control, delivery, inventory, and machine performance. If cost accounting practices related to factory automation are improved, the ability of American manufacturing firms to compete in world markets should improve.

Many of the respondents in this survey are aware of the cost accounting problems, are studying them, and are planning to make appropriate changes. But progress is slow, reflecting the fact that much of the movement toward factory automation has occurred in the last three to five years. Management accountants must be a positive force for progress by being aware of the automation occurring in their companies and adapting their accounting procedures and systems to it. ■

James A. Hendricks is professor of accountancy at Northern Illinois University. A CPA, he holds a Ph.D. degree in accountancy from the University of Illinois. He is a member of the Rockford Chapter, through which this article was submitted.

[1]Robert A. Howell, James D. Brown, Stephen R. Soucy, and Allen H. Seed, III, *Management Accounting in the New Manufacturing Environment*, National Association of Accountants, Montvale, N.J., 1987.
[2]Robin Cooper and Robert S. Kaplan, "How Cost Accounting Distorts Product Costs," *Management Accounting*, April 1988, p. 21.
[3]Henry R. Schwarzbach and Richard G. Vangermeersch, "Why We Should Account for the 4th Cost of Manufacturing," *Management Accounting*, July 1983.
[4]Ibid, Cooper and Kaplan, pp. 22-23.
[5]Robert A. Howell and Stephen R. Soucy, "Operating Controls in the New Manufacturing Environment," *Management Accounting*, October 1987, pp. 25-26.
[6]Ibid, Howell and Soucy, p. 26.
[7]Harold P. Roth and Wayne J. Morse, "Let's Help Measure and Report Quality Costs," *Management Accounting*, August 1983, p. 50.
[8]Ibid, Howell and Soucy, pp. 29-30.
[9]Ibid, Howell, Brown, Soucy, and Seed, pp. 54, 60.
[10]Ibid, Howell and Soucy, p. 29.

Xerox Corp.

Xerox automated warehouse.

Bibliography

Akers, Michael D. and Grover L. Porter. "Expert Systems for Management Accountants." March 1986, pp. 30-34.

Barton, M. Frank, Surendra P. Agrawal, and L. Mason Rockwell, Jr. "Meeting the Challenge of Japanese Management Concepts." September 1988, pp. 49-53.

Barton, Thomas L. and Robert J. Fox. "Evolution at American Transtech." April 1988, pp. 49-52.

Bennett, Robert E. and James A. Hendricks. "Justifying the Acquisition of Automated Equipment." July 1987, pp. 39-46.

Biggs, Joseph R. and Ellen J. Long. "Gaining the Competitive Edge with MRP/MRP II." May 1988, pp. 27-32.

Brayton, Gary N. "Productivity Measure Aids in Profit Analysis." January 1985, pp. 54-58.

Brunton, Nancy M. "Evaluation of Overhead Allocations." July 1988, pp. 22-26.

Calvasina, Richard V., Eugene J. Calvasina, and Gerald E. Calvasina. "Beware the New Accounting Myths." December 1989, pp. 41-45.

Campbell, Robert J. "Pricing Strategy in the Automotive Glass Industry." July 1989, pp. 26-34.

Campi, John P. "Total Cost Management at Parker Hannifin." January 1989, pp. 51-53.

Cardullo, J. Patrick and Richard A. Moellenberndt. "The Cost Allocation Problem in a Telecommunications Company." September 1987, pp. 39-44.

Clark, John. "Costing for Quality at Celanese." March 1985, pp. 42-46.

Clark, Ronald L. and James B. McLaughlin. "Controlling the Cost of Product Defects." August 1986, pp. 32-35.

Dietemann, Gerard J. "Measuring Productivity in a Service Company." February 1988, pp. 48-54.

Doost, Roger K. and Evans Pappas. "Frozen-to-Current Cost Variance." March 1988, pp. 41-43.

Edwards, James B. "At the Crossroads." September 1985, pp. 44-50.

Fox, Robert J. and Thomas L. Barton. "Management Control at American Transtech." September 1986, pp. 37-47.

Frank, Gary B., Steven A. Fisher, and Allen R. Wilkie.

"Linking Cost to Price and Profit." June 1989, pp. 22-26.

Gass, Gerald L., Grover McMakin, and Roger Bentson. "White Collar Productivity." September 1987, pp. 33-38.

Hakala, Gregory. "Measuring Costs with Machine Hours." October 1985, pp. 57-61.

Jayson, Susan. "Goldratt and Fox: Revolutionizing the Factory Floor." May 1987, pp. 18-22.

Johansson, Henry J. "Preparing for Accounting System Changes." July 1990, pp. 37-41.

Johnson, H. Thomas and Dennis A. Loewe. "How Weyerhaeuser Manages Corporate Overhead Costs." August 1987, pp. 20-26.

Keegan, Daniel P., Robert G. Eiler, and Charles R. Jones. "Are Your Performance Measures Obsolete?" June 1989, pp. 45-50.

Keller, Donald E. and Paul Krause. "'World-Class' Down on the Farm." May 1990, pp. 39-45.

Keys, David E. "Six Problems in Accounting for N/C Machines." November 1986, pp. 38-47.

Krause, Paul and Donald E. Keller. "Bringing World-Class Manufacturing Accounting to a Small Company." November 1988, pp. 28-33.

Lammert, Thomas B. and Robert Ehrsam. "The Human Element: The Real Challenge in Modernizing Cost Systems." July 1987, pp. 32-37.

Lippa, Victor. "Measuring Performance with Synchronous Management." February 1990, pp. 54-59.

Mackey, James T. "Eleven Key Issues in Manufacturing Accounting." January 1987, pp. 32-37.

Michaels, Lawrence T. "A Control Framework for Factory Automation." May 1988, pp. 37-42.

Mielcarz, Richard J. and Aida Shekib. "Telecommunications for the Factory Floor." April 1990, pp. 42-44.

Morse, Wayne J. and Harold P. Roth. "Why Quality Costs Are Important." November 1987, pp. 42-43.

Pipkin, Al. "The 21st Century Controller." February 1989, pp. 21-25.

Porter, Grover L. and Michael D. Akers. "In Defense of Management Accounting." November 1987, pp. 58-62.

Robinson, Michael A. and John E. Timmerman. "How Vendor Analysis Supports JIT Manufacturing." December 1987, pp. 20-24.

Roth, Harold P. and A. Faye Borthick. "Getting Closer to Real Product Costs." May 1989, pp. 28-33.

Sadhwani, Arjan T. and M. H. Sarhan. "Electronic Systems Enhance JIT Operations." December 1987, pp. 25-30.

Sadhwani, Arjan T., M. H. Sarhan, and Dayal Kiringoda. "Just-In-Time: An Inventory System Whose Time Has Come." December 1985, pp. 36-44.

Sadhwani, Arjan T. and Thomas Tyson. "Does Your Firm Need Bar Coding?" April 1990, pp. 45-48.

Sauers, Dale G. "Analyzing Inventory Systems." May 1986, pp. 30-36.

Schiff, Jonathan B. and Allen I. Schiff. "High-Tech Cost Accounting for the F-16." September 1988, pp. 43-48.

Schwarzbach, Henry R. "The Impact of Automation on Accounting for Indirect Costs." December 1985, pp. 45-50.

Seed, Allen H., III. "Improving Cost Management." February 1990, pp. 27-30.

Smith, Gene L. "Improving Productivity in the Controller's Organization." January 1986, pp. 49-51.

Stec, Stanley F. "Manufacturing Control Through Bar Coding at Target Products." April 1988, p. 47.

Sullivan, William G. and James M. Reeve.

"XVENTURE: Expert Systems to the Rescue." October 1988, pp. 51-58.

Tatikonda, Lakshmi U. "Production Managers Need a Course in Cost Accounting." June 1987, pp. 26-29.

Taussig, Russell A. and William L. Shaw. "Accounting for Productivity: A Practical Approach." May 1985, pp. 48-52.

Tietze, Armin R. and Delphine R. Shaw. "OPUS: A New Concept for Mastering Cost." August 1986, pp. 27-31.

Tyson, Thomas N. "Quality and Profitability: Have Controllers Made the Connection?" November 1987, pp. 38-42.

Vangermeersch, Richard. "Reviewing Our Heritage." July 1987, pp. 47-49.

Wagner, James. "Operating Rhythm." June 1986, pp. 36-39.

Whitt, Sue Y. and Jerry D. Whitt. "What Professional Service Firms Can Learn from Manufacturing." November 1988, pp. 39-42.

Williams, Kathy. "CAM-I: On the Leading Edge." June 1989, pp. 18-21.

Woods, Michael D. "How We Changed Our Accounting." February 1989, pp. 42-45.

Wright, Michael A. and John W. Jonez. "Material Burdening: Management Accounting Can Support Competitive Strategy." August 1987, pp. 27-31.